The

Sanctifier

A Translation by SISTER M. AQUINAS, O. S. U.
OF THE WORK "EL ESPIRITU SANTO" BY LUIS M. MARTINEZ
Late Archbishop of Mexico

ST. PAUL EDITIONS

NIHIL OBSTAT:
Bede Babo, O.S.B.
    Censor Librorum

IMPRIMATUR:
+ James A. McNulty
    Bishop of Paterson

Reprinted and photographed with the kind permission of St. Anthony's Guild, Paterson, New Jersey.

Liturgical Designs by Jose de Vinck

With a few exceptions, duly noted in the text, the Scriptures are quoted in the Confraternity of Christian Doctrine translations, as follows: the New Testament (copyright 1941); and the books of Genesis (copyright 1952) and Psalms, Ecclesiastes, Canticle of Canticles, Wisdom, Sirach (all copyright 1955). Sources for quotations other than Scriptural are listed at the end of the book.

ISBN 0-8198-6804-3 (paper)

TRANSLATOR'S PREFACE

Surprisingly, very few of the writings of the late Archbishop of Mexico, Luis M. Martinez, have as yet been translated into English. This will not be the case for very long, however, in view of the fact that friends and close acquaintances have been very active in circulating more and more of his works and in making known his great personality.

Since the work was begun, the beloved Archbishop of the Mexican people has left them to return to the embrace of the Father whose Spirit he has done so much to make known among them. Always revered by the Mexicans and all those whose privilege it was to know him, the Archbishop will remain an inspiration to all who will yet come under his influence through the writings that he has left us.

A close and lifelong friend of the Archbishop refers to his personality as "a diamond of multiple facets." He is seen as a philosopher, a theologian, a teacher, an educator, a superior, a sociologist, a sacred orator, a writer, a poet, a director of souls, a humorist. "But," continues his friend, "there is perhaps one aspect that has remained in shadow until now, in spite of the fact that it is the most important: it is the interior man, his spiritual life, his intimate relationship with God; in a word, it is the mystic, . . . the experimental mystic, who speaks and writes about what has happened to him personally, in the style of St. Teresa — or better, of St. John of the Cross."[1] May the passing of time and the gradual clarification of knowledge regarding this saintly man give us this true picture.

We can understand a little the Archbishop's intense dedication to his people, his devotion to their needs, his longing for sacrifice, from these words summing up the sermon he gave in the Cathedral of Mexico on the occasion of assuming his position as head of the Archdiocese of Mexico City: "I come to promise you but one thing: I come to give you my life."[2] Those who read his work on the Holy Spirit will surely learn where he acquired the love and the knowledge that made him the tremendous force he was in a wide circle of souls.

The help of many kind friends was necessary in order to bring this translation of a sublime and masterful work to completion. I wish to express my sincere thanks to them for enabling me to share its spiritual treasures with others.

Because the termination of the translation nearly coincides with the Ursuline celebration of one hundred years in Kentucky, this work is offered in thanksgiving to God for the blessings we have received.

SISTER M. AQUINAS, O. S. U.

Feast of Pentecost
May, 1957

---

1. J. G. Trevino: "Monsenor Martinez," *La Cruz*, No. 428, p. 205.
2. Ibid: No. 427, p. 175.

CONTENTS

PART I
TRUE DEVOTION TO
THE SPIRIT

PART II
THE GIFTS

PART III
THE FRUITS

PART IV
THE BEATITUDES

PART I
TRUE DEVOTION TO THE SPIRIT

CHAPTER I: INTRODUCTORY

ONE FORTUNATE TENDENCY OF our times has been that which seeks to establish the supernatural life on the solid basis of dogma. Nothing is more right and necessary than this. Life ought to be based on truth; or rather, it is truth itself that descends, so to speak, from the heights of the understanding to pour itself out over the affections, the works, and all the activity of man.

The truths that we beg God to reveal to us are not only "light," but "spirit and life." They are not only a sublime and complete doctrinal system, they are also "words of eternal life"; the exceedingly fruitful seeds that transform souls when the intelligence and the heart are opened to them as to the very substance of life.

Love is the essence of the Christian life. It is the charity poured by the Holy Spirit into souls, the charity which embodies the perfection of all the virtues. But it is a very ordered love, because virtue, according to the beautiful and profound words of St. Augustine, is order in love. And that order is the fruit of light, of dogmatic truth, for, as St. Thomas teaches, it belongs to wisdom to set things in order.

The influence of dogma in the Christian life puts each thing in its place, and thus avoids those pietistic deviations caused by mere personal inclination or lack of instruction. Such deviations, though devout and well-intentioned, hinder the prompt and rich flowering of Christian perfection in souls. It is more important than we sometimes realize to put things in their proper place in the spiritual life.

St. Grignon de Montfort, in his excellent little treatises, *True Devotion to the Most Holy Virgin* and *The Secret of Mary,* which are fortunately circulating among us with a marvelous effect on souls, has done no more than establish the most holy Virgin in her place in Christian piety. The merit of these works consists in this, that they show an understanding of the universal and indispensable function of Mary Immaculate in the sanctification of souls: a traditional doctrine of the Church which obtained the magnificent confirmation of the Holy Apostolic See in modern times when the feast of Mary, Mediatrix of All Graces, was introduced into the liturgy.

St. Grignon de Montfort understood so clearly the place that belongs to Mary in the work of sanctification that he made devotion to this sweet Mother, not something superficial or intermittent, consisting of isolated practices with a special place and hour in our day, but constant and essential, reaching to the very depths of our heart and filling our whole being and all our life like a heavenly perfume.

The method of Grignon de Montfort is not artificial. It does not impose on Christian life the particular note of filial tenderness that the saint himself professed for the Blessed Virgin. It simply shows how to bring to Christian life the traditional Catholic teaching about Mary. That is, it gives her her proper place as universal Mediatrix of the graces of God.

With even greater reason, then — because He is more forgotten — the Holy Spirit must be given His proper place, the place which rightfully belongs to Him in Christian life and Christian perfection. Devotion to the Holy Spirit must become what St. Grignon de Montfort made of devotion to Mary: something not superficial and intermittent, but constant and profound, filling the depths of souls and impregnating lives with the sweet unction of infinite love.

CHRISTIAN LIFE is the reproduction of Jesus in souls; and PERFECTION, the most faithful and perfect reproduction, consists in the transformation of souls into Jesus. This is the doctrine of St. Paul, set forth time and again in his Epistles: "Do you not know yourselves that Christ Jesus is in you?"[1] "For all you who have been baptized into Christ, have put on Christ."[2] "... Christ dwelling through faith in your hearts."[3] "Those whom He has foreknown He has also predestined to become conformed to the image of His Son."[4] These are some of the many expressions of the Apostle relative to CHRISTIAN LIFE.

As for PERFECTION, these profoundly comprehensive words are well known: "It is now no longer I that live, but Christ lives in me."[5] The word "transformation" is also from St. Paul: "But we all, with faces unveiled, reflecting as in a mirror the glory of the Lord, are being transformed into His very image from glory to glory."[6]

Now, how will this mystical reproduction be brought about in souls? In the same way in which Jesus was brought into the world, for God gives a wonderful mark of unity to all His works. Divine acts have a wealth of variety because they are the work of omnipotence; nevertheless, a most perfect unity always shines forth from them because they are the fruit of wisdom; and this divine contrast of unity and variety stamps the works of God with sublime and unutterable beauty.

In His miraculous birth, Jesus was the fruit of heaven and earth. Isaias foretold this in words breathing forth the poetry of an age-old desire and a unique hope, words which the Church lovingly repeats during Advent: "Drop down dew, ye heavens, from above, and let the clouds rain the Just: let the

1. 2 Cor. 13:5.
2. Gal. 3:27.
3. Eph. 3:17.
4. Rom. 8:29.
5. Gal. 2:20.
6. 2 Cor. 3:18.

earth be opened and bud forth a Saviour."[7] The Holy Spirit conveyed the divine fruitfulness of the Father to Mary, and this virginal soil brought forth in an ineffable manner our most loving Saviour, the divine Seed, as the prophets called Him.

This is what we are taught regarding Jesus, with the conciseness and the precision of an article of faith: "who was conceived by the Holy Ghost, ... of the Virgin Mary." That is the way Jesus is always conceived. That is the way He is reproduced in souls. He is always the fruit of heaven and earth. Two artisans must concur in the work that is at once God's masterpiece and humanity's supreme product: the Holy Spirit and the most holy Virgin Mary. Two sanctifiers are necessary to souls, the Holy Spirit and the Virgin Mary, for they are the only ones who can reproduce Christ.

Undoubtedly, the Holy Spirit and the Virgin Mary sanctify us in different ways. The first is the Sanctifier by essence: because He is God, who is infinite sanctity; because He is the personal Love that completes, so to speak, the sanctity of God, consummating His life and His unity, and it belongs to Him to communicate to souls the mystery of that sanctity. The Virgin Mary, for her part, is the co-operator, the indispensable instrument in and by God's design. From Mary's maternal relation to the human body of Christ is derived her relation to His Mystical Body which is being formed through all the centuries until the end of time, when it will be lifted up to the heavens, beautiful, splendid, complete, and glorious.

These two, then, the Holy Spirit and Mary, are the indispensable artificers of Jesus, the indispensable sanctifiers of souls. Any saint in heaven can co-operate in the sanctification of a soul, but his co-operation is not necessary, not profound, not constant; while the co-operation of these two artisans of

---

7. Isa. 45:8.

Jesus of whom we have just been speaking is so necessary that without it souls are not sanctified (and this by the actual design of Providence), and so intimate that it reaches to the very depths of our soul. For the Holy Spirit pours charity into our heart, makes a habitation of our soul, and directs our spiritual life by means of His gifts. The Virgin Mary has the efficacious influence of Mediatrix in the most profound and delicate operations of grace in our souls. And, finally, the action of the Holy Spirit and the co-operation of the most holy Virgin Mary are constant; without them, not one single character of Jesus would be traced on our souls, no virtue grow, no gift be developed, no grace increase, no bond of union with God be strengthened in the rich flowering of the spiritual life.

Such is the place that the Holy Spirit and the Virgin Mary have in the order of sanctification. Therefore, Christian piety should put these two artisans of Christ in their true place, making devotion to them something necessary, profound, and constant.

But all the dogmatic richness and all the practical influence, the treasures of light and life, that are contained in this synthesis, must be brought out by analysis. With divine help, then, let us attempt it in the following pages.

CHAPTER II: THE SOUL'S DELIGHT-FUL GUEST

HOW WONDERFUL IS THE WORK OF the artist! By efforts both ardent and gentle he can penetrate hard and shapeless materials with the light of his soul. The instruments he uses, though often crude, can impart to these materials exquisite proportions and shapes.

That is the way one may conceive the sanctifying work of the Holy Spirit, Artist of souls. Is not sanctity the supreme art? God has only one ideal which, in its prodigious unity and because it is divine, encompasses all the highest forms of beauty. This ideal is Jesus. The Holy Spirit loves Him more than an artist loves his ideal. That love is His being, because the Holy Spirit is nothing but love, the personal Love of the Father and of the Word. With divine enthusiasm He comes to the soul — the soul, breath of the Most High, spiritual light that can merge with uncreated Light, exquisite essence that can be transformed into Jesus, reproducing the eternal ideal.

That which the human artist dreams of without ever being able to attain, the divine Artist accomplishes because He is perfect and infinite. His action is not exterior nor intermittent, but intimate and constant. He enters into the depths of our souls, penetrates the innermost recesses, takes up His permanent dwelling there, to produce later on His magnificent work.

To the Artist of souls, sanctification and possession are the same act: for sanctification is the work of love, and love is possession. The very lowest degree of sanctity demands that the Holy Spirit dwell in our souls, possess them; while supreme sanctity is the supreme possession that the Spirit attains in the soul, the full and perfect possession of love.

Therefore the first relationship that the Holy Spirit has with souls is that of being the delightful Guest — "dulcis Hospes animae" — as the Church calls Him in the inspired prose of the Mass of Pentecost. Without doubt, the entire Blessed Trinity dwells within the soul living the life of grace, as it is to dwell eternally within the soul living the life of glory, which is the full and joyous expansion of the life of grace. Thus Jesus taught us on the night before His death, that night of intimate secrets and sweet effusions: "If anyone love Me he will keep My word, and My Father will love him, and We will come to him and make Our abode with him."[1] Fortunately, this consoling doctrine is familiar to the faithful of our times. But attention should be given to the fact that the Scriptures attribute, in a special manner, this indwelling to the Holy Spirit.

"Do you not know that you are the temple of God and that the Spirit of God dwells in you?"[2] Without this dwelling of the Holy Spirit in us we cannot "become Christ." "If anyone does not have the Spirit of Christ, he does not belong to Christ."[3] Grace and charity, that are the life of our souls, have relationship with the Spirit who dwells in us, because "the charity of God is poured forth in our hearts by the Holy Spirit, who has been given to us."[4] Even the resurrection of the flesh is a consequence of this indwelling of the Holy Spirit, who converts our bodies into His temple. "If the Spirit of Him who raised Jesus from the dead dwells in you, then He who raised Jesus Christ from the dead will also bring to life

---

1. John 14:23.
2. 1 Cor. 3:16.
3. Rom. 8:9.
4. Ibid. 5:5.

your mortal bodies, because of His Spirit who dwells in you."[5]
And the Holy Spirit does not come to us in a transitory manner; infinite Love is not a passing visitor who pays us a call
and then goes away. He establishes in us His permanent
dwelling and lives in intimate union with our souls as their
eternal Guest. Jesus promised this to us on the last night of
His mortal life: "And I will ask the Father and He will give
you another Advocate to dwell with you forever, the Spirit of
truth whom the world cannot receive, because it neither sees
Him nor knows Him. But you shall know Him because He
will dwell with you, and be in you."[6]

Undoubtedly, as we have already said, this permanent and
intimate dwelling in our souls which is attributed by appropriation to the Holy Spirit pertains to all the divine Persons;
but the appropriation is made by the Scriptures, by Jesus Christ
Himself, so we know that it is perfectly founded and admirably efficacious for revealing the Blessed Trinity to us.
And why is this indwelling in souls attributed to the Holy
Spirit? Because it is a work of love. God is in our souls in a
most particular manner because He loves us.

What delight in the thought! It is not because of the
exigencies of His immensity, nor only because our wretchedness demands it, that God establishes His dwelling in souls;
love, which attracts, allures, and makes one overcome all difficulties, makes the God of heaven, who is in love with souls,
come down to them and unite Himself to them in an intimate
and permanent manner. This is love: union or desire of union;
and as the Holy Spirit is the infinite Love of God, to Him is
appropriated this happy name: "the soul's delightful Guest."

The Holy Books give us a foundation for exploring this
mystery of love. We have already seen St. Paul establish a

---

5. Ibid. 8:11.
6. John 14:16-17.

close bond between the Holy Spirit and charity. And St. John, the master of love, completes in a wonderful way the teachings of St. Paul. In his First Epistle, the Beloved Disciple explains the intimate relation that exists between the Holy Spirit and charity. This virtue is the image of God, because "God is love"[7]; and for this reason charity accomplishes the prodigy that "he who abides in love abides in God, and God in him."[8] But the unmistakable sign of the mutual and sweet possession is that we have received the Holy Spirit: "In this we know that we abide in Him and He in us, because He has given us of His Spirit."[9]

The first gift of love is love itself, and all the other gifts emanate from this supreme gift, as from their source. Therefore, the Gift of the love of God is the Holy Spirit. Loving us with the love of friendship and giving us His Spirit is for God one and the same thing. And through His Gift, He gives us all the gifts of His munificence. "Through the Gift, which is the Holy Spirit, are distributed many gifts proper to the members of Christ," says St. Augustine. But of all the gifts which God gives us through His Gift, the most excellent and precious, the created gift which cannot be separated from the uncreated, is charity, the image of the Holy Spirit.

The love of friendship is mutual. God loves us through the Holy Spirit; and that we may correspond to that infinite love with a love created, to be sure, but also supernatural and divine, the Holy Spirit when giving Himself to us pours into our souls the likeness of Himself, which is charity; and this can become so perfect that it can be said that God and we

---

7. 1 John 4:16.
8. Ibid.
9. Ibid. 13.

form one same love, one same spirit, as St. Paul teaches: "He who cleaves to the Lord is one spirit with Him."[10]

There is, then, a very close union between the Holy Spirit and charity: the Holy Spirit does not give Himself to us without pouring charity into our hearts, nor can there be the love of charity in us without the Holy Spirit's coming to us by the very act of loving.

Consequently, the basic reason why God dwells in us, why He remains in us and we in Him, is love. The love of God that descends to the depths of our souls, our love which by its irresistible needs attracts the God of heaven and captivates Him in the bonds of charity — these are two loves that seek each other, find each other, and fuse together in a divine unity. On the part of God it is the Holy Spirit who gives Himself to us, and on our part it is charity, the image of the Holy Spirit, that cannot be separated from the divine Original. Therefore the inspired expression of the Church, "delightful Guest of the soul," encloses a mystery of love.

Undoubtedly, knowledge also makes God dwell in us as in His temple: though not knowledge as such, even of the supernatural order, but only that knowledge called wisdom, which is, as it were, experienced, and which proceeds from love and produces love. "The Son," says St. Thomas Aquinas, "is the Word; not any sort of word, but one who breathes forth Love." Thus too, St. Augustine says that the Son is sent "when He is known and perceived by someone. But the perception signifies experimental knowledge. And this is properly called wisdom."

Some profound considerations result from this doctrine, revealing to us the important part played by the Holy Spirit in the spiritual life.

---

10. 1 Cor. 6:17.

The divine gifts that belong to the understanding make us resemble the Word of God, who is Wisdom engendered by the understanding of the Father, and the gifts that pertain to the will make us resemble the Holy Spirit, who is infinite Love.

Now, on earth, the most perfect gift is charity; consequently, our assimilation with the Holy Spirit is more perfect than our assimilation with the Word of God. But from charity, by which the gifts of the Holy Spirit are ordered in their progress and development, springs that loving wisdom which, according to St. Thomas, accomplishes our resemblance to the Word of God, our transformation into Christ, which is the work of light, and consummates holiness on earth.

In the supernatural order love leads to light; the Holy Spirit leads us to the Word, and through the Word we go to the Father, in whom all life is completed and all movement is converted into rest. And in Him every creature finds its perfection and its happiness, because all things are completed when they return to their principle.

The development of these ideas will reveal to us the economy of the work of sanctification; but in the present chapter it is sufficient for our purpose to establish upon a firm foundation this consoling doctrine: that the Holy Spirit is, in a unique sense, the soul's delightful Guest.

CHAPTER III: THE SUPREME DIRECTOR

THE SOUL'S DELIGHTFUL GUEST does not remain idle in His intimate sanctuary. Being, as the Church calls Him, fire and light, He hardly takes possession of the soul before His beneficent influence extends itself to the whole being and begins with divine activity its work of transformation.

The Holy Spirit lives in the center of the soul, in that profound region of the will where He Himself has diffused charity; and from that center He pours Himself out, so to speak, over the whole man with a divine unction, like the sacred perfume of which the Scriptures speak, which descended from the head of Aaron down his flowing beard and over his vestment to the tassel of his mantle.

Like the victor who, on taking possession of a kingdom, places in each city men to execute his orders and act as his regents governing the place he has conquered, so the Holy Spirit, the loving Conquistador of souls, places some divine gifts in each of the human faculties, that through His holy inspirations the whole man may receive His vivifying influence. Into the intelligence, the supreme faculty of the spirit from which radiates light and order over the whole human being, He pours the gifts of wisdom, of understanding, of counsel, and of knowledge; into the will, the gift of piety; and into the inferior region of the sensible appetites, the gifts of fortitude and fear of God. By means of these gifts the Holy Spirit moves the whole man, becomes Director of the supernatural life, and more — becomes the very soul of our soul and life of our life.

If man had but to accomplish a work of moral perfection according to his human nature, then human reason, a spark from the light of God, would be enough to direct the life of the spirit; but the work that has to be accomplished in man, as we have already said, is divine. It is the reproduction of Jesus, the masterpiece of God, and for such an exalted undertaking the direction of the Holy Spirit is necessary. Sanctity is impossible without this direction, as it is impossible to obtain a finished and perfect work of art without the direction of a master.

The intimate Master of our souls is the Holy Spirit; thus Jesus taught in His discourse at the Last Supper: "The Advocate, the Holy Spirit, whom the Father will send in My name, ... will teach you all things, and bring to your mind whatever I have said to you."[1]

The Holy Spirit teaches everything, not only as earthly masters do, by projecting the light of their explications on the subject of their teaching, but intimately, by communicating a new light, a divine light, to the intelligence itself. "His anointing teaches you concerning all things,"[2] said the Apostle St. John. His teaching is unction. He teaches us by pouring Himself into us gently and penetratingly. His teaching is as a divine caress of love. He teaches us as mothers teach their children, with kisses of love, with an indefinable outpouring of tenderness. We learn from Him as we perceive the fragrance of a perfume, as we savor the sweetness of a fruit, or enjoy the caress of a breeze that enfolds us.

The light of the Holy Spirit is the fruit of love; it is the happy consequence of union. United intimately to divine things through the work of the Holy Spirit, the soul tastes them by a direct divine experience. How profoundly do the

1. John 14:26.
2. 1 John 2:27.

words quoted above from St. John express this: "His anointing teaches you concerning all things."

But light is not the only mark of the direction of the Spirit; there is also sanctity. As the artist is not content with explaining to his pupil the secrets of art, but takes the uncertain hand of the beginner and gently but firmly moves and guides it in order that the beauty of his ideal may be expressed on the canvas, even thus does the Holy Spirit take our faculties and move and guide them, so firmly that they do not stray, and at the same time so gently that our activities continue to be vital, spontaneous, and free. Only the Creator can reach in this way to the depths of our acts and, so far from changing their properties, rather marvelously perfect and elevate them.

The supplications of the Church to the Holy Spirit admirably detail this work of His; in the Sequence of the Mass of Pentecost:

> *Wash the stains of guilt away,*
> *Bend the stubborn heart and will;*
> *Melt the frozen, warm the chill,*
> *Guide the steps that go astray;*

in the hymn "Veni Creator":

> *Kindle with fire from above*
> *Each sense, and fill our hearts with love;*
> *Grant to our flesh, so weak and frail,*
> *That strength of Thine which cannot fail.*

All these, in addition to many other delicate and marvelous operations, are contained in that sweet and firm movement that the Holy Spirit exercises in every human faculty, by reason of which He is called the soul of our soul.

The seven gifts are a divine means for making our soul fit to receive the motion of the Spirit. The celestial influence of this intimate Guest is called inspiration; its action is the breath of wind, delicately soft and irresistibly strong, that impels our life toward heaven, the warm and powerful wind of love that cleanses, eases, rectifies, consoles, refreshes — but also moves, carrying along all that is before it.

Imagine a fine lyre whose strings, perfectly harmonized, vibrate at the blowing of the wind, each giving its own sound and all together composing a beautiful symphony. This is the soul of a just man when the Holy Spirit possesses it fully and has harmonized all the faculties by means of His gifts. Each one of them, like the strings of a living lyre, gives its own sound when the wind of the Spirit blows.

What else would the Holy Spirit, the personal love of God, produce but a song if it is proper to love to sing? And what shall love sing but the Beloved — the divine obsession of the one who loves? What is to be sung but the name of the Beloved, the unique word holding all beauty, that love pronounces? The earth and the heavens sing because love passes through; because the immaculate wings of the Spirit soar above them.

But the song of souls is a new song, because the Spirit infuses new love in them. The song of souls is free. It is not like the song of nature, which is harmonious but compelled, the automatic reproduction, as it were, of the impression the Spirit made in the beginning of time when He moved triumphantly over the fruitful waters. The song of souls is theirs and the Spirit's conjointly, as the sounds given off by the strings of a lyre come also from the artist who makes them vibrate.

Nevertheless, nature and souls sing to the same Beloved, saying the same thing, each in its own language. To live spiritually is to sing, because living spiritually is loving. For the song to be perfect, all the human faculties must be rectified and harmonized, like the strings of a lyre, and the Holy Spirit must inspire the unique song of a unique love.

The true Director of souls, the intimate Master, the soul of the spiritual life, is the Holy Spirit. Without Him, as we have already said, there is no sanctity. The perfection of a soul is measured by its docility to the movement of the Spirit, by the promptitude and fidelity with which its strings produce the divine notes of the song of love. A soul is perfectly holy when the Spirit of love has taken full possession of it, when the divine Artist finds no resistance or dissonance in the strings of that living lyre, but only celestial strains coming forth from it, limpid, ardent, and delightfully harmonized.

The inspirations of the Holy Spirit are not, then, something extraordinary and superfluous in the spiritual life; they are its vital, perfect impulse. Undoubtedly, their infrequency at the beginning of the spiritual life is due precisely to the imperfection of that life — just as the direction of reason is not frequent nor strong in the early years of man's natural life because his development is still imperfect. As the spiritual life grows, the strings of the living lyre of the soul, which before were weak and inharmonious, are attuned and harmonized; the soul becomes marvelously sensible to the movement of the Spirit, and life becomes intense, rich, perfect, holy.

St. Paul expressed this action of the Holy Spirit in souls very well when he said: "For whoever are led by the Spirit of God, they are the sons of God."[3] The Apostle thus makes known a mysterious bond between the movement of the Holy Spirit and the divine adoption. Through the Spirit we become sons of God, and because we are sons we are moved by the Spirit. Thus He is called in the Scriptures "Spirit of adoption . . . by virtue of which we cry, 'Abba! Father!' For the Spirit Himself gives testimony to our spirit that we are sons of God."[4] Without doubt we are sons by grace, and this

---

3. Rom. 8:14.
4. Ibid. 15-16.

precious gift, the true participation in the divine nature, puts us in intimate and special relationship with the divine Persons: it makes us sons of the Father, incorporates us with Jesus, and the Spirit of God becomes in a certain manner our spirit. These relationships are simultaneous; but, in the order of appropriation, the mission of the Holy Spirit is the first in our soul, because the first gift, intimately connected with grace, is charity. The Holy Spirit brings to our souls the fruitfulness of the Father and binds us lovingly to the Son.

And because of this, the Spirit of the Father and of the Son becomes ours in an ineffable way. And just as it is our natural spirit that directs and moves temporal life, so this Spirit of God, ours by the mystery of adoption, moves and directs our life that is for eternity. Because we are sons we are heirs, and "none can receive the inheritance of that land of the blessed, except he be moved and led thither by the Holy Ghost." Thus St. Thomas teaches when he interprets in this sense the words of the Psalmist: "May Your good Spirit guide me on level ground."[5]

This intimate direction of our souls accomplished by the Holy Spirit is something profoundly bound up with the mystery of the spiritual life; it is something which that life demands essentially, just as our natural life demands the movement of our soul. Consequently, the Holy Spirit is truly the soul of our soul and the life of our life.

---

5. Ps. 142:10.

CHAPTER IV: THE GIFT OF GOD

N<small>OT ONLY TO POSSESS US DOES</small> the Holy Spirit live in us, but also to be possessed by us, to be ours. For love must possess, as well as be possessed. He is the Gift of God — "Altissimi Donum Dei." Now, the gift which belonged to the giver becomes the possession of the one who receives it. The Gift of God is ours through the stupendous prodigy of love.

Almost every time that Sacred Scripture speaks of the mission of the Holy Spirit in our souls, we find the word *give.* "I will ask the Father and He will give you another Advocate." "In this we know that we abide in Him and He in us, because He has given us of His Spirit." "For the Spirit had not yet been given, since Jesus had not yet been glorified."[1] "Giving them the Holy Spirit just as He did to us."[2]

The word "give," "gift," has a meaning proper to the Holy Spirit. The Father gave us His Son because He loves us: "God so loved the world that He gave His only-begotten Son."[3] "Through [Him] He has granted us the very great and precious promises."[4] It is characteristic of love to give gifts, but the first gift, the gift par excellence, is love itself. The Holy Spirit is the Love of God; therefore He is the Gift of God. God gave His Son to us through love; consequently, that inexpressible gift is through the first Gift, through the Gift of all gifts.

Now to the giving on the part of God corresponds possession on our part. We have what God has given us. The

---

1. John 7:39.
2. Acts 15:8.
3. John 3:16.
4. 2 Pet. 1:4.

Holy Spirit is then something of our own, and we can call Him, according to St. Thomas, "the spirit of man, or a gift bestowed on man."

Have we thought of what possession of the Gift of God means in our souls? Have we thought of the divine significance of that rigorously exact phrase: "The Holy Spirit is ours"? Possession is proper to love. In its first stage it is a desire of possession; perfect love is the joy of possession, and love that is consummated is the abyss of possession.

In earthly love how imperfect, how ephemeral, how inconstant our possession is! In divine love, however, the one who is loved is necessarily possessed and with a more profound intimacy than we know, and so unchangingly — on God's part always and on ours when love attains its perfection — that St. Paul exclaims: "I am sure that neither death, nor life, nor angels, nor principalities, nor things present, nor things to come, nor powers, nor height, nor depth, nor any other creature will be able to separate us from the love of God, which is in Christ Jesus our Lord."[5]

The soul in grace has this ineffable intimacy with the three Persons of the Most Holy Trinity. But the first intimacy is with the Holy Spirit, because He is the first Gift. Charity, on which this close intimacy is founded, is a disposition for receiving the Holy Spirit and assimilation with Him.

Undoubtedly the root of our intimacy with God is grace, as St. Thomas teaches: "By the gift of sanctifying grace the rational creature is perfected so that it can freely use not only the created gift itself, but enjoy also the divine Person Himself; and so the invisible mission[6] takes place according to the

---

5. Rom. 8:38-39.
6. The word "mission" as it is used with regard to the Holy Spirit implies a new and special mode of presence of the Person who is sent, in those who receive Him, as St. Thomas observes (cf. Ia, q. 43).

gift of sanctifying grace; and yet the divine Person Himself
is given."

But grace is only the root. The immediate reason why any
of the divine Persons gives Himself to us is a gift which
emanates from grace and which our soul assimilates with the
Person we possess. "The soul is made like to God by grace.
Hence for a divine Person to be sent to anyone by grace, there
must needs be a likening of the soul to the divine Person who
is sent, by some gift of grace." And as the Holy Ghost is Love,
the soul is assimilated to the Holy Ghost by charity.

We possess God because He gives Himself to us, but His
first Gift is the Holy Spirit. Our first intimacy, then, is with
the Holy Spirit. This does not mean that we can possess one
divine Person without possessing the others, for They are inseparable; but, according to the order of appropriation, we
possess the Father and the Son because we possess the Holy
Spirit, who is the first Gift of God.

But let us note the just-quoted teaching of St. Thomas,
whose austere precision, entirely free from the exaggerations
of enthusiasm, gives to his words an admirably profound
meaning: Through grace, the soul can not only use the created
gift freely, but can also *enjoy the divine Person.* And this is
not a light phrase that escaped the holy Doctor without his
measuring its profundity. It is a doctrine that he sets forth
fully when he explains the term *gift* as applied to the Holy
Spirit: "The word *gift* imports an aptitude for being given.
And what is given has an aptitude or relation both to the giver
and to that to which it is given. For it would not be given by
anyone, unless it was his to give; and it is given to someone to
be his. Now a divine Person is said to belong to another,
either by origin, as the Son belongs to the Father, or as possessed by another. But we are said to possess what we can
freely use or enjoy as we please: and in this way a divine

Person cannot be possessed, except by a rational creature united to God. Other creatures can be moved by a divine Person, not, however, in such a way as to be able to enjoy the divine Person, and to use the effect thereof. The rational creature does sometimes attain thereto, as when it is made partaker of the divine Word and of the Love proceeding, so as freely to know God truly and to love God rightly. Hence the rational creature alone can possess the divine Person. Nevertheless, in order that it may possess him in this manner, its own power avails nothing: hence this must be given it from above; for that is said to be given to us which we have from another source."

What profound and consoling truths! The Holy Spirit is ours. We can enjoy Him and use His effects. It is in our power to use Him; we can enjoy Him when we wish. Each one of these truths deserves to be extensively and lovingly meditated upon.

We have already said that possession is the ideal of love: mutual, perfect, enduring possession. God, in loving us and permitting us to love Him, divinely satisfied this exigency of love: He wished to be ours and He wished us to be His.

But this possession is not superficial and transient, as in human love. It is something very serious, very profound and lasting. God gives Himself to us with ardor and vehemence, with the deep truth of His infinite love. He does not live *with* us, but *in* us. He does not wish to come only at our call to satisfy our desires, like those who love each other on earth; He gives Himself to us, delivers Himself to us, makes us the Gift of Himself, that we may use it according to our pleasure.

To use that Gift is to enjoy it for it is the supreme end of our being, our life's happiness; and no other use can be made of happiness than to enjoy it. We are able to *make use of* His other gifts, the effects of His love; we can only *enjoy* His Gift.

It is in our power to enjoy that happiness which we carry within our souls whenever we wish to, for what is ours is ours to dispose of. The Gift that has been given to us, that we possess, is ours, and we may freely make use of God. The sweet familiarity with which the saints treat God, as well as their confident boldness in drawing near to Him, attracts our attention. There is nothing strange about it; the wonderful, the amazing, thing is that God loves us and that He wants to be loved by us; the rest is the logical consequence of that love, because, as Lacordaire has so profoundly said: "Love in heaven and on earth has the same name, the same essence, the same law." From the moment in which God determined to love, He became ours. What is strange about our using freely and trustingly that which belongs to us?

Heaven itself is a natural consequence of this love. There our joy will be perfect and complete, while the joy that we have in our exile is imperfect, mixed with pain and hope. For the same gift is enjoyed in a different manner when conditions change, and especially when the capacity of the one who possesses it changes. But the root of both joys, that of heaven and that of earth, is the same. It is the Gift of love.

To enjoy God is to know Him and to love Him. But it is not just any sort of knowledge or any sort of love that gives this joy. It is the intimate knowledge that penetrates His truth and the profound love which unites us with His sovereign goodness. For us to attain such a knowledge and such a love, our own strength is not sufficient; we need to receive from God Himself His gifts: participation in the divine Word and personal Love.

To enjoy the Holy Spirit is to love; to enjoy the Word is to know. But just as the divine Persons are inseparable, those

divine joys are also intimately bound together. Intimate knowledge produces love; profound love is a source of light. Whoever enjoys the Son and the Holy Spirit attains to the joy of
the Father, plunging himself, so to speak, into the bosom
of immense tenderness, into the ocean from which all good
proceeds.

"If thou didst know the Gift of God!" said Jesus to the
Samaritan woman.[7] If only we knew the treasures that are
hidden in the higher life of the soul, the riches of that divine
world into which the Gift of God introduces us! The world
cannot receive these holy realities, nor does it even suspect
them, because "it neither sees nor knows" the Gift of God.
But from how many souls that could know the divine Gift are
God's wonders hidden!

Undoubtedly that full participation in the Word and in
the Holy Spirit that makes us know Him intimately and love
Him profoundly, is sanctity, is union. But hardly does the life
of grace begin in souls when God gives His gifts to them and
they begin to find their joy in Him. The spiritual life is always
substantially the same from the beginning until the magnificence of its full flowering.

Before the soul reaches the maturity of union it possesses
the Gift of God, but as one possessing a treasure whose value
is unknown and whose advantages cannot be fully enjoyed
immediately. This imperfect spiritual life is the true life, but
it does not yet have full consciousness nor full possession of
itself. There are such heavy shadows in the understanding!
There is still such a mixture of earthly affections in the heart!
The soul is so bound to creatures! It does not know what it
possesses, nor has it the holy liberty of the children of God
to lift its wings and soar aloft to the enjoyment of Him.

_____

7. John 4:10.

This is precisely the work of the Holy Spirit in souls: to bring to holy maturity, to happy plenitude, that germ of life which He Himself deposited in them.

The spiritual life is the mutual possession of God and the soul, because it is essentially their mutual love. When the Holy Spirit possesses a soul completely, and the soul attains the full possession of the Gift of God, this is union, perfection, sanctity.

Then the soul participates in such a way in the divine Word, and in the Love that proceeds from the Word, that it can freely know God with an intimate and true knowledge, and love Him with a true and profound love. Then the soul belongs wholly to God, and God to the soul. Then God works in the soul as one would work in that which belongs to him completely, and the soul enjoys God with confidence, with liberty, with the sweet intimacy that we use with our own.

If only we knew the Gift of God! If only we knew the goodness and love of God, and the happiness and riches that are contained for us in this profound invocation of the Church: "Gift of God most high!"

CHAPTER V: THE DIVINE CYCLE

AS WE HAVE SEEN, OUR FIRST INTIMACY is with the Holy Spirit because He is the first Gift of God, the excelling Gift. Through the Holy Spirit, the Father gave us His Son, for He gave Him to us through love. The Spirit brought to the Virgin Mary the divine fecundity of the Father, and the Word was made flesh. "The Holy Spirit shall come upon thee and the power of the Most High shall overshadow thee,"[1] said the archangel to Mary.

The Evangelists are careful to show us the Holy Spirit in the principal mysteries of Jesus, to make us understand that each time Jesus is given, the giving is inspired and, as it were, preceded by the divine Gift par excellence. The Holy Spirit leads Jesus to the desert when He begins His public life.[2] He appears in the form of a dove over the head of Jesus in the Jordan, and as a luminous cloud on Thabor.[3] That same Love impelled the eternal Priest to perform the supreme act of His life: the double immolation of the Last Supper and of Calvary. For St. Paul tells us that Christ "through the Holy Spirit offered Himself unblemished unto God."[4]

And Jesus returns to the Father, taking with Him regenerated humanity. As His life on earth is about to end, He gives us a synthesis of His divine mission: "I have glorified Thee on earth; I have accomplished the work that Thou hast given Me to do. . . . I have manifested Thy name to the men whom Thou hast given Me out of the world. . . . But now I am coming to

---

1. Luke 1:35.
2. Cf. Matt. 4:1.
3. Cf. Luke 3:22; Matt. 17:5.
4. Hebr. 9:14.

Thee ... that they may be perfected in unity ... Father, I will that where I am, they also whom Thou hast given Me may be with Me; in order that they may behold My glory, which Thou hast given Me, because Thou hast loved Me before the creation of the world."[5] The cycle of love is completed in the Father, for all things find their full perfection when they return to their origin.

But that divine cycle must be repeated; always commencing, always ending, until the end of time. The Holy Spirit comes down again on the feast of Pentecost, not only in the bosom of the Most Pure Virgin, but over all flesh, in order to reproduce Jesus mystically in the Church, and to renew in her, across the centuries, the mysteries of His life. At the end of time the Church will have the right to exclaim, like Jesus in the Cenacle: "I have glorified Thee on earth.... But now I am coming to Thee ... that they may be perfected in unity." And in the splendid glory of the last day, the great cycle of love will be consummated in the bosom of the Father.

Now the divine cycle must be reproduced in each soul, for this is the glorious destiny of souls. The Gift of God will come to each one of them as it came to the Virgin Mary; and since, after Love itself, the Gift of divine love is Jesus, the Holy Spirit will bring to each soul the divine fecundity of the Father; in each the Word will take flesh mystically, and Jesus will sing the poem of His divine mysteries; and each, through Him, will go to the Father. Nobody goes to the Father except through Him. By returning to its origin and completing the divine cycle, each soul will find its happiness in the loving bosom of the Father.

Many souls, resisting until the end, will weep over their eternal sterility in desolation, hopelessly removed from Love. Others, not docile enough to Love nor very generous in their

5. John 17:4, 6, 13, 23-24.

correspondence to it, departing from this world bearing but a trace of the likeness of Jesus, will be perfected in the fire of purgatory that they may enter into the joy of the Lord. Only the souls of the saints, letting themselves be possessed by "Christ's bestowal,"[6] will fully accomplish the designs of God, and in them the work of the Holy Spirit will appear splendidly finished and perfected. The divine cycle will have been completed in all its majestic fullness.

Let us contemplate carefully this perfect work of infinite love.

All the economy of the supernatural order, the whole magnificent plan of God for repairing the dignity of human nature even more admirably than when He elevated it in the beginning, is expressed in those beautiful words of the Canon of the Mass: "Through Him, and with Him, and in Him, be unto Thee, O God the Father almighty, in the unity of the Holy Spirit, all honor and glory." The glory of the Father: a new glory, superior to that of the natural order because it is of the supernatural, the divine order — this is the end of the Incarnation and of the Redemption, of the Church and of the sanctification of souls. The whole mystery of Christ has this most exalted end. He Himself teaches us that He came to glorify the Father; and when He had completed the divine poem to the glory of the Father by completing His mortal life, He wished, in the immensity of His filial tenderness, that this poem of glory should not end, that its harmonies should continue to resound, strong and immortal, throughout eternity.

But only the voice of Jesus can intone that canticle; only through Him can the Father receive that glory. All those who in time and eternity will glorify the Father will do it through Him. Through Him the men of the Old Testament glorified

---

6. Eph. 4:7.

God; through Him the Church has glorified Him and will con‑
tinue to glorify Him.

It is necessary, then, for the voices of souls to be united to
the voice of Jesus that they may ascend to the Father, that they
may ring with the divine accent that is pleasing to Him. All
glorification of the Father is done through Jesus. "Without
Me you can do nothing."[7] Without Him there is no spotless
purity, no selfless love, no heroic sacrifice. Without Him noth‑
ing exists, nothing is of value in the divine order.

In His desire to glorify the Father, in His tenderness for
souls, Jesus did more than give them His merits and unite Him‑
self with them to intone the hymn of glorification: He united
Himself with souls in an ineffable manner so that every voice
might be His voice, every love His love, and all glory His
glory; that in Him the heavenly Father might receive all honor
and glory.

Fully to glorify the Father, it is necessary to be transformed
into Jesus; because the glorification of the Father is His work,
and "in order to do the work of Jesus it is necessary to be
Jesus," according to the profound words of Monsignor Gay.

The end of the sanctification of souls is the glory of the
Father; the essence of that marvelous work is transformation
into Jesus. This is a work of light, of wisdom; for the Word
of God is the Wisdom of the Father, the Light of light, the
Brightness of eternal light. To be transformed into Jesus is to
bear His image, uncreated Wisdom, graven in our souls with
strokes of divine light.

Undoubtedly, through sanctifying grace itself, which is a
participation in the divine nature, we resemble God and pos‑
sess Him; but the further, special assimilation with each one
of the divine Persons and individual possession of them comes

---

7. John 15:5.

from supernatural gifts that have sanctifying grace as their origin. Light and its beneficence come to us from a heavenly body; but its richness, the caress of its warmth, its ultimate efficacy, come from the different elements in the ray. So also grace, with its retinue of gifts, produces all the supernatural wonders in our soul, makes us resemble the divine Son, and, more marvelous than the sun's ray, brings us to the very focal point from whence it springs.

The gifts that make us resemble each one of the divine Persons are distinct. The gifts of understanding trace on the soul the image of the Word, who is the Light of wisdom, and by a special mission make us possess uncreated Wisdom. The gifts of love make us resemble the Holy Spirit, who is infinite Love, and by opening the way to His mission, put us in the most happy possession of Him. That is the way St. Thomas teaches this truth:

"The soul is made like to God by grace. Hence for a divine Person to be sent to anyone by grace, there must needs be a likening of the soul to the divine Person who is sent, by some gift of grace. Because the Holy Ghost is Love, the soul is assimilated to the Holy Ghost by the gift of charity. Hence the mission of the Holy Ghost is according to the mode of charity. Whereas the Son is the Word; not any sort of word, but one who breathes forth Love. . . . Thus the Son is sent, not in accordance with every and any kind of intellectual perfection, but according to the intellectual illumination which breaks forth into the affection of love."

As St. Thomas notes above, the divine likeness of the Word does not shine on the soul from any source of light as such, but only from the light of love: from the loving knowledge which gives us in a certain sense the sweet experience of God, and which inflames the heart with the fire of holy affections. Therefore St. Thomas adds: "Hence St. Augustine plainly says

(*De Trinitate,* IV, 20) 'The Son is sent whenever He is known and perceived by anyone.' Now, perception implies a certain experimental knowledge; and this is properly called wisdom, as it were a sweet knowledge."

The image of the Word — uncreated Wisdom — is the participated Wisdom which communicates to us the most excellent of the gifts of the Spirit. "Now men are called the children of God in so far as they participate in the likeness of the only-begotten and natural Son of God, according to Rom. 8:29, 'whom He foreknew . . . to be made conformable to the image of His Son,' who is wisdom begotten. Hence by participating in the gift of wisdom, man attains to the sonship of God."

Through the gift of wisdom the soul becomes like to the Word and possesses Him, for by that gift there is a mission of the Son of God. To be transformed into Jesus is therefore to share fully the gift of wisdom. But this gift has its roots in charity; it is the light that springs forth from love, that grows when love increases, that reaches the fullness of its splendor when charity has attained its perfect development. One who possesses the gift of wisdom sees because he loves; he knows divine things because he is intimately united to them, because he savors and enjoys them in an ineffable way. He sees because "he looks through the eyes of his beloved," as someone has said in the inimitable language of love. St. Thomas says in his austere and very exact style: "The infused wisdom which is a gift, is not the cause but the effect of charity."

Charity, created likeness of the Holy Spirit and foundation for the possession of infinite Love and intimacy with Him, leads us to wisdom, which gives us the image, the possession, and the intimacy of the Word of God. The Holy Spirit takes us to Jesus; He makes us Jesus by transforming us into Him. This is His work; nobody can be conformed to Jesus except in the unity of the Holy Spirit. "Likewise," says St. Thomas, "the Holy Ghost is called the Spirit of adoption in so far as we receive from Him the likeness of the natural Son, who is the begotten Wisdom."

This is the divine cycle in the sanctification of souls: nobody can go to the Father except through Jesus; nobody can go to Jesus except through the Holy Spirit. Through Jesus, with Jesus, and in Jesus souls glorify the Father in the unity of the Holy Spirit forever and ever.

All the supernatural virtues and all the gifts of the Holy Spirit come to the soul with Him. It is through the virtues, first of all, that the Holy Spirit purifies souls so that charity may freely develop in them and the Spirit Himself may be able to strengthen and to perfect in them His loving possession. When the soul has been purified through the virtues, the Holy Spirit more surely possesses it. Now, by means of His gifts, He purifies it more thoroughly and harmonizes everything until, in perfect peace, penetrated with charity, now sovereign in it, and fully possessed by the Holy Spirit, the soul is transformed into Jesus through the fullness of the gift of wisdom.

The peak of this divine ascension of the soul is *transforming union,* which is characterized by a very intimate relation with the Word of God, through a transformation into the Word Incarnate. This transformation, which is the fruit of love, is essentially a transformation of light. We have seen that St. Paul speaks of it thus: "But we all, with faces unveiled, reflecting as in a mirror the glory of the Lord, are being transformed into His very image from glory to glory, as through the Spirit of the Lord." It is accomplished through the fullness of the gift of wisdom, which undoubtedly brings with it a particular mission of the Son, and consequently a special and perfect possession of Him.

When the soul has attained this most perfect union, it understands completely these words of St. Thomas Aquinas, already quoted: "The rational creature does sometimes attain thereto, as when it is made partaker of the divine Word and of the Love proceeding, so as freely to know God truly and to love God rightly." Therefore, the saints are able to enjoy God; intimate familiarity with the divine Persons is something habitual and proper to their state.

This life of Jesus in souls is like a mystical prolongation of His mortal life; it is like a mystical incarnation in souls by which He renews, mystically also, the mysteries of His life — now those of His infancy, sometimes those of His public life, at times those of His passion, and again, those of His Eucharistic life — according to the profound and loving designs of God in His saints.

But let us note the marvelous unity of the works of God. This mystical incarnation in souls is produced in the image and likeness of the divine Incarnation of the Word in the immaculate bosom of Mary. The transforming union is the work of the Holy Spirit, who brings to souls the divine fecundity of the Father. But in this mystic work, as in the divine Incarnation, the Holy Spirit requires the co-operation of the creature; the soul overshadowed by the Holy Spirit, guided and moved and made fruitful, so to say, by Him, forms Jesus in itself. The soul that has arrived at divine union experiences all the noble and legitimate manifestations of human love because the love of God condenses them all in its eminent perfection; that soul can be called mystically "mother of Jesus," as the divine Master Himself taught us with these words: "Whoever does the will of My Father in heaven, he is My brother and sister and mother."[8] And the passive character

8. Matt. 12:50.

belonging to the soul in the mystic formation of Jesus — not because it does not work but because it is moved by the Holy Spirit — leads us to recognize this mystical maternity. Thus Father Thery, O. P., when explaining the character of fourteenth-century Dominican mysticism, cited these words as the proper doctrine for that spiritual school: "In the spiritual life, in the generation of the Word in us, we are 'mothers,' that is, the passive element."

In the mortal life of Christ, as in His mystic life in the Church and in souls, the divine procedure does not vary. St. Thomas summarizes it: "The Holy Ghost manifests the Son, as the Son manifests the Father."

The soul transformed into Jesus can do the work of Jesus, which is to glorify the Father. Thus the divine Jesus leads souls to the Father, in whom all perfection is consummated, because all things find their happiness when they return to their beginning.

CHAPTER VI: THE MOTION OF THE HOLY SPIRIT THROUGH THE GIFTS

E HAVE COMPARED THE sanctifying work of the Holy Spirit to the artist's delicate reproduction of his ideal on canvas or in marble. We know the intimate sanctuary where the divine Artist works, His spiritual instruments, and His marvelous technique. To put it briefly, we may say that the Holy Spirit enters into the most interior part of our being, possesses us, lets Himself be possessed by us, and, in an embrace of divine love, produces in our souls the radiant transformation He desires.

On the night of love when Jesus made us His friends, He revealed His secrets to us, and we heard from His own lips the unfathomable promise that the Spirit of Truth would teach us all things.

The operation of the Holy Spirit in our souls is motion. He sanctifies us by directing all our activities with the sweetness of love and the efficacy of omnipotence. He is the only One who can move us in this way because He alone can penetrate into the hidden sanctuary of the soul, the enclosed garden, invisible to creatures. He is the only One who can move us in this way because, being omnipotent, He possesses the divine secret of touching the source of human activities without depriving them of their vitality or their freedom.

This sanctifying movement of the Holy Spirit is something special, even among the movements of the supernatural order. In the other movements, the Holy Spirit assists our weakness but leaves the management of our acts to our superior faculties: the reason directs and deliberates, the will works in the region of its own activity. But in this very special movement the Holy Spirit takes up His abode in the deepest, the most intimate and most active part of our being. He constitutes Himself the immediate director of the soul, which in its full strength and freedom moves only under His inspiration.

This intimate and very special movement is the work of love. It is founded on love, caused by love, and leads to love.

The Holy Spirit must be intimately united to a soul in order to move it. He moves us because He loves us and is loved by us. He moves us in the measure of our mutual possession. We might say that His movement is the caress of infinite Love; that the Holy Spirit moves us because in His intimate fusion with our soul, which is the work of charity, His divine movements, His holy palpitations, make themselves felt throughout the whole man, who is one with Him.

Without this movement of the Holy Spirit it is impossible, normally, to save our souls and especially to attain Christian perfection. Man's reason, even assisted by God's light and enriched with the supernatural virtues, is no more than a pupil in the divine art. Now, the pupil will never accomplish such a work of art as the reproduction of Jesus if he does not depend on the direction and immediate intervention of the Master, who alone is in possession of the ideal in its magnificent fullness and of the secret procedure of His art.

Undoubtedly it is the part of the pupil, under the careful direction of the Master, to prepare the canvas on which the fine lines of Jesus will be sketched by the Artist's hand; it is his part to make ready the marble so that the Holy Spirit can breathe into it the light of His ideal, for God disposes all things with admirable gentleness. But the exquisite work, the delicate and perfect art, the masterful strokes, the touch of divine light, the immaterial form, the living palpitation, the *quid divinum,* only the Master's hand can impart to the stainless canvas, the immaculate marble, of our souls. In every art there is something incommunicable that belongs only to genius; in the divine art there is something incommunicable and infinite that belongs only to God.

Both the Master and the disciple have their own instruments of work. For the disciple, they are the virtues; for the Master, the seven gifts. The virtues are undoubtedly the precious means of sanctification, but they are our means; the gifts are the instruments of the Holy Spirit. The virtues are divine brushes, but they are managed by man. If the gifts did not come to their aid, the pupil's work could hardly be accomplished. The handiwork of the Master is achieved by these divine, mysterious instruments, the gifts.

Now this is the essential difference between the virtues and the gifts: the first are made to be exercised under the direction of reason; the second are exercised under the immediate direction of the Holy Spirit.

The virtues in the supernatural order are without doubt divine; as to their origin, for God infuses them; as to their end, for they lead to God; as to their object, for they produce the work of sanctification. But the virtues are managed by men, and they have consequently a human mark, just as the pupil's timid, faltering style is revealed in his first hesitating lines. They do not yet show the mark of genius, the fullness, the boldness, the sublimity, of the Master, the divine stamp of Him who is called "the Finger of God's right hand."

The gifts, on the contrary, do bear this stamp. Without the gifts the work of perfection is impossible. As we have said, it requires the immediate direction of the Holy Spirit; and the human faculties could not receive the motion of the

Spirit without the gifts that He Himself places at the fountainhead of our activity to receive His sanctifying motion, His divine inspirations, His vivifying breath.

The gifts of the Holy Spirit have been forgotten, like the Spirit Himself. Many desiring to be "practical and solid" think too much about the work of man, and little, much too little, about the work of God. They exalt the virtues, and that is well; but they forget the gifts, and that is ingratitude and baseness. The gifts are also necessary to salvation, and furthermore the finest, the most exquisite part of the work of sanctification belongs to them. Perhaps it is because the gifts are forgotten that so many souls miss the designs of God, and so many others, capable of high perfection, drag themselves along in effortless mediocrity.

But let us continue our study of the movement of the Holy Spirit. Is it possible to determine the meaning and direction of that movement? Jesus said to Nicodemus: "The wind blows where it will."[1] It is certainly impossible to determine the precise operations of the Holy Spirit in souls, they are so hidden, so mysterious, so unexpected! But let us supplicate Him to reveal to us the general direction of His holy movements.

The course of the Spirit is invariable and immense; with His immaculate wings the divine Dove always describes a circle loving and infinite. He comes from the Father and from the Son, and back to these divine Persons He bends His majestic flight, drawing after Him in gentle impetuosity the souls that are docile to His inspirations. From whence is Love to come if not from the bosom of Love? And where is Love to complete its magnificent circular movement if not in its own unfathomable breast?

The ideal of the Holy Spirit when moving a soul with His gifts is not, we have said, the same as the ideal of the reason

---

1. John 3:8.

when it moves the faculties by means of the virtues. St. Thomas Aquinas teaches that the acts of the virtues and the acts of the gifts conform to distinct rules: human in the first, divine in the second.

Each artist has his ideal; each movement, its principle and its rule. When the pupil moves the brush the rule that inspires the movement is the ideal of the master, although the pupil understands it but poorly, his mind not being completely open to its beauty. But when the master, transported by inspiration, himself moves the brush, the norm of the movement is higher, broader, more beautiful. It is the sublime, luminous, fruitful ideal of genius.

When reason directs the acts of the virtues, its norm is human; or rather, the divine ideal is adjusted to the narrow mold of reason. But when the Holy Spirit moves by means of His gifts, the norm is enlarged. It is the norm without the veils of humanity, the ideal in all its magnificent brilliance. It is God Himself shared by man; as if man, under the impulse of the Spirit, no longer worked humanly, but became God by participation, as St. Thomas boldly puts it.

And, continues the holy Doctor, as the method corresponds to the rule, as the ideal leaves its unmistakable stamp on the works that it inspires, so man's work bears the particular character of the human ideal, with the limitations, the timidity, and the uncertainty that belong to human nature. But when man works illuminated by the divine ideal of the Spirit, his acts have the unmistakable mark of the divine; they show the gentle operation of the divine Dove that lifts the soul to heaven on its shining wings.

With reference to the divine appropriations, we might say that the ideal of the acts performed under the inspiration of the Holy Spirit corresponds to the Father. The ideal is the first exemplar of the work. The Father is the beginning; the work of sanctification is a work of paternity and adoption; from the Father "all fatherhood in heaven and on earth receives its name."[2] And the end of perfection is Jesus, for Jesus is the image of the Father. During the days of His mortal life He sought the ideal of His acts in the bosom of the Father. The will of the Father, which He came upon earth to accomplish, and the glory of the Father, which formed the one great desire of His soul, appear in the Holy Gospel as His supreme norms. In the most solemn moments of His life the Son lifted His profoundly understanding eyes to the Father, and seemed to gaze with all intentness and sweetness upon that ocean of light.

In order to reach us, this unique light has to be dispersed. It has to be adjusted to the capacity of each one of the seven gifts, as the ray is diffused in the colors of the spectrum. Only God can contain Himself in His infinite unity; in us, especially in exile, the facets of His unique beauty must appear one by one. In the gift of fear, He is the sovereign we revere as the Master of life and death; in fortitude, He is the omnipotent force that delivers itself into the hands of weakness; in piety, He is the Father to whom we must adhere with filial affection, extolling His glory; in counsel, He is the eternal and supreme norm of human action; in knowledge, the inexhaustible exemplar of creatures; in understanding, the supernatural end that sheds light on all knowledge. And in wisdom, He is the focal point that illumines the soul because He is the focal point of love, and because He and Wisdom, united in an embrace of love, have revealed with love's gentleness the secret of all truth.

But under all its indescribable aspects it is the same ideal: it is God, it is the Father, from whose loving bosom comes the Spirit bringing divine fruitfulness to the soul. Like heavenly

---

2. Eph. 3:15.

dew the divine fecundity fructifies the earth of the soul that it may produce a celestial harvest. And note well that the soul does not remain idle. Its activity is more intense and complete under the impulse of the gifts than when it is exercising the virtues. The soul does not move itself through the gifts, it is moved by the Holy Spirit. Therefore, as we have previously said, the acts of the gifts have a certain passive character, and the soul is as a mother, fruitful under the divine fecundity of the Holy Spirit.

The spiritual life in its most exalted and perfect sense consists in the adaptation of the soul to the divine norm, to the ideal of the Father. The Holy Spirit is the Artist who unites in a kiss of love the Father and the transformed soul.

Little by little, under the vivifying influence of the Spirit, under the divine action of the gifts, the soul adapts itself more and more perfectly to the infinite Exemplar, as under the inspired blows of the chisel, the life of the ideal becomes alive in the resplendent whiteness of the marble. One after another the gifts by their cleansing action will take away from the soul the impurities characteristic of human misery. The gentle brilliance of heavenly light will descend upon the purified soul and the pale outlines of the ideal will begin to appear, as the stars come out in the quiet splendor of twilight. Then all is harmony in the soul; all desires are fused in the oneness of a conquered love; all the scattered lights are unified in the gloriously divine theme. The work is about to appear in its magnificent beauty. The realization of the ideal in the soul is but the image of the Father; the created yet supernatural reproduction, full of light and truth, of that unique, infinite, and consubstantial image of the Father, the Word, who on taking flesh willed to be called Jesus.

By a miracle of love, the ideal and the work of art seem to be one. The scene of Thabor is reproduced; in the midst of the luminous cloud of the Spirit, the soul transformed into Jesus reflects in its white vesture the brilliance of glory. In the silence there echoes over that happy soul, like a beautiful canticle, the voice of the Father exclaiming with divine tenderness: "This is My beloved Son."[3]

The Spirit has completed the divine circle of His flight. The Father and the Son, uniting in Their eternal kiss of love, join the soul to Their embrace. . . .

---

3 Matt. 3:17, 17:5; Mark 9:6; Luke 9:35; 2 Pet. 1:17.

CHAPTER VII: THE SOUL'S RE-SPONSE

ASSUREDLY, WE MIGHT STUDY AT MUCH greater length the marvelous action of the Holy Spirit in souls. But since it is our purpose merely to establish the dogmatic foundations for this devotion, and not to set forth now in full the beautiful and inexhaustible theology of the Holy Spirit, it will be helpful to examine these foundations as a whole before starting to build on them.

Like the traveler pitching his tent in the desert, the Holy Spirit takes possession of souls as their most sweet Guest. But unlike the traveler, who folds his tent as morning breaks, the eternal Guest stays on. The tent He pitches on the soil of our barrenness is something divine, a sketch, a reflection, of our heavenly home: grace that divinizes the soul; divine charity, the supernatural image of the Spirit who pours Himself into our hearts; all the virtues and gifts. These are the conditions of His indwelling, that He may begin His work of sanctification, and direct us with the strong, gentle influence of love.

His ideal is to produce Jesus in us, and through Jesus and with Jesus, to take us to the bosom of the Trinity and glorify the Father with the supreme glorification of Jesus. Through the shadows of faith we will try to get a glimpse of this divine work; to see how, under the influence of the Holy Spirit, souls are purified, illuminated, and enkindled until they are transformed into Jesus, who is the ultimate ideal of God's love and of the aspirations of the soul, the glorious summit of the mystical ascent where we find peace and happiness: where we find God.

What is devotion to the Holy Spirit but a loving and constant co-operation with His divine influence, with His sanctifying work? To be devoted to the Holy Spirit is to open our soul for Him to dwell there, to dilate our heart that He may anoint it with His divine charity, to deliver our whole being up to Him that He may possess it with His gifts, to give Him our life that He may transform it into a divine one, to put into His hands the shapeless block of our imperfection that He may mold it to the divine image of Jesus.

To be devoted to the Holy Spirit is to possess Him and to let ourselves be loved and moved according to His good pleasure; to permit the divine Artist to destroy in us all that is opposed to His holy designs: all the bad, all the earthly, and all the humanly weak; and to let Him infuse into us a new life, the marvelous participation in the life of God.

What broad and heavenly vistas spread before us if we meditate on these truths with the help of God's light!

We have seen the action of the Holy Spirit in our souls. Now we shall examine our co-operation with His wonderful influence. This co-operation must be a "consecration" — a word sometimes taken in a very superficial sense. Some think that in order to consecrate themselves to the Holy Spirit, it is enough for them to recite devoutly some prescribed prayer. The prayer may be beautiful and meaningful, but the wealth of thought and beauty it embodies will often remain unrealized; its influence will be only ephemeral and transitory. It is a good and holy thing to say the prayer provided it is said, not as a mere formula, but as a sincere expression of the promises we intend to fulfill during our whole life: provided it is truly the beginning of a new life.

When a temple is consecrated to God it is a place set apart for Him alone. The greatest possible purity and solidity, the truest art, are used in its construction; and after it is magnificently ornamented, it is offered to God, to be His forever. All around the temple is the land that belongs to the children of men. The temple is the gate of heaven, the house of God; outside it one can do all that is lawful; within, one can only give glory to God.

Now the Scriptures tell us very definitely that we are temples of the Holy Spirit. St. Paul says: "Do you not know that you are the temple of God and that the Spirit of God dwells in you?"

We were consecrated temples of the Holy Spirit on the day of our baptism. This is clearly set down in the ritual prescribed for the administration of the sacrament: the priest breathes three times in the face of the one who is going to be baptized and says: "Go out from him, unclean spirit, and give place to the Most Holy Spirit." And making the sign of the cross on the forehead and breast, he says: "Be faithful to the heavenly precepts, and may your actions be such that you may now enter the temple of God." In a later exorcism, he orders the devil to go out from the creature of God whom the Lord has deigned to call "in order that he may become a temple of the living God and the Holy Spirit may dwell in him."

Before the regenerating water is poured, the catechumen is freed from the empire of the devil and made to renounce the satanic works and pomps; then, when his will is confirmed in its consecration to God, he is baptized, and the Holy Spirit takes possession of His temple.

Every Christian is a temple of the Holy Spirit; every Christian is consecrated to Him; and nothing else may be done in that temple in which God dwells except that which will give glory to Him. The Apostle St. Paul taught that even the most ordinary actions of the Christian should be done to this end: "Therefore, whether you eat or drink, or do anything else, do all for the glory of God."[1]

Is not this the ratification of the baptismal offering, the renewal of the promises made at that time, the free and loving acceptance of the life that God infused in our souls when the Church received us into her maternal bosom? True devotion to the Holy Spirit is not something distinct from the Christian life; it *is* the Christian life thoroughly understood, seriously practiced, and deeply enjoyed.

To be a devotee of the Holy Spirit is to comprehend the august dignity of the Christian, his holy mission, and his arduous duties that are sweetened by love. It is to establish oneself in truth, to be faithful to the sacred promises of baptism, to be what one ought to be, and then to strive for that perfection to which every Christian should aspire.

For, like all consecrations, our consecration to the Holy Spirit must be total. He is master of our whole being because of His divine sovereignty, because of our loving surrender of ourselves at baptism, and because our love gives Him full possession of all that belongs to Him. Infinite Love wishes to possess us totally, without anyone sharing with Him. Therefore St. Paul has said: "What fellowship has light with darkness? What harmony is there between Christ and Belial? Or what part has the believer with the unbeliever? And what agreement has the temple of God with idols? For you are the temple of the living God."[2]

If, then, we are to belong to the Holy Spirit, all idols must be thrown out of His temple; all darkness must be dispelled in order that God's light may shine there; all ties that bind us to Belial must be destroyed; there must be separation

---

1. 1 Cor. 10:31.
2. 2 Cor. 6:14-16.

from all that is impure and earthly. Then we may become in truth "a chosen race, a royal priesthood, a holy nation, a purchased people"; one fit to "proclaim the perfections of Him" who has called us "out of darkness into His marvelous light."[3]

Consecration to the Holy Spirit must be total: nothing must draw us away from His loving possession. Undoubtedly vacillations and deficiencies are part of our imperfection, but even so, our love must not be extinguished. Rather, it must lift its divine flame toward infinite love in the midst of all human vicissitudes.

True devotion to the Holy Spirit, therefore, is not something superficial and intermittent, but something profound and constant, like Christian life itself; it is the love of the soul that corresponds to the love of God, the gift of the creature who tries to be grateful for the divine Gift, the human co-operation that receives the loving and efficacious action of God. As divine love is eternal, its gift without repentance and its action constant, it is our part to have our heart always open to love, ready to receive the unspeakable gift, and to keep all our powers docile to the divine movement.

---

3. Cf. 1 Pet. 2:9.

CHAPTER VIII: DETACHMENT AND LOVING ATTENTION

B Y ITS VERY ESSENCE, THE CHRISTIAN life is the mutual possession of God and the soul; true devotion to the Holy Spirit, as already noted, is the loving acceptance of that life and its full realization. It follows that, in order to be truly devoted to the Holy Spirit, we must continue perfecting that mutual possession, adapting ourselves to the divine exigencies: our love to His love, our activity to His gifts, our efforts to His action.

That we may grasp consecration to the Holy Spirit in all its fullness, it is necessary to analyze what is demanded of us by each one of the sanctifying offices, as we call them, that the Holy Spirit exercises in our souls. If He is our Guest, we must give Him a place in which to dwell; if He is our Director, we must submit to His inspirations; if He is our Gift, we must possess Him; if He is the Artisan who, in a divine way, brings our soul to its perfection, we must let Him work, we must be submissive to His loving designs.

Each aspect of His mission in our souls imposes special duties on us; each one of His gifts demands the loving adaptation of our soul. Let us begin by examining what the divine Spirit, as the most delightful Guest of our soul, asks of us.

Our duty toward a guest is to remain with him while he is in our house. The Holy Spirit dwells permanently in our souls, which have been consecrated as His temples. He is not our Guest of a single day, but our eternal Guest. Consequently, our duty is to live with Him, to live always in His presence. How sweet and fruitful, then, our lives would be! for there is no bitterness in His treatment of us, and His divine conversation causes no weariness.

The intimate life with the Holy Spirit is, in reality, love. If He is our Guest, it is because He loves us. The Scriptures, as we have seen, speak of charity and of the Holy Spirit's dwelling in our souls as being the same thing. St. Thomas says very clearly: "The Holy Spirit dwells in us by charity." In the same way, we live with the Holy Spirit if we love Him; and our life with Him will be perfect in proportion to our love.

Nothing is more just than to love Him, for He is infinite Love. "Love is not loved," Jacopone da Todi used to cry through the streets in the excess of his love. Love is not loved! Is it not the lack of a living faith as well as the deep misery of our hearts that explains this anomaly?

To love Love is to live with Him, it is to allow ourself to be possessed by Him, it is to impregnate ourself with His divine fire and to let ourself be consumed by it. At first that fire is hidden in the depths of the soul, under the ashes of our wretchedness. Our heart is God's, but the greater part of our thoughts and acts escape His loving dominion. The soul has, as it were, the principle of the presence of God, but this is not yet developed, and our spirit wanders among creatures without ever fixing itself complacently on God.

But love, like fire, is absorbent; little by little it extends its sweet demands until it pervades our whole being with its victorious influence. Each day our thoughts and our acts get nearer and nearer to love's source, until the thought of God and His loving presence becomes a divine obsession.

Is not love the obsession that enslaves all our faculties, that absorbs our life, admits no rival, and is satisfied with nothing less than our whole being? Is not love the fortunate conqueror who entered through the gates of our heart, we knew not when, and after having gained possession of us, inch by inch, planted his triumphant standard to wave above us, leaving in his victorious path the bleeding shreds of what we formerly loved, casting from the soul all that is not his, to become the only master of our thoughts?

What a mysterious thing is love! Nothing is so strong and nothing so gentle. It is death and it is life; it ruthlessly kills all thoughts that do not correspond to its unique thought, all affections that are not fused in its unique flame, all acts that are not the pedestal of its greatness. And when it destroys, it builds; when it kills, it gives life, new life, full and fruitful.

When love has accomplished its work, there is perfect harmony in the human soul; all is united, all is blended in its marvelous unity. Therefore, for one who loves God perfectly, it is imperative to live in His presence. When our eyes do not behold the Beloved everywhere, and our thoughts do not go to Him as the sunflower turns to the sun; when our heart does not rest in presence of the Beloved, or does not search for Him with torturing anxiety when He seems to go away; when all the strength of our being does not throw itself upon the divine Beloved as the impetuous torrent that rushes toward the ocean — then love has not yet attained its perfect development; it still has not succeeded in pouring the fullness of its life upon the mortal remains of the old affections.

If we are to obtain intimate life with the Holy Spirit, and to have the sweet presence of the divine Guest, there is only one definitive and efficacious means: it is love. "Where thy treasure is, there also will thy heart be,"[1] said Jesus. And we may add: Where your heart is, there is your whole being. The secret of recollection and of the presence of God is in the heart; if one is dissipated among many concerns, it is because his heart has not yet found its treasure; other affections dispute

---

1. Matt. 6:21.

with the true one for dominion over the soul; love has not yet fully accomplished its work of death and destruction.

Happy the soul that is emptied of all affection for created things, and that lets itself be invaded by the divine obsession of love. Its life is celestial, even in exile, for it lives on love; in intimate communion with infinite Love!

CHAPTER IX: THE EXERCISE OF THE THEOLOGICAL VIRTUES: FAITH

E HAVE SPOKEN OF THE negative part of our duties to the Holy Spirit as our Guest, namely, of the necessity of emptying our soul that the divine Spirit may enter there. When God wishes to fill a heart with His greatness, all that is created must go out of it. This emptiness is demanded by the Holy Spirit, who aspires to fullness of possession; it is required by the holy exigencies of a "love . . . strong as death,"[1] which separates and mercilessly roots out everything else from the soul and leaves the profound and delightful solitude of union.

But if love separates, it is in order to unite; if it roots out, it is in order to plant; if it empties, it is to fill; if it puts the soul in solitude, it is to bring plenitude. Those who love should be left alone to look at each other without interference, to love without disturbance, to speak without witnesses, to pour out their hearts in isolation, in the most pure and intimate union.

The delightful Guest of our soul aspires to this union, and the mystery of it is accomplished by the theological virtues.

Our natural intelligence, no matter how clear, profound, and brilliant it may be, is not sufficient to enable us to discern the Holy Spirit; our human heart, no matter how tender and ardent, is not sufficient to enable us to love Him; our weakness is powerless to touch Him, to embrace Him. More penetrating eyes are needed, a new heart and stronger arms to

---

1. Cant. 8:6 (Douay trans.).

reach out to Him. The natural prerogatives of the most perfect of the seraphim are not enough to enable them to touch
God in the supernatural and divine manner to which He has
condescended to call us in the excess of His mercy and of His
love.

For we must not forget that the intimacy with God which
the Holy Spirit communicates to the soul, that intimacy whose
germ comes with grace, whose fullness is sanctity, and whose
consummation is heaven, is something divine, above all created
strength, and requiring supernatural and divine principles of
activity.

While these principles that the Holy Spirit communicates
to the soul in taking possession of it are many and varied,
only the theological virtues can touch God intimately. The
other virtues purify the soul, remove from it the obstacles to
union, draw it nearer to God, adorn it, beautify it; but none
of these other virtues nor even all of them together can make
the soul touch God, because God is not their proper object.

Even the gifts of the Holy Spirit, the exceedingly noble
instruments of the heavenly Artist, exquisite supernatural
realities which elevate the soul to divine regions, and are
superior to the infused moral virtues — even these cannot of
themselves touch God. Rather, they are at the service of the
theological virtues, regulated and directed by these superior
forces which have God for their proper object, and consequently the ineffable privilege of touching Him.

Without doubt the theological virtues need the precious
aid of the gifts to accomplish the lofty and wonderful operations of the spiritual life; but the essence of the intimacy of
the soul with God is in the exercise of the theological virtues
and especially in the exercise of charity, queen and formative
principle of all virtues, the bond of perfection that unites and
harmonizes the virtues and the gifts in the divine unity of

love, and constitutes the basis for the mutual possession of the Holy Spirit and the soul.

The foundation of prayer, the root of recollection, the essence of the interior life, is the exercise of the theological virtues. Perhaps sufficient thought is not given to their importance. It may be that they are not granted the place belonging to them in the spiritual life. It may be that, for lack of solid instruction, through exaggerated concern for the practical, and through a false humility, these virtues are at times neglected in the pursuit of more human ends. Nevertheless, the theological virtues are supreme, not only by their excellence, but also by their practical importance, by the solidity of their foundation, and because they are the beginning of our intimacy with God.

Our chief concern and duty toward the divine Guest is to try to be with Him. It is good to wash the feet of a guest, to seat him at table, to prepare a banquet for him. But it is even better to treat him affectionately, to be with him while he is under our roof, to look at him, to speak to him and listen to him, to give him signs of friendship and love. And if He is the Beloved, the only Love of our heart, may our eyes never lift from His beautiful countenance, our hands never rest from caressing Him, our loving heart never cease to pour itself out into His heart.

Now this loving intimacy that the Spirit longs for and the soul sighs for, cannot be brought about except by the theological virtues. To repeat: the other virtues empty the soul, place it in the desired solitude, cleanse and adorn it; but for communicating with the Beloved in this solitude, the theological virtues are necessary. The eyes of faith contemplate Him among the shadows; the arms of hope reach Him beyond time in the triumph of eternity; the heart of charity loves Him with a created love made to the image and likeness of love uncreated. This is the bond that ties the soul close to the Holy Spirit, this is the essence of all perfection and the form of all virtue.

The presence of the Holy Spirit in our souls demands that we know it; that we have the sweet conviction of His indwelling, of our living under His very glance, of His seeking our own. How sweet to live in the light of that mutual glance! — a light at times so penetrating that it seems to plunge into the bosom of God, so bright that it resembles the dawn of the eternal day, so gentle that it seems to radiate from heaven. Then life is easy and pleasant in the depths of the soul, in loving intimacy with the divine Guest.

At times, however, the soul's heaven grows dark, and in the great stretches of solitude there cannot be found a single ray of light nor a vestige of the former sweetness. It seems that the heart is empty, that the soul has lost its priceless treasure. How difficult it is to be recollected; with what tedium the hours pass; and with what bitterness the soul drags itself along the path that leads to God! But in the midst of these necessary vicissitudes of the spiritual life there is something that does not change nor end; something very solid that does not permit the soul to get lost, and which, like a sure compass, marks out its divine course. It is faith that always reveals the divine to us wherever it is; it is faith that makes us look at the delightful Guest, both in the shadows of desolation and in the full, celestial brilliance of consolation.

The Scriptures tell us that "He who is just lives by faith."[2] It is for this reason that St. John of the Cross recommends so emphatically, for souls aspiring to union with God, this life of faith as the straight and sure path to the summit.

Our devotion to the Holy Spirit, then, must be founded on faith. It is the basis of the Christian life; it accomplished our

---

2. Rom. 1:17.

first communication with God, and it initiates our intimacy with the Holy Spirit, producing in our soul that glance which unites us with the Spirit of Light called by the Church "Most blessed Light! Most happy Light!"

Faith by its very nature is imperfect; but to help correct its imperfections as far as possible, we have the intellectual gifts of the Holy Spirit. With their aid the glance of faith becomes more penetrating, more comprehensive, and more divine.

CHAPTER X: THE EXERCISE OF THE THEOLOGICAL VIRTUES: HOPE

EVEN THOUGH FAITH IS OUR FIRST and fundamental communication with God, for intimacy with Him faith is not enough. Such intimacy is attained through the heart more than through the intelligence; because the Holy Spirit is Love, and, as St. Thomas Aquinas teaches, in this life it is better to love God than to know Him, and love is more unifying than knowledge. Man receives the virtues of hope and charity so that he may achieve intimate contact with God.

Through the theological virtue of hope we tend toward God, our end, our good, our happiness. And we tend toward Him not with the uncertainty and inconstancy of human hope, but with the unshakable support of His loving strength. The terminus of our hope is in the heavenly fatherland, for there we shall have eternal and full possession of God. We have the divine promise that cannot deceive: heaven and earth shall pass away but not the word of God. And if, together with hope, we have charity in our soul, we have more than the promise: we possess in substance the Good that we shall possess fully in heaven. The Holy Spirit, our Guest, our Gift, is the pledge of our inheritance. As St. Paul says: "And in Him you too, when you had heard the word of truth, the good news of your salvation, and believed in it, were sealed with the Holy Spirit of the promise, who is the pledge of our inheritance."[1]

How secure is the hope that has for its pledge possession of that very Good which it aspires to enjoy for eternity! What

---

1. Eph. 1:13-14.

happiness to carry in our soul the seed of glory, the substance of heaven! Our spiritual life is truly the eternal life. Therefore does Jesus say: "He who believes in the Son has everlasting life."[2] He does not say "he will have," but "he has." In truth, the life of grace and the life of glory are the same supernatural life: the germ of it is in grace, and its fullness is in the life to come. Therefore, the Church also teaches us, in the Preface of the Mass for the Dead, that when we die our spiritual life is not lost, but transformed. "The life of the faithful is changed, not taken away."

There should follow, as a legitimate consequence from the firmness with which we hope for eternal life, equal firmness in hoping for all the necessary means to attain it. We do not travel haphazardly on our voyage to heaven. Faith points out the definite route for us, hope gives us unfailing support; faith gives us light, hope imparts confidence.

To understand the practical importance of the virtue of hope, let us note the most common and most dangerous obstacle in the way of perfection. This is discouragement resulting from the faults, the temptations, the aridities, found in every spiritual life. It reduces fervor and generosity, and impedes progress to perfection. While we have confidence, any obstacle can be overcome, any sacrifice is easily made, and our struggles are crowned with victory. But when discouragement invades the soul it is without energy or support, and thus easily deterred, misguided, and confused. Therefore St. Thomas teaches that, although despair is not the greatest of sins (for infidelity and hatred of God, which are opposed to faith and charity, are graver considered in themselves), yet so far as we are concerned despair is the most dangerous of sins. Here he cites St. Isidore: "To commit a crime is death to the soul; but to despair is to descend into hell."

---

2. John 3:36.

The more we advance in the spiritual life, the stronger must be our hope, for the struggles become more terrible, the sacrifices greater, and the intimate operations of grace more profound and more difficult to understand.

Let us now analyze the relationship between the Holy Spirit and the virtue of hope. The Spirit is not only light and fire, He is also strength; He is the spiritual unction that invigorates those who struggle on earth, the strength of the Most High, the Gift of the omnipotent right hand of the Father. If we wish to consecrate ourselves to Him, it is not enough that we never take our eyes off His light and that our heart be always open to the holy effusions of His love: it is necessary also that our arm receive the support of His most strong arm, that, like the spouse of the Canticles, we come out of the desert of our need by the luminous path of faith, enraptured by the delights of charity and supported on the arm of the Beloved, the arm of hope.

Faith and charity enrich us with the light and love of the Spirit. Hope puts us in communion with the strength of the Most High and opens our soul to all the supernatural aids of which the Spirit is the living and inexhaustible source.

Hope is a supernatural capacity for receiving the Holy Spirit, who aids and sanctifies, with all the divine streams that spring from this fountain. When He Himself has satisfied the thirst of our soul, our hope is fulfilled, for He is the Spirit of the promise and the pledge of our inheritance, as we have heard from the lips of St. Paul.

CHAPTER XI: THE EXERCISE OF THE THEOLOGICAL VIRTUES: CHARITY

WHAT WE HAVE SAID ABOUT detachment and loving attention to the Guest of our souls, and about the exercise of faith and hope, has been but a preparation for that which constitutes the foundation of devotion to the Holy Spirit: namely, love. Love is essential in this devotion because the Holy Spirit is the infinite and personal Love of God. His work is a work of love. What He seeks and longs for is to establish the reign of love. How can we meet love except with love? How can we fulfill its desires and satisfy its divine requirements, co-operate with its plans and utilize its gifts, except by love?

Now, the most perfect and excellent love is that of charity. The divine Spirit pours into our hearts the third theological virtue, that we may have this love. St. Paul composed a magnificent eulogy on the virtue of charity in the thirteenth chapter of the First Epistle to the Corinthians. There he shows that charity is the most excellent of the gifts of God, the form of all the virtues, something divine and celestial that does not end with life but accompanies the soul into eternity.

Charity is the most perfect image of the Holy Spirit, with whom it has a very close relationship. When charity is in the soul, the Holy Spirit lives in it; and when the Spirit gives Himself to a soul, He pours charity into it. The degree of charity in any soul is the measure of the mutual possession that exists between itself and the Spirit. It is the measure of all the infused virtues and of the gifts of the Spirit. It is the measure of grace and of glory.

True devotion to the Holy Spirit is the mutual possession between Him and the soul. Clearly, then, charity is the foundation of this devotion, as it is the formal element of Christian perfection. All other things either pave the way for the full reign of charity, or are its precious consequences. St. John of the Cross teaches that "it is a great thing for the soul to exercise itself constantly in love, so that, when it is perfected here below, it may not stay long, either in this world or in the next, before seeing God face to face." And so highly did this saint esteem charity that he writes: "Even one of them [these acts of love of the soul] is of greater merit and worth than all that the soul may have done in its life apart from this transformation, however much this may be."

Some there are who think that the exercising of oneself in love is proper only to him who is perfect. Assuredly it is true that in the heights of the spiritual life the soul does nothing else but love, as St. John of the Cross expresses it:

> *My soul has employed itself*
> *And all my possessions in His service.*
> *Now I guard no flock,*
> *Nor have I now other office,*
> *For now my exercise is in loving alone.*

But love must be exercised in all the stages of the spiritual life. Charity is in the soul from the moment of the entrance of grace, it always remains as the form of the virtues and the bond of perfection; that is, it moves, impels, directs, and co-ordinates all the virtues and all the spiritual gifts. Whatever work the soul has to do, whether to purify itself, to progress, or to unite itself intimately with God, charity is always the principle, impeller, and director. Love takes many forms and accomplishes many tasks: in the first days of the spiritual life, it cleanses the soul and roots out by means of the moral virtues all that is opposed to its reign; later, it directs the gifts of the Holy Spirit so that they may complete the purification of the soul, illumine it, and prepare it for union with God. Finally, it unites the soul with God and enriches it with light, adorns it with virtues, accomplishes in it a divine work of harmony and perfection.

The exercise of charity is a brief and delightful road for the attainment of sanctity; brief, because everything is simplified when it is treated thoroughly; delightful, because love facilitates every effort and sweetens every sacrifice. How easy is the way when one loves! How courageous, how strong, and how filled with consolation is the soul that is sustained by love!

One virtue cannot increase, of course, without the others, and any one of them can be the road by which to attain the others, since all the infused virtues are united in charity, as St. Thomas teaches. However, there is no doubt that, since charity is the form of all the virtues, to possess the queen is to acquire rapidly and sweetly all that follow in her train.

"Love and do what you will," said St. Augustine. Is humility lacking? The most forceful motive, the most fruitful effort, toward humility will be found in love. Is it poverty we need? Nothing is poorer than a love that leaves all to gain all. Do we seek to acquire obedience? Nothing is sweeter than to submit ourself through love to a representative of the Beloved. And so it is with the other virtues, as St. Paul says: "Charity is patient, is kind; does not envy, is not pretentious, is not puffed up, is not ambitious, is not self-seeking, is not provoked; thinks no evil, does not rejoice over wickedness, but rejoices with the truth; bears with all things, believes all things, hopes all things, endures all things."[1]

It is the practice of charity that specifically develops the gifts of the Holy Spirit, for these precious instruments are

---

1. 1 Cor. 13:4-7.

deeply rooted in this virtue. Prayer, recollection, the spirit of mortification, all the most efficacious and necessary recourses for advancing in perfection, have their fecund roots and powerful stimulus in charity.

But why go on analyzing the principles of the spiritual life? In order to understand the importance of charity, it is sufficient to dwell on the consideration we have already stated: the more we love with the love of charity, the more we shall possess the Holy Spirit and the more we shall be possessed by Him, the Sanctifier, the supreme Director of all our supernatural activities.

This does not mean that we need not exercise all the virtues carefully and constantly, for they prepare the soul for perfect love and later produce works of love; but we should give charity the importance it deserves in the work of sanctification. In physical life, for example, to insist on the importance of sound nerves because the nerves rule all our vital functions, is not to deny that care must be given to the other organs, but simply to call attention to the singular importance of the nervous system.

This interesting point of the spiritual life can also be considered under another aspect. Frequently souls lack the guidance of a clear ideal, the impulse of a powerful force, in the constant struggles, vicissitudes, and sacrifices of the spiritual life. They recognize their needs, they know the remedies, they see, imperfectly at least, the path they must follow. But they are so weak, their courage fails at each step, they let time slip by without taking advantage of it; and they sadly behold the years passing with no personal progress in spite of their good desires and holy intentions. What is it they lack? A precise ideal, an impelling force. If they would love, they would have an extraordinary power. Charity, when it unites us to God, our end, fixes our attention on the true ideal of our life; and, because it is love, it communicates the supreme strength, the only strength, one might say, that exists in heaven or on earth.

More than this, charity joins us closely to the Holy Spirit. It puts us in contact with the divine flame, the unique source of holiness. Who would not burn if led into a glowing furnace? Who can escape being sanctified if he throws himself into the very essence of sanctity?

But people have so many preoccupations, fruits of a narrow spiritual criterion and of inaccurate conceptions of divine things. All these concerns are, no doubt, encouraged by the devil to prevent souls from attaining their proper good. How can I dare to love God if I am full of misery and of sin? How can God love me in that condition? How can there be the mutual correspondence that love demands?

The answer is, that loving God is not only a most precious right that we all have, but a most happy duty. Is it not the first and principal commandment? — "Thou shalt love the Lord thy God with thy whole heart, and with thy whole soul, and with thy whole strength, and with thy whole mind."[2] In order that God be loved, He must be good; not necessarily we. The fact that we are wretched and imperfect does not diminish His incomprehensible beauty, His infinite goodness, His boundless mercy, nor any other of the titles that He has to our love. Rather, our imperfections, if we consider them well, are a stimulus to love, for they cry out to us that we must look outside of ourselves for that which our heart desires; that we must lift our eyes and our soul to merciful Love, to the only One who can take pity on our miseries and tenderly cure them. For our miseries are a testimony of the immense goodness of God. Lowly as we are, He loves us, and not only gives us the right but imposes on us the duty of loving Him.

---

2. Luke 10:27; cf. Mark 12:30.

How is it that God loves us as we are? Because His love is not like ours, poor and indigent, seeking in the beloved what is lacking in ourself. No, God's love is a love of infinite fullness and looks for nothing except a void to fill, for poor beings to make happy, for miseries to cure, because He is infinite Goodness and infinite Mercy. Like the ocean that seeks a bed in which to pour its fullness, the infinite God seeks the immensity of our misery in order to fill it.

If we waited to love God and to be loved by Him until we were clean, strong, good, we could wait forever. Rather, we could despair forever. All the good that we have we receive from the love of God. He does not love us because we are pure or good; rather, if we are pure or good, it is because God loves us. Our love, an imperfect love, looks for certain qualities in the loved object; the love of God, the perfect love, does not look for these qualities, but gives them. He does not ask, but gives and gives Himself, communicates Himself without reserve.

It was precisely our love, the love of His poor creatures, that God came on earth to seek in the midst of the sorrows and sufferings of His mortal life; it is what He asks of us, what He demands of us. He came filled with gifts for the poor ones of earth whose hearts were miserable and broken, but capable of loving. He came to ask them to love Him. He came to oblige them to love Him by the extreme tenderness and ardor of His love. After speaking of suffering and dying for love, He remained in the Tabernacle asking for our love; even as, at an earlier time, He sat on the curb of Jacob's well and said to every soul coming into this world what He said to the Samaritan woman: "I thirst. Give Me to drink!"[3]

---

3. Cf. John 4:8.

CHAPTER XII: CHARACTERISTICS OF THE LOVE OF THE SPIRIT: HE POSSESSES US

L OVE, WE HAVE SAID, IS THE FOUNDATION of devotion to the Holy Spirit, as it is also the foundation of Christian perfection. But love as a reflection of God, as His own image, is something that encloses within its simplicity a boundless wealth and a variety of forms. Who can fathom the depths of love?

Human love in all its manifestations is admirably in harmony with the love of charity; it is confident in filial love, trusting in friendship, sweet and fruitful in the love of husband and wife, disinterested and tender in the love of a mother. Our love of God must include all these forms of human love; every fiber of our heart must vibrate when the harmonious and full canticle of love bursts forth from it. But since God is one in essence and triune in Persons, our love for Him takes on a particular aspect accordingly as it is directed to each one of the divine Persons.

Our love for the Father is tender and confident like that of children; eager to glorify Him as His only-begotten Son taught us to do by word and example. Love for the Father is the intense desire to have His will fulfilled on earth as it is in heaven. Our love for the Son, who willed to become flesh for us, is characterized by the tendency to union with Him and transformation into Him; by imitation of His example, participation in His life, and the sharing of His sufferings and His

Cross. The Eucharist, mystery of love, of sorrow, and of union, reveals the characteristics of this love.

Love for the Holy Spirit also has its special character, which we should study in order completely to understand devotion to Him. We have explained how the Holy Spirit loves us, how He moves us like a divine breath that draws us to the bosom of God, like a sacred fire that transforms us into fire, like a divine artist who forms Jesus in us. Surely, then, our love for the Holy Spirit should be marked by loving docility, by full surrender, and by a constant fidelity that permits us to be moved, directed, and transformed by His sanctifying action.

Our love for the Father tends to *glorify* Him; our love for the Son, to *transform* ourselves into Him; our love for the Holy Spirit, to *let ourselves be possessed and moved by Him.*

In order to attain this holy docility to the motions of the Spirit, the soul must be so silent and recollected that it can hear His voice; so pure and so filled with light that it can clearly perceive the meaning of the divine inspiration; so surrendered to the will of God that it embraces that will without hesitation; and so selfless that it performs that will without stopping at any sacrifice. Love accomplishes all this alone, or through the virtues and gifts which it co-ordinates and directs; for love, as St. Paul teaches, "believes all things, hopes all things, endures all things."

Love brings recollection and silence to the soul. Whosoever loves, distinguishes among thousands of voices the voice of the beloved. Does not a mother know the voice of her child among all other sounds, does she not hear it even when she is asleep? Love causes silence because it brings solitude and recollection; because it concentrates all its activity and desire on the beloved. The Holy Spirit frequently speaks to souls, breathes upon them, and inspires them. But they do not hear

Him except in the measure of their love for Him, in the proportion in which love has anointed them with silence. Closely united with the Holy Spirit through love, souls feel the secret palpitation of the heart of God.

One of the characteristics, then, that love for the Holy Spirit should have is this solicitous attention to the sound of His voice, to His inspirations, to His most delicate touches. We should struggle against all disturbances, all distracting noises; we must bravely detach ourselves from all creatures, from every affection. Little by little, love will have power over our heart and spread its deep influence through all our faculties.

The voice of the Spirit is gentle; His movement is very delicate. To perceive them, the soul needs silence and peace. But it is not enough to hear: the divine language must be understood. "The sensual man does not perceive the things that are of the Spirit of God, for it is foolishness to him and he cannot understand, because it is examined spiritually. But the spiritual man judges all things, and he himself is judged by no man. For 'who has known the mind of the Lord, that he might instruct him?' But we have the mind of Christ."[1]

Therefore, the things of the Spirit have a spiritual and secret sense that not everyone perceives. To know divine things, the soul has to be pure, and in proportion to its purity it judges spiritual things and penetrates inspirations. Such purity is produced by love and wondrously brought to perfection by it, for purity considered negatively is withdrawal from earthly things, while under its positive aspect it is deification; and love deifies by uniting the soul to God.

Human love, by the union it produces between those who love each other, makes one penetrate the mind of the other, and in a certain manner guess his hidden thoughts. Who has

---

1. 1 Cor. 2:14-16.

not admired the amazing intuitions of the mother discovering what her little one suffers from its all but unintelligible cry? Even so, divine love, leading the soul into the intimacies of God and bringing God to the soul, produces that marvelous understanding of spiritual things which we see in the lives of the saints.

When Jesus, risen from the dead, appeared on the shores of Tiberias to the disciples who were fishing in Peter's boat, He was recognized by only one of them. It was John, the Apostle of purity and love, who said to Peter: "It is the Lord."[2] Pure and loving souls have the secret of discovering Jesus in whatever way He shows Himself to them, for the clean of heart see God, and love penetrates all veils. Whether Jesus comes radiant in glory, or humiliated and covered with ignominy; whether He brings divine consolations, or bestows bitter things, these souls catch the enchantment of the divine perfume and exclaim, like the beloved disciple: "It is the Lord!"

The loving soul perceives through silence the divine inspirations, and by its own purity discovers their deep meaning, allowing itself to be taken along, docile and gentle, by the breath of the Spirit. Love offers no resistance to that divine breath, because to give and to let itself be possessed, to surrender to the exigencies of infinite Love, are of its very essence. By its nature, love is the union of wills, the fusion of affections, of identical inclinations. Holy Scripture speaks clearly, as we have seen, about the docility of souls that love: "For whoever are led by the Spirit of God, they are the sons of God."

One of the most intense and delicate joys of love is precisely this abandonment to the dispositions and action of the beloved, this sweet slavery that makes the soul lose its own

---

2. John 21:7.

sovereignty in order to surrender itself to love; this ineffable happiness of having a Master — sweeter perhaps than knowing oneself to be master of the Beloved. O mystery of love which we cannot explain, but which the heart understands! To love is to disappear, to efface oneself to the point of transformation into and fusion with the Beloved.

This sweet abandonment to all the movements of love is the characteristic mark of devotion to the Spirit. To love this divine Spirit is to let ourselves be taken along by Him, as the feather is carried along by the wind; to let ourselves be possessed by Him, as the dry branch is possessed by the fire that burns it; to let ourselves be animated by Him, as the sensitive strings of a lyre-take life from the artist's touch.

The degrees of this abandonment are degrees, not only of love, but of Christian perfection, the height of which is characterized precisely by the extension and constancy of the movements of the Spirit in the soul He possesses. St. John of the Cross often taught this truth, as in the following passage: "For the soul, like the true daughter of God that it now is, is moved wholly by the Spirit of God, even as St. Paul says: 'That they that are moved by the Spirit of God are sons of God.' So the understanding of the soul is now the understanding of God; and its will is the will of God; and its memory is the memory of God; and its delight is the delight of God; and the substance of the soul, although it is not the substance of God, for into this it cannot be changed, is nevertheless united in Him and absorbed in Him, and is thus God by participation in God, which comes to pass in this perfect state of the spiritual life. . . . "

Undoubtedly this docility requires abnegation, for it will always be true that love and pain are proportionate, and that the perfection of the one cannot be attained without the perfection of the other. The soul abandoned to the Holy Spirit exposes itself to every sacrifice, every immolation. The soul of Jesus was possessed by the Holy Spirit in a singular manner. We shall never comprehend to what depths of pain He was led thereby.

The path of the divine Dove is ever the same. His flight is always toward Calvary. The shining white wings can always be described above the blessed Cross, for that is where love is to be found on earth, as in heaven it is found in the bosom of the Father.

CHAPTER XIII: CHARACTERISTICS OF THE LOVE OF THE SPIRIT: WE POSSESS HIM

LOVE OF THE HOLY SPIRIT CONSISTS IN letting oneself be possessed by Him with complete docility, with perfect purity, and with total abnegation. This is true devotion to the Holy Spirit, but it is only one aspect of love: the other, essential also, is to possess. *Yours and mine:* the whole essence of love is in these two words. Thus the spouse of the Canticles sings: "My Lover belongs to me, and I to Him."[1] And this is the way that Jesus expresses the mystery of infinite love in His magnificent prayer to His Father on the night of the Last Supper: "And all things that are Mine are Thine, and Thine are Mine; and I am glorified in them."[2] In the same prayer He tells of His immense love for men: "I in them and Thou in Me; that they may be perfected in unity."

No one can let himself be possessed without at the same time possessing. These two aspects of love, which our imperfect understanding must keep separate, constitute the reality and unity of love. To love the Holy Spirit, then, is both to let oneself be possessed by Him and to possess Him; He is not only the Director of our life, but also the Gift of God, our Gift.

Let us recall the teaching of St. Thomas Aquinas previously quoted: "By the gift of sanctifying grace the rational creature is perfected so that it can freely use not only the created

---

1. Cant. 2:16.
2. John 17:10.

gift itself, but *enjoy also the divine Person Himself*. The rational creature does sometimes attain thereto, as when it is made partaker of the divine Word and of the Love proceeding so as freely to know God truly and to love God rightly."

To possess Love is to love Him; it is to allow oneself to be penetrated by His fire, and to receive the ardent effusions of love, and in them, to receive Love itself.

This possession has its degrees. For the lowest degree of charity, it is enough to possess the Holy Spirit because He and charity are inseparable, according to the words of the Apostle St. Paul: "The charity of God is poured forth in our hearts by the Holy Spirit who has been given to us." Only the Holy Spirit can pour charity into our souls; together with created love, we are given uncreated love, so that the principle and germ of charity is the Holy Spirit.

In proportion as the soul grows in charity, this happy possession of the Gift of God increases. The more we love the Holy Spirit, the more He is ours; and the more we love Him, the more we are His. In other words, the more perfectly the Holy Spirit is the principle of our love, the more perfectly He is the completion of that love, the more perfectly He is our Gift.

To have an idea of the degrees of possession, it is helpful to consider the perfect degree, for ordinarily the perfect leads us to a knowledge of the imperfect, as we judge what a seed is like from the ripe fruit. In the works of the mystics, expressions like these are frequently found: "To love with the heart of God"; "To love with the Holy Spirit." Some saints, like Catherine of Siena, tell us that God gave them His heart in exchange for theirs. Certainly these expressions should not be taken literally. On the other hand, we should not consider them as mere figures, like those we use to express our poor earthly sentiments, to tell the intensity of our affections or the ardor of our desires. It would be profitable for us to examine the mysterious realities hidden under the symbolical words of the saints.

Every act of charity proceeds from the habit of that virtue which the Holy Spirit infuses into our hearts. No matter how imperfect an act of love may be, we love with charity, the most perfect supernatural gift that we receive on earth. It is the created, but most faithful, image of the Holy Spirit.

We can use this charity in two ways: by moving ourselves to perform an act of love, or by being moved to it by the Holy Spirit with that special movement explained in Chapter VI of this study. When we love under the special movement of the Holy Spirit, it can be said with theological exactness that we love with the Holy Spirit. For, as St. Thomas teaches: "The operation of an effect is not attributed to the thing moved but to the mover. Hence in that effect in which our mind is moved and does not move, but in which God is the sole mover, the operation is attributed to God." And such is the case of the soul that works under the special movement of the Holy Spirit, as the holy Doctor himself assures us: "The spiritual man is not inclined to do anything as by a movement of his own will principally, but by the inspiration of the Spirit."

The mystics call this love produced by the special movement of the Spirit, *passive love.* Not because the soul does not move: for indeed, the soul is never so active as then. It is called passive because the soul does not move itself. The Holy Spirit moves it and it works under His divine impulse. The act of passive love belongs to the Holy Spirit and the soul, but more to the Spirit than to the soul. Therefore it can truly be said that the Holy Spirit loves in the soul and that the soul loves with the Holy Spirit, especially when this passive love has reached its perfection.

It will help us to understand this doctrine if we recall a comparison used by St. John of the Cross to explain something similar: A piece of wood is thrown into the fire. The fire envelops, penetrates, possesses it. To the wood, being possessed by the fire and burning are the same thing. But at first the wood is not wholly burned because the fire has not penetrated it completely. Penetration and possession come about little by little as the wood burns, until, perfectly penetrated by the fire, it is converted into it and burns with the same fire and has all the characteristics of fire.

The Holy Spirit is rightly called fire, living fountain, charity, because He is Love. The spiritual life is nothing else but the penetration of the soul by that divine fire. The Holy Spirit possesses the soul and the soul burns, that is, it loves. Charity is the intimate fire that burns the soul, but the Holy Spirit, quite as intimately present in the soul, is both the cause of that fire and its glorious end. At first the soul does not burn totally because it needs to be purified in order that the divine fire may perfectly penetrate and possess it. Little by little the divine penetration is effected and the soul gradually burns more thoroughly, more profoundly. The divine penetration becomes so perfect, the spiritual combustion so complete, that the soul is "deified"; one might say that it is changed into fire, into love. It may be said to burn with the fire of God, and to love with the Holy Spirit, for the divine Spirit moves it to love so intimately and fully that, in all truth, this love is attributed to the Holy Spirit. The Spirit of God loves in the soul, and the soul loves with that Holy Spirit.

As the wood when perfectly penetrated by the fire takes on the very character of fire, so the soul that loves with the love of the Holy Spirit participates in the divine characteristics of eternal Love. Who can describe this love? As the Scriptures say, it is "intelligent, holy, unique, manifold, subtle, agile, clear, unstained, certain, not baneful, loving the good, keen, unhampered, beneficent, kindly, firm, secure, tranquil, all-powerful, all-seeing, and pervading all spirits, though they be intelligent, pure and very subtle."[3] Is not Love perhaps the Spirit of Wisdom?

A beautiful and profitable commentary could be made on this passage from the Scriptures. How easy it would be to find in perfect love all the participated characteristics of infinite Love! We would see all the multiple kinds of love in that perfect Love! By understanding it, how well we would comprehend the new life, the life "hidden with Christ in God"[4] of which St. Paul speaks to us, and which is nothing but participation in eternal love — unutterable intimacy with the Holy Trinity! How well we would understand the divinity, the fruitfulness, the abnegation, the heroism, the tenderness, and all the goodness of love of neighbor if we understood how we ought to love in the Holy Spirit!

When this acme of love is reached, the soul is perfectly possessed by the Holy Spirit, for He moves it entirely at His good pleasure; and the soul possesses the Holy Spirit perfectly for, in the sense already explained, it loves with Him. The mystery of love is completed, the soul has attained with love the most perfect union that is possible on earth. What else is love but aspiration toward unity, fruition of unity, expansion of unity?

Then the soul fully enjoys the Gift of God. The words of St. Thomas are realized to their fullest: the soul shares in eternal love in such a way that it freely loves God with complete rectitude. This glorious liberty and holy rightness are the result of the wondrous unity brought about between the Holy Spirit and the soul.

---

3. Wis. 7:22-23.
4. Col. 3:3.

From the heights of this perfection the degrees of the mutual possession of the Holy Spirit and the soul can be contemplated, as from a mountaintop one looks down on the winding paths that lead up to it. In each stage of the mystic ascension the soul is letting itself be possessed by the Holy Spirit, and possesses Him exactly in the proportion in which it is possessed; for the Holy Spirit is the soul's Gift in the degree in which He directs it, in the measure in which He moves and possesses it. This mystical possession, these two aspects of a unique possession, form a sort of divine ring: love, which as it grows greater, as it becomes perfect, unifies, simplifies, deifies the soul; for all these ineffable things, love, simplicity, unity, are reflections of God, who is unutterable unity, infinite simplicity, and eternal charity.

CHAPTER XIV: THE HOLY SPIRIT
TAKES US TO THE WORD

D EVOTION TO THE HOLY SPIRIT IS not properly understood if we do not see that it is closely related with devotion to the Father and to the Word, and that by a divine logic it leads to these two devotions, and also contains them in their essential elements.

In a beam of sunshine there are light, heat, and energy, which can be separated, studied, and utilized, though they are actually one in their natural state. In the same way, devotion to the three divine Persons must form a single supernatural reality, although when passing through the prism of our limited understanding each seems separate, adapting itself to the imperfection of our intelligence, which is unable to embrace the whole in one single glance.

The Holy Spirit, being the love of the Father and of the Son, pours into the soul He moves and into the heart He possesses a love for the Father similar to that of the Son, and a love for the Word similar to that of the Father. Even more: in the soul that possesses the Holy Spirit and is possessed by Him, there is, as explained above, a limited but ineffable image of the mystery of the love of the Trinity. For the soul loves the Father as it loves the Word, and it loves the Word as it loves the Father.

The Scriptures teach us this mystery in a marvelously simple way, telling us, as we have already seen, that through the Spirit we cry to the Father — "You have received a spirit of adoption as sons, by virtue of which we cry, 'Abba! Father!' "; and that through the Spirit we pronounce the name of Jesus: "And no one can say 'Jesus is Lord,' except in the Holy Spirit."[1] To cry to the Father is to have a knowledge of our filiation and to feel in our innermost being the tenderness of children. To say "Lord Jesus" is not simply to pronounce with our lips that most sweet name, but to utter it in the intimacy of our souls as the fruit of our contemplation, as a cry of love from our heart. Therefore, the Spirit reveals to us our relations with the other divine Persons and makes us love those Persons whose loving bond He is.

"The Holy Ghost," explains St. Thomas, "is called the Spirit of adoption in so far as we receive from Him the likeness of the natural Son, who is the begotten Wisdom."

We do not need to dwell on this point because in Chapter VI of this study we showed how all the sanctifying action of the Spirit is reduced to reproducing the ideal of the Father in the soul, transforming it into Jesus. But we must explain the co-operation the soul has to give to this divine work.

We have compared the Holy Spirit to an artist who expresses his ideal in some material thing. The comparison, though exact, is imperfect. Matter is inert; marble cannot know the transformation that is going to be accomplished in it, nor is it aware of the artistic form and beauty it will have. It is powerless to do anything but let itself be used. On the other hand, the soul in which the divine Artist works has knowledge and love; it can receive from God the revelation of His designs and love them with the incredible strength of the love it has received from Him. It can be the marble and the chisel at the same time, capable of being transformed into an intelligent and free instrument in the hands of God.

---

1. 1 Cor. 12:3.

The soul knows that it is going to "become Jesus," and it loves Him with whom it is to unite itself. Not only does it permit itself to be chiseled and polished by the tools of the Holy Spirit, but it strips itself of all that can impede its divine transformation, and places at the disposition of the Artist its love and its desire of immolation.

When the soul is said to be passive under the intimate operations of grace, this does not mean that it is idle, or that it is not free. Rather, it means that those operations are so directed by the Spirit of God that, according to the teaching of St. Thomas already quoted, they should be attributed more to the Holy Spirit than to the soul.

The soul should know the ideal of the Holy Spirit as precisely and clearly as possible. How many retard His action by failure to grasp that ideal! Travelers who journey life's whole length without knowing where they are going, mariners without compass lost in the solitude of the sea, these souls that do not know their ideal wander aimlessly, working much, accomplishing little, making their way painfully without finding a secure port. As St. Thomas says, souls who are looking for perfection should know in what it consists, so as not to go along aimlessly, fighting haphazardly, beating the air in vain.

Of course, not all souls need to know the nature of Christian perfection with the exactitude of a theologian; but souls of good will, in the simplicity of their faith, with the intuitions of love, find their course with admirable precision and certainty; just as the bird with its marvelous instinct finds its nest more easily than a wise man provided with the best instruments could find it.

Souls must know their ideal, and their directors should help them in this most important matter. Many wish to be saints; but having only a vague and inexact concept of sanctity, they journey on without a realized destination, at the risk of being lost or of straying far from the road.

Jesus Himself has told us that He is the ideal: "I am the way, and the truth, and the life."[2] He is the light that guides by His teaching. He is the road because of His divine example. And He is the true life that leads us into the ocean of infinite life. Through Jesus we go to the Father in whom all things are perfected, as St. Paul says in speaking of the order established by God in human things: "All are yours, and you are Christ's, and Christ is God's."[3] All things are ordered to us, we to Christ, and Christ to God. This is perfection: to transform ourselves into Jesus in order to produce the ideal of the Father and to clothe ourselves with His glory; for Jesus is the ideal and the glory of the Father.

Now it is to this end that the Holy Spirit leads us; when He takes possession of a soul He infuses into it the ideal, and the desire of attaining it. Like the wind that carries the leaf along in its course, even so the Spirit, compared in Scripture to a strong wind, attracts souls and leads them to the Father and the Son. We have already noted that He describes an immense and invariable course: He comes from the Father and the Son, and He wings His way back toward Them taking souls along with Him. Devotion to Him cannot, therefore, reach its full development without this divine orientation to the Father and the Son.

But let us observe that, although all souls are destined to reproduce Jesus, not all of them do it in the same manner, for the Holy Spirit distributes His gifts as He pleases: "All these things are the work of one and the same Spirit, who allots to everyone according as He will."[4] In this passage

2. John 14:6.
3. 1 Cor. 3:22-23.
4. 1 Cor. 12:11.

the Apostle refers to the charisms, but the words can be applied also to the gifts. Though all of them are communicated to the just, they are not given in the same form and with the same measure, as the Apostle tells us in the Epistle to the Ephesians: "But to each one of us grace was given according to the measure of Christ's bestowal."

The ideal of reproducing Jesus is so sublime that no one can fulfill it adequately, not even the Blessed Virgin. She who is the most faithful and perfect reproduction of Jesus does not equal nor exhaust the divine ideal. Our heavenly Father, in His loving desire to see the image of His Son reproduced, has willed that each soul reproduce Him in its own way, copying one or more of His divine characteristics.

Someone has said that, since God could not create an infinite being, He brought into existence an endless variety of creatures to show His divine perfections and to give glory to Him. What He has done in the natural order He has done with greater perfection in the supernatural. It is true that the material universe is the reproduction of the Word: from each created thing shines forth some likeness to this ideal of the Father. But in the supernatural order, not only do souls reproduce the appearance of the Word Incarnate: they are its actual image. Not that any soul can duplicate it perfectly, but in every holy soul there is represented some aspect of the divine Jesus. O beautiful vision of the heavens! There one sees nothing but the reproduction of Jesus among the blessed: each soul a different image of Jesus, all presenting a magnificent variety and a most perfect unity.

Some souls are destined to reproduce the Infant of the crib with childlike virtues; others, Jesus of Nazareth, silent and contemplative; still others, the Apostle and Master who teaches and comforts, consoles and saves. Then there are those who are to reproduce Jesus of the Cenacle, transfigured with love,

Jesus of the tabernacle, loving in silence and mystically offering Himself in sacrifice; those, too, who are to reproduce the unutterable agony of Gethsemani; and others, the bloody sacrifice of Calvary.

But why continue? It is quite impossible to give all the ways in which souls reflect Jesus.

To discover and to fix its ideal, each soul must seek to learn in what way God wants it to reproduce His Son. It is of no little importance for each one to find its own particular path and to determine its course. How many souls fail because they have taken the wrong road! Would the beloved disciple St. John have been able to follow in the footprints of the Apostle of the Gentiles? Would St. Augustine and the first hermit, St. Paul, have traveled the same paths? Do you think that St. Francis Xavier would have attained the same glory by following St. Joseph of Cupertino? Teresa of Jesus is not Joan of Arc, nor is Gemma Galgani Thérèse of Lisieux. All the saints are admirable, but each is unique. In order to become holy, they all had to find their individual course. In their lives we read of many hesitations and waverings until they became docile to the Holy Spirit and took their own precise road.

Let no one believe that only great souls have their mission and their particular course to follow; all souls have both these things perfectly determined for them. Not all have the spectacular, hard mission of the great saints. In the Mystical Body of Jesus we are not all meant to be the heart brimming with love, the eyes aglow with intimate light; some will be the hands that bless, the feet that evangelize; others will remain hidden by divine concealment. But all are members of that Body and have a particular place and function.

The first thing that souls aspiring to perfection should do is fix the ideal and discover the special designs of God in their regard. For this, they need to be instructed and well directed.

But, above all, they need to be docile to the intimate direction of the Holy Spirit, who communicates Himself to the simple and reveals His secrets to souls of good will.

The Holy Spirit will show Jesus to them: "He will glorify Me."[5] The Holy Spirit will glorify Jesus and reveal all His beauty. And He will present Him to each soul accordingly as the soul is prepared to receive Him, and under that aspect which the soul must reproduce, and in those mysteries in which it must share in a particular manner. When the Holy Spirit shows the divine ideal to them, He infuses in them the kind of love of Jesus which is in accord with God's designs for them, together with a particular spiritual attraction that is peculiar to each individual soul. Aided by divine light and superhuman love, the soul will co-operate with the Spirit in its own transformation. It will not be mere lifeless marble being cut and polished by the chisel: rather, permitting itself to be moved by the divine Artist, it will put all its energy at His service, and will tear from itself all that opposes its transformation into Jesus. With its eyes on the divine Model, in perfect docility to holy inspirations, it will work and suffer constantly to attain the ineffable likeness to Jesus.

Is it not true, then, that devotion to the Holy Spirit brings with it devotion to Jesus?

---

5. John 16:14.

CHAPTER XV: THE HOLY SPIRIT TAKES US TO THE FATHER

ESIDES TAKING US TO THE WORD, THE Holy Spirit leads us to the knowledge, the love, and the repose of the Father. Love is not understandable without unity. Eternal love is the ineffable unity that exists between the Father and the Word and joins them, as we would say, in an infinite embrace. Created love is the great aspiration for unity that is fulfilled only when it is lost in the infinite ocean of God's unity.

Therefore charity is perfected when the soul is united to God and enters into the joy of the Lord. For this reason Jesus prayed so earnestly that we would all be perfected in unity; and this is why the first and last aspiration of the soul in love is expressed in the first versicle of the Canticle of Canticles: "Let Him kiss me with kisses of His mouth."[1] The mouth of the Father is the Word; His kiss is the Holy Spirit. Through that mysterious kiss the entire Trinity is communicated to the soul and the soul to the Trinity. The consummation of unity, the consummation of love, consists in this: that the soul, transformed into Jesus, reposes in the bosom of the Father, in the unity of the Holy Spirit.

These are the three stages of divine love: the soul is possessed by the Holy Spirit; the soul is transformed into the Word made flesh; and the soul rests in the bosom of the heavenly Father. They are three aspects of the same love, three forms of one devotion, three depths of one abyss of life and happiness.

---

1. 1:2.

We cannot possess the Holy Spirit without having in the depths of our heart that aspiration to the Father which is as natural in the supernatural realm, as logical in the life of grace, as it is natural and logical for the flame to rise upward, for water to flow to the ocean. As St. Augustine says: "The Father is the beginning of all divinity, or, if it is better so expressed, of all deity." Although it is common to the three divine Persons to be the beginning of the universe, it is attributed to the Father by appropriation. And since the Father is the beginning, He is also the end in whom everything finds its consummation and its rest. The charity poured into our hearts by the Holy Spirit raises in us an immense aspiration to the Father.

There can be no transformation into Jesus if one does not aspire to the Father and bear the very sentiments of Jesus in his heart. For is not the Heart of Jesus one divine aspiration to the Father? The whole Gospel bears witness to this. The ideal of Jesus is to glorify the Father, His passion is to love the Father, His food is to do the Father's will. The soul transformed into Jesus has this same ideal, this divine passion, and this heavenly food. Therefore, devotion to the Father is the logical consummation of devotion to the Holy Spirit.

Perhaps the faithful have forgotten about devotion to the Father. But the Church has not forgotten, for the greater part of her prayers are directed to the Father, through Jesus Christ, in the Holy Spirit. In the sacrifice of the Mass, which is the center of her liturgy, the Church, particularly in the Canon, addresses our heavenly Father. Jesus, through the ministry of the priest, offers Himself to the Father, and the Holy Spirit completes the offering.

Why do we not enter fully into the spirit of the Church, into the spirit of Jesus? Jesus asked the Father to sanctify us in truth.. The supreme truth, the fount of all truth, is the ineffable mystery of the life of God, the august mystery of the

Trinity, the beginning of our spiritual life and its most felici-
tous end in heaven. And the whole essence of our supernatural
life is a reflection of the infinite life of God. We shall be
sanctified fully when we get to the heart of the ineffable mystery, when our spiritual life becomes a solid devotion to the
Father, to the Son, and to the Holy Spirit.

What in very truth is the liturgical life, the life of the
Church, but the divinely profound and wondrously artistic
realization of these three devotions that must form a solid
supernatural reality in the light of one faith, in the fire of one
love, in the consummation of one sacrifice?

Let us examine the principal characteristics of devotion to
the Father. There are three: *adoration* in spirit and in truth
of the divine majesty resplendent in the Father; *filial love,*
respectful and tender, because its object is the Father; and
the *desire to fulfill the Father's will* even to abandonment,
because His will is the supreme norm of our life.

We have already said that the life of the Son, which is a
full, perfect, and living devotion to the Father, has these three
characteristics. To adore and love the Father and to fulfill
His most holy will was the whole life of Jesus. It should also
be our life.

As Jesus has taught us, we must adore in spirit and in truth
the infinite majesty that shines forth from the Father. "But the
hour is coming, and is now here, when the true worshipers will
worship the Father in spirit and in truth. For the Father also
seeks such to worship Him. God is spirit, and they who worship Him must worship in spirit and in truth."[2] The Father
must be adored in light and love: in light, the reflection of
eternal light; in love, the image of infinite love. And He must
be adored in *Jesus who is Truth, and in the Holy Spirit who
is Love.* To adore the Father in spirit and in truth is to share,

---

2. John 4:23-24.

as much as a creature can, in the mystery of the Trinity, contemplating the Father with the eyes of Jesus and effacing ourselves lovingly before His majesty under the impulse of infinite Love.

The intimate life of Jesus is the perfect adoration of the
Father in spirit and in truth; from deep within the soul of
Jesus comes the adoration which is the perfect glorification
of the Father and the source of the words of life, of the perfect sacrifice with which Jesus glorified the Father in His
mortal life and now glorifies Him in His heavenly and mystical
life. Is there anyone who can search the depths of this abyss?
His divine lips spoke from the abundance of His heart, and
whenever they referred to the Father, seemed to distill heavenly
honey. The divine joy hidden in His heart appeared exteriorly
on those occasions: "In that very hour He rejoiced in the Holy
Spirit and said, 'I praise Thee, Father, Lord of heaven and
earth.' "[3] What a mystery of gladness these words hold: "He
rejoiced in the Holy Spirit." In the sacerdotal prayer in the
Cenacle, Jesus, always moderate in speech, multiplies epithets
when addressing His Father: "Holy Father. . . . Just Father."[4]
His eyes, sweetly and lovingly raised to the Father, tell us more
than His words. If only we could contemplate and understand
those frequent glances of Jesus, His poem of love and adoration of the Father!

As with Jesus, the foundation of our interior life must be
this profound adoration of the Father. We must adore Him
in spirit and in truth, for this is what He expects. Without
this interior adoration our exterior acts are nothing, or very
little. For the Father to be pleased with and glorified in them
they must come forth from the abundance of our heart, the
overflow of our own sentiments of adoration and love.

---

3. Luke 10:21.
4. John 17:11, 25.

We must adore the Father in truth and especially in the Truth, that is, in Jesus. What are our poor prayers worth without Him? The blessed in heaven adore the Father through Jesus: "Through whom the angels praise Thy majesty, the dominations adore it," as the Church sings in the Preface of almost every Mass. We must adore the Father in spirit, and above all in the Holy Spirit, because in Him we cry: "Abba! Father!" Only the light that the Holy Spirit diffuses in our souls can reveal to us the ineffable majesty of the Father; only His divine breath can diffuse in our hearts the self-effacement of adoration and love.

Before His agony, Jesus gave the Father this description of His wonderful life: "I have glorified Thee on earth." God grant that our life, like that of Jesus, may be nothing else but a perpetual, living glorification of the Father; that this may have its roots in interior adoration and be diffused like a divine sap in our words and works!

One might think that devotion to the Father would exclude confidence and love for Him in as much as it is based on profound respect. Because of the limitations of our nature, we think that respect and confidence, adoration and love, are incompatible in ourselves, just as we think that majesty and tenderness are incompatible in God. On the contrary, majesty is wondrously harmonized with tenderness in the Father. Even further (if one may venture to utter what he is firmly convinced is the truth even though he does not completely understand it), devotion to the Father is a devotion of confidence precisely because it is one of respect; because it is a most profound adoration, it is a tender love; and because the Father is majestic, He is tender.

Tenderness is not weakness, but plenitude. It is the height of greatness because it is the height of love. Perhaps there are certain sensible forms of tenderness that might be attributed to weakness, but true tenderness coming from the depths of the heart is found only in love that has attained a rich fullness, in pure and disinterested love, in love that has become an ocean, and overflows. In the natural order, tenderness is characteristic of great love, of the pure love of noble souls. There is no affection more tender than a father's or, supremely, a mother's; these loves give more than they receive; they overflow because of their fullness. They show a beautiful union of majesty and tenderness that remains even when time has diminished the ardor of their affections. That is why tenderness, as Christians know it, was hardly to be found among the pagans. Jesus brought this secret to earth, because He brought the fullness of love.

No tenderness on earth is like the tenderness of Jesus. Astonished humanity has been contemplating it for twenty centuries with untiring admiration — and without understanding. Jesus caressed little children. He allowed John's head to rest on His breast. He sweetly pardoned sinners. He permitted a repentant woman to cover His feet with perfume and kisses. And He let His own tears of divine tenderness fall without disguise or shame.

The human tenderness of Jesus is a reflection of the divine tenderness of the Father. Precisely because God is infinite love, He is infinite tenderness. He overflows without measure because He is plenitude without limit. He has the perfection of tenderness because in Him is the perfection of majesty. He alone who is perfect worth can love that which is worth nothing. He alone who has everything can fill what is empty. He alone who is supremely exalted can come down to the abyss of our lowliness. The depth of His loving condescension is measured by the exaltation of His greatness.

In creatures, tenderness is limited because their love is limited, and because they are not plenitude. In God, the abyss of tenderness is one with the abyss of majesty — our intelligence does not understand but our heart tells us this is true. It is impossible for mere creatures to scrutinize the mystery of the infinite tenderness of the Father, but Jesus has revealed it to us in His own. Thus we understand the words that He spoke to Philip: "He who sees Me sees also the Father."[5] Therefore, when the Spirit of adoption in us cries to the Father, we feel our heart dilated and ourselves submerged in an immense ocean of tenderness. We know from the Holy Gospel that whenever the voice of the Father has been heard on earth, it has pronounced words of tenderness: "This is My beloved Son"; "I have both glorified [Thy name], and I will glorify it again."[6] These words tell us of the tenderness of the Father for His only-begotten Son, as well as for the children adopted through Jesus and in Jesus.

It belonged to the Apostle St. John to give us the supreme revelation of the tenderness of Jesus: "In this has the love of God been shown in our case, that God has sent His only-begotten Son into the world that we may live through Him."[7]

And just as in the Father majesty and tenderness are one, so in our souls respect harmonizes with confidence, adoration with love. Fundamentally, all these things have the same root: the infinite. Our respect is most profound for the same reason that our confidence is unlimited; our adoration is perfect precisely because our love is immense.

Adoration, when it has attained its plenitude, is love, and love, when it has attained its perfection, is adoration. Therefore the only full and perfect love, the only love that completely satisfies the heart, is the love of God: it is the only love that can become adoration. If God were not so great,

---

5. John 14:9.
6. Ibid. 12:28.
7. 1 John 4:9.

if He were not infinite, if we could comprehend Him or exhaust Him, we would not love Him as we do; He would not satisfy our heart. The supreme enchantment of divine love lies precisely in this, that God is a truth never to be encompassed, a good never to be exhausted, a beauty ever renewed. The most lovable, the most exquisite thing about God is that "I know not what," according to the expression of St. John of the Cross; He is the One whom language cannot express, nor intelligence explain, but whom the intuitions of love discover in a divine vision of happiness. This "I know not what" is infinite majesty, ineffable tenderness; and the homage our soul renders to Him is, at the same time, respect and confidence, adoration and love.

Was there not in the soul of Jesus a love for the Father intense and tender, a love that seems to throb in every page of the Gospel; that became a divine explosion on Calvary, and lives on victorious and immortal in the Eucharist? Let us not weary of repeating it: the foundation of all the mysteries of Jesus is His love for the Father. It is the center of His intimate feelings, the root of His prodigious works, the source of His words of eternal life, the secret of His immolations, the fountain of His fecundity; in a word, the supreme reason for His life and death, for His glory in heaven and His abiding presence on earth until the end of time.

CHAPTER XVI: THE WILL OF THE FATHER

F THE THREE CHARACTERISTICS of devotion to the first Person of the Blessed Trinity, the most outstanding in Jesus is His passion for fulfilling the Father's will. Jesus hid His profound adoration in the mystery of His intimate thoughts, and, ordinarily, He hid His tenderness with a veil of divine serenity, though it escaped at times in the brilliance of His glance, in the tone of His voice, in His sudden emotion; but when it was a question of His Father's will, far from concealing His desire to fulfill it, He was pleased to show it in all the circumstances of His life.

The secrets of the soul of Jesus in the beginning of His life can only be glimpsed by privileged souls, but there is one that He willed to reveal to us as a prophecy in the Old Testament and as a fundamental reality in the New. St. Paul makes this splendid revelation to us by taking the words of the Psalms and disclosing their meaning: "Therefore in coming into the world, He says, 'Sacrifice and oblation Thou wouldst not, but a body Thou hast fitted to Me. In holocausts and sin-offerings Thou hast had no pleasure. Then said I, "Behold, I come — in the head of the book it is written of Me — to do Thy will, O God." ' In saying in the first place, 'Sacrifices and oblations and holocausts and sin-offerings Thou wouldst not, neither hast Thou had pleasure in them' (which are offered according to the Law), and then saying, 'Behold, I come to do Thy will, O God,' He annuls the first covenant in order to establish the second. It is in this 'will' that we have been sanctified through the offering of the body of Jesus Christ

once for all."[1] In these words we have, as it were, a revelation
of the depths within Jesus: we know what He felt, what He
said, and what He longed for in the beginning of His life;
He came to do the will of His Father, and the full accomplishment of that will was His oblation on Calvary. In this
accomplishment we have been sanctified.

Jesus Himself has told us that He came to do the will of
His Father: "For I have come down from heaven, not to do
My own will, but the will of Him who sent Me."[2] He did
the will of the Father without ceasing and even when it was
repugnant to His humanity, as in Gethsemani: "I do always
the things that are pleasing to Him."[3] For Jesus, the will of
His Father was the foundation of His relationship with souls
and the root of His holy affections: "For whoever does the
will of My Father in heaven, he is My brother and sister and
mother." In the prayer to His Father in which He made a
sort of summary of His desires to teach us what ours should be,
we find these words that seem to come forth as a triumphant
cry from the depths of His soul: "Thy will be done on earth,
as it is in heaven."[4] He wished to tell us in our own language
how avidly He sought to do the Father's will and how that
will was His very life: with undisguised emotion He said to
the Apostles at Jacob's well: "I have food to eat of which
you do not know. . . . My food is to do the will of Him who
sent Me."[5] What could be the will of the Father if Jesus
loved it so, if He was always seeking it, and making it the
very center of His life, the very foundation of His soul?
The will of God is the norm of perfection, the secret of happiness, and the repose of love. It would be very good and
profitable for our souls to examine this last point.

1. Hebr. 10:5-10.
2. John 6:38.
3. Ibid. 8:29.
4. Matt. 6:10.
5. John 4:32, 34.

The most perfect kind of love demands that we seek the good of the beloved. But when the beloved is God, it is the infinite Good, the fullness of good that lacks nothing, to which nothing can be added. Therefore, the first act of love of God is to rejoice in that ocean of Good and to praise it without rest. The happiness of the blessed consists in rejoicing in the infinite perfections of God, in His inexpressible goodness, in His resplendent beauty. By their profound and loving adoration they are eternally intoning the canticle of praise.

Love might console itself for not being able to do good to the Beloved by having complacency in the fact that the Beloved has the fullness of good and lacks nothing. But it has pleased God that souls who are in love with Him should do to Him the good that the impetuous exigencies and immense necessities of love demand. We certainly cannot add one iota to His goodness and felicity; the Psalmist is lovingly complacent in the knowledge of his inability to do so when he says: "My Lord are You. Apart from You I have no good."[6] But there is a good that we *can* do to God, accidental and extrinsic to His fullness: we can lovingly fulfill His will. The will of God is to reflect Himself in creatures; it is to communicate Himself to them; it is to fill them with His goodness and His happiness. The fulfillment of that will is His glory: the end of all His works and the end of all His creatures. Their happiness consists in co-operating in its accomplishment.

The love of God, so rich in its shades, so varied in its tenderness, so admirable in its manifestations, has in reality but two fundamental acts to which all the others can be reduced. Since love (we refer to the love of benevolence) consists in willing the good of the beloved, and God has only two goods — one essential, which is His infinite fullness, the other accidental and extrinsic, which is His glory — therefore our

6. Ps. 15:2.

love for Him also has two fundamental acts: complacency in the infinite good and accomplishment of the accidental good by the fulfillment of His most holy will. The divine flowering of love in the saints, their desire for perfection, their longing to suffer, their ardent zeal for the salvation of souls, are but manifestations of these two fundamental acts. And it is likewise true that all the things which are good for us and which we may legitimately seek are intimately connected with these two acts, for we find our happiness in the possession of God, in the enjoyment of the infinite good, and in the reflection of the glory of God within us.

Therefore Jesus, who loves the Father with a divine passion, had, as a secret nourishment, the fulfillment of the will of Him who sent Him. And therefore also, true devotion to the Father consists in a filial love which rejoices in loving adoration of the divine goodness, and aspires with all its strength to fulfill the divine will.

The Holy Spirit alone can give us a share of Jesus' hunger to do the will of God, because this hunger is love and all true love comes from infinite Love. Being the love of the Father and the Son, the Spirit is the infinite and personal complacency of love in the fullness of good. When He is reflected in souls, when He communicates Himself to them, when He possesses and deifies them, He pours into them an image, limited, but divine, of Himself, pure Love; and by impressing this unutterable image, He communicates to souls the two essential complacencies of love.

For worldly people, the will of God is often a tragic hardship; for imperfect souls, it is a motive for resignation; for saints, it is heaven. Why so many diverse effects from one thing? Simply because each soul receives the will of God according to its relations with the Holy Spirit. The world neither knows nor loves the will of God and despairs many

times on account of it. Imperfect souls already possess the
Holy Spirit; but since their love is imperfect, they receive the
will of God with resignation, a mixture of joy and sorrow.
The Spirit has not yet attained complete possession of them,
nor do they enjoy that entire harmony and fullness of peace
that love brings, because all their inclinations have not yet
been co-ordinated in the unity of love.

In the saints, however, all is harmony, peace, unity, for all
is love. The Holy Spirit has penetrated, possessed and transformed them. With divine light they see in the divine will
the good of God, which is their own good, and with all the
impetuosity of love, with all the vehemence of the Spirit's
motion, they give themselves up to that will.

Only the Holy Spirit can infuse in our hearts such passion
for the divine will, for only He can bring us to know the
Father and teach us to love Him, by transforming us into Jesus.

Therefore the Church prays in the "Veni Creator," part of
the liturgy of Pentecost, "that we may know the Father through
Thee." If we could devise a beautiful and perfectly graded
scale of all the forms of acceptance of the will of God, from
the most imperfect resignation to the purest joy, we would
have at the same time a scale indicating the different degrees
of possession that the Holy Spirit can achieve in souls. He is
the great unifier, or rather, He is unity, because He is Love.
The Father and the Son embrace lovingly in the unity of the
Holy Spirit; and the blessed souls who let themselves be possessed and moved by eternal Love, share in this divine unity,
according to the prayer of Jesus to the Father: "That they may
be one, even as We are."

Jesus laid bare the fundamental longing of His soul when
He taught us to say: "Thy will be done on earth as it is in
heaven." But that desire of Jesus is not fulfilled until the Holy
Spirit takes possession of souls and, by revealing the Father
to them, lovingly unifies them in His divine will.

CHAPTER XVII: THE CROSS

A TRUE DEVOTION TO THE FATHER, THE Son, and the Holy Spirit leads to one end, the Cross: the true and supreme glorification of the Father, the highest expression of love on earth, the central point of the will of God. Let us examine carefully this doctrine that brings us to the core of Christianity, whose greatest revelation is the mystery of the Cross, whose life-giving source is the Eucharist, the divine perpetuation of that mystery, and whose secret means of leading souls to God is participation in the sacrifice of Jesus.

St. Paul did not wish to know anything "except Jesus Christ and Him crucified,"[1] nor did he wish to glory in anything but the Cross of Christ, in which is our salvation, our life, and our resurrection.[2]

To glorify God is to recognize and to proclaim His infinite excellence and omnipotent sovereignty over all creation. Irrational creatures that display the divine marks given them by the hand of the Creator, glorify God indirectly, as St. John of the Cross expresses it in the inimitable lines of his "Spiritual Canticle":

> *Scattering a thousand graces*
> *He passed through these groves in haste,*
> *And, looking upon them as He went,*
> *Left them, by His glance alone,*
> *Clothed with beauty.*

---

1. 1. Cor. 2:2.
2. Cf. Gal. 6:14.

And the Scriptures tell us "the heavens declare the glory of God"[3] and "the earth is full of His praise."[4] But only rational creatures glorify God directly, for they alone can know, or at least have a glimpse of, infinite grandeur, and be led to praise it, and to efface themselves before it in loving subjection. Scriptures present the saints prostrating themselves before God's majesty. The clearer the knowledge of God and the more profound the self-effacement of the creature, the more perfect is the glorification.

After the fall, the glorification of God was tinged, so to speak, with the color of expiation required by divine justice, and the self-effacement of the creature was changed into the humiliation of pain and death. The people of Israel, instructed by God, and other peoples of the world, guided by the remains of primitive revelation, understood that supreme glorification required sacrifice, in which the victim was destroyed in honor of the supreme Being.

But those ancient sacrifices were not sufficient in themselves for either expiation or glorification. How could sin-stained creatures satisfy divine justice? How could they who had not received the perfect revelation of infinite greatness, perfectly glorify God?

God rejected the ancient sacrifices and accomplished a stupendous prodigy of justice and mercy, of wisdom and love, in the sublime sacrifice of Calvary in which Jesus — most pure Victim, capable of offering a sacrifice of infinite value — offered to God a complete and superabundant expiation for sin, and, at the same time, gave Him the most perfect glorification.

---

3. Ps. 18:2.
4. Hab. 3:3.

God dies to glorify God! Jesus, knowing infinite goodness better than anyone, immolated Himself on the Cross with unfathomable love! Who but God can know the sublime fullness, the ineffable perfection, of this supreme glorification? And once the divine mystery is accomplished, there remains but to perpetuate it, to crystallize it, to make it immortal. Jesus has done this by giving us the incredible miracle of the Eucharist.

Perhaps in heaven we shall see that glorification and love are the same: that only love glorifies God, and that in glorification alone does love find its rest and its peace. On earth we do not see this. We have to separate the things of God and painfully examine their various aspects, and only then rebuild the divine reality in our imperfect way, by bringing together our scattered concepts.

The Cross, the supreme glorification of God, is also the supreme expression of love. Love is surrender, it is giving, it is the sweet communication of our whole being with that of the Beloved; it is the divine strength that makes us efface ourselves in honor of the One we love; the power to lose all so as to give all; the knowledge of the exquisite delight of our incredible poverty, of our perfect divestment, of our ineffable humility. In these, the Beloved will become our wealth, our happiness, our glory, our all.

We read in the Holy Gospel that the kingdom of heaven is like a man who sells all he has in order to buy a precious pearl, or a field in which a great treasure is hidden. These are symbols of love. Supreme love is the infinite surrender, the complete communication, the ineffable giving, of the three divine Persons in the bosom of God. God is charity and His intimate life is the mystery of the unutterable donations of love.

The love of the creature, since it is a reflection of eternal love, is also a total and most sweet donation. The angels accomplish it in the peace and joy of their spiritual and immaculate nature. On earth, the supreme donation of love cannot be made except in pain and death. This might seem to be an imperfection; yet this wretchedness of ours is the occasion of exquisite happiness, singular glory. Give me a lover, says Augustine, and he will understand what I am saying! To know that we die for the One we love, that our destruction is His joy, that we can purchase a smile from His lips at the price of death and sorrow — is not this the highest delight and joy of love? Love without pain is truly insipid and imperfect.

It is not that we have chosen this way of love. The God of heaven who enjoys the delights of infinite love willed to love in this way, and He performed prodigies in order to die of love and pain on the Cross. "In this we have come to know His love, that He laid down His life for us," said St. John,[5] and his words have been repeated by all souls in love with God.

By dying on the Cross for us, Jesus showed to what lengths God would go in His love for man; by dying for the glory of the Father, He expressed the depth of the love of man for God. The Cross is the supreme symbol of this love.

In the Epistle to the Hebrews, quoted earlier, St. Paul reveals the mystery of the will of God: "Therefore in coming into the world, He says, 'Sacrifice and oblation Thou wouldst not, but a body Thou hast fitted to Me. In holocausts and sin-offerings Thou hast had no pleasure. Then said I, "Behold, I come . . . to do Thy will, O God!" ' " And in this will, adds St. Paul, we were sanctified, in the unique offering of the body of Jesus Christ.

---

5. 1 John 3:16.

Each one of the mysteries of Jesus, each instant of His life, is the fulfillment of His Father's will, but we have St. Paul's revelation that the co-ordinating center of all the divine dispositions is the Cross.

God wills many things that are in reality but one thing. For unity is the mark of all that is His, a rich unity that holds the universe in magnificent harmony. The human artist, in his masterpiece, wills and arranges all the elements, lights and shadows, colors and figures, seeking in this variety a central theme which will unify and harmonize the artistic elements, and which is the key to the work and the reason for its beauty. The divine Artist has willed many things: the earth with all its marvels, history and all its vicissitudes, the supernatural order with all its prodigies. Yet among this immense variety, His gaze, His search, His love, are only for Jesus Crucified. The Cross is the key to God's magnificent work, the secret of its unity and beauty, the co-ordinating principle of the world and history, of time and eternity. Therefore St. Paul could say that the will of the Father was accomplished by the oblation of the body of Christ, and that we are sanctified in that will.

The devotion to the Father that filled the soul of Jesus, that soul great beyond measure, had the Cross for its terminus. Only on the Cross was His longing to glorify the Father satisfied, His immense hunger for doing the will of the Father appeased, only there did His infinite love attain rest.

The loving dream of Jesus during His mortal life was the Cross; He longed for it as only the heart of the Man-God could long for the culmination of all His infinite aspirations. Although He hid His supreme secret under the mantle of divine serenity, it escaped Him as a perfume escapes its containing vial. It undoubtedly revealed itself at Nazareth, to be received in Mary's heart; and again, in intimate conversations with His Apostles, as when He said: "I have a baptism to be baptized with; and how distressed I am until it is accomplished";[6] and that other time in the Cenacle, when He told His disciples of His ardent desire to celebrate the Pasch with them.

Jesus carried in His heart for thirty-three years the cruel, torturing martyrdom of longing for sacrifice, and of waiting for the hour appointed by the heavenly Father. Therefore, His devotion to the Father had a definitive form — sacrifice; a clear symbol—the Cross; and a precise formula—"Christ . . . through the Holy Spirit offered Himself unblemished unto God."

---

6. Luke 12:50.

CHAPTER XVIII: THE CON-SUMMATION

IF THE CROSS WAS FOR JESUS THE CENTER of devotion to the Father, it should hold the same place for us. We have seen that the sacrifice of the Cross was the perfect glorification of the Father, the supreme act of love for Him, and the perfect fulfillment of His will. Once this supreme sacrifice was accomplished, there remained nothing more for Jesus to do but to perpetuate it. As Lacordaire says, once the word of love has been pronounced, the only thing to do is to repeat it. So Jesus perpetuated His sacrifice in two ways on earth: in the Eucharist and in souls. Therefore, the center of Catholic worship — which in the Church is the devotion of Jesus to the Father in the Holy Spirit — is the Mass; and the center of Christian life — which is this same devotion in souls — is the mystic participation in the sacrifice of Jesus by each soul.

In the liturgy of the Church there are many sacraments, many blessings, many songs of praise, many fervent prayers; but all of them are grouped around the Mass, of which they are either the preparation or the consequence. In the same way, there are in the Christian life many virtues and many gifts, numerous intimate communications with God and a multitude of holy and heroic acts; but all of them are grouped around the Cross, for they are the preparation or the consequence of the intimate, loving sacrifice.

A Calvary, or a martyrdom, is the peak of perfection. And the happy soul that carries the Cross of Christ, traveling the rough path that leads to divine union, asks for no other reward, aspires to no other happiness, than to be crucified with Jesus. This is the highest happiness on earth, as the Master tells us in the eighth beatitude, which crowns and synthesizes His wonderful doctrine of happiness.

The Church celebrates as a feast day the occasion of the finding of the true Cross by St. Helena. In the same way each soul should celebrate its personal discovery of the Cross. Until it has done this the soul is restless, desirous of perfection and of happiness, longing for the reward of its efforts and the realization of its ideal. But when God permits it the celebration of this feast, it rests in perfect happiness and offers in its intimate sanctuary the mystic Mass of its loving sacrifice to "fill up what is lacking of the sufferings of Christ," according to the bold expression of St. Paul.[1]

There was a bishop of early Christian times who made the Lord an oblation of his martyrdom, using almost the very words of the Canon in the offering of the Eucharistic sacrifice. He was right: martyrdom was his personal Mass, the heroic reflection and echo of all the Masses he had celebrated, the correspondence of his ardent love to the immense love with which Jesus had so many times sacrificed Himself in the bishop's anointed hands.

Each priest, each soul, must carry within that intimate reflection of the Cross, that echo of Calvary. Each priest, each soul, must answer the sacrifice of Jesus with his own. The solemn and glorious martyrdom of blood is not the only one; there are personal martyrdoms, meritorious and cruel, unseen by man but seen by God. Each virtue can have its own martyrs. Charity, queen of them all, has many very great ones.

But whether one exclaims with St. Paul, "I bear the marks of the Lord Jesus in my body";[2] or says with St. Ignatius of Antioch, "I am the wheat of Christ, and I must be crushed

---

1. Col. 1:24.
2. Gal. 6:17.

by the teeth of wild beasts so that I may be converted into immaculate bread"; or longs with St. Teresa of Jesus to give one's life in testimony against the enemies of Christ — every soul should aspire to martyrdom; the Cross should be the center of its life, the goal of all its aspirations. It is the cross that satisfies the Father completely, and it is His Crucified Son that He longs to behold in each soul. What complacency is His when He beholds the sacrifice of Jesus in that "clean Oblation" which is immolated and offered "in every place"![3] And how He is pleased by those personal hosts that pure and loving souls ceaselessly offer to Him! This does not mean that other acts of devotion do not please the Father. He accepts and is pleased with all of them that have been performed "in spirit and in truth"; but nothing satisfies Him like loving sacrifice; just as all liturgical acts are pleasing to Him, but none so much as the sacrifice of the Mass.

Let us repeat that the supreme glorification of the Father, the highest love for Him, the completest accomplishment of His will, is perfect and personal participation by every soul in the sacrifice of Jesus. But the divine science of the Cross, the love of the Cross, and the intimate participation in the Cross are precious jewels that only the Holy Spirit can communicate to souls. "The doctrine of the Cross," says St. Paul, "is foolishness to those who perish, but to those who are saved, that is, to us, it is the power of God."[4] And he adds: "We, for our part, preach a crucified Christ — to the Jews indeed a stumbling block and to the Gentiles foolishness, but to those who are called, both Jews and Greeks, Christ, the power of God and the wisdom of God."[5]

In chapter two of the same Epistle he explains this radical difference of opinion. The knowledge of Jesus Crucified is a

3. Mal. 1:11.
4. 1 Cor. 1:18.
5. Ibid. 23-24.

hidden wisdom that escapes the princes of this world but has been revealed to us by the Holy Spirit. Only the Spirit of God knows the secrets of God. And we have received this Spirit that we may be able to know the gifts of God. Therefore, while the worldly man does not perceive the action of the Spirit of God, the spiritual man judges all things, for he has received the profound meaning of the mystery of Christ, of which the Cross is the depth and the marrow.

From faith we have the substance of the revelation of the Cross; but in order to penetrate it, to discover the unknown wealth contained in it, the divine treasures hidden under its bitterness, the ineffable sweetness it holds within the sharpness of its pain, we must submit this faith to be enlivened and corrected by that deep and penetrating light that the Holy Spirit communicates to souls through His gifts.

Experience tells us that as souls progress in the spiritual life, the love of sacrifice, the desire to suffer, and the deep appreciation of pain increase in them, without their knowing how or why. A divine instinct, a supernatural intuition, progressively discovers for them the treasures of the Cross, and teaches them that it is the root of all virtues, the foundation of love, the closest bond of union, the sweetest reward loving souls can receive on earth. This is because the Holy Spirit, while He more and more takes possession of souls, reveals to them His secrets and removes little by little the veil that hides from human eyes the holy, the unutterable and divine revelation of the Cross.

When the Holy Spirit fills souls with light to help them penetrate the mystery of the Cross, He also enkindles in them an ardent and passionate love for suffering. Can human nature be led by its own power to the love of pain? Philosophers may convince us that we should suffer: but the most they can do is produce in us the cold, proud attitude of the Stoics.

Such an attitude is not human, because it opposes all our natural inclinations; nor is it divine, because it does not lift us up from the earth but only plunges us deeper in the abyss of pride.

No: Philosophy will never teach us to love pain; only eternal Love can infuse such love into our souls. Before pain can be loved, it must be transmuted into love, and Jesus alone has succeeded in doing this. To love the Cross, we must see Jesus on it and understand the personal and indestructible ties that bind Him to it. To love the Cross, we must experience the sweet and strong attraction which Jesus Crucified exercises over souls, as He Himself promised: "And I, if I be lifted up from the earth, will draw all things to Myself."[6] Man, abandoned to himself, hates nothing so much as pain; when the fire of the Holy Spirit burns within his soul, there is nothing he loves so intensely.

Let us remember the incomprehensible aspirations of the saints: the irrepressible longing of St. Ignatius Martyr for the supreme sacrifice; the disconcerting alternatives of St. Teresa of Jesus: "To suffer or to die"; the eagerness of the virgin of Lisieux to embrace in her loving heart all martyrdoms and all pain.

Madness? Undoubtedly. A divine madness, the madness of a God in love, who willed to die for man and who left on earth the precious seed of this sublime folly. Is love itself perhaps not madness? Do not all the bold deeds of genius and heroism appear to be madness? Does not all that falls outside of the narrow mold of mediocrity seem madness? There are some who never fail to proclaim that saints are abnormal. They believe that human normality consists in living to its fullest the animal life of man, ennobled with the refinements of what they call culture. Viewing that cramped and narrow criterion, how well we understand the truth of

6. John 12:32.

the Apostle's words: "The sensual man does not perceive the things that are of the Spirit of God." All the great and noble things which make us proud of our heritage, and without which the world would be plunged into the deepest degradation, are the result of that madness of the Cross.

Against modern paganism, worse in a way than the old paganism, there is no other remedy than the Holy Spirit, pouring Himself copiously into souls and renewing the face of the earth, revealing the mystery of pain and enkindling in hearts the rarest, most intense of all loves, the supreme love that saves: the love of suffering.

The Holy Spirit, who communicates the science of the Cross and infuses love for it in souls, also gives to chosen souls a participation in it, according to His loving designs. Jesus Himself offered His sacrifice under the divine influence of the Holy Spirit, as the oft-quoted Scriptural passage tells us: "Christ . . . through the Holy Spirit offered Himself unblemished unto God."

It is not our sacrifice itself that has value and merit, greatness and power to glorify God; its power and its life are in the love that impregnates and inspires it. The Apostle has said that martyrdom itself avails nothing without love. Is not hell the greatest suffering? Why is it so sterile, so desolate, so full of despair? Because love has gone forever from that accursed place. And if those eternal pains glorify God, it is because the former love of the damned, now turned into hate, still gives glory to Him.

For sacrifice to have value, it must be the fruit of love; to have infinite value, it must be the fruit of infinite love. Therefore Jesus offered Himself through the Holy Spirit, the personal Love of God. And all the souls who wish to share in the sacrifice of Jesus, all who wish, like Him, to offer themselves to the Father, must offer themselves through the Spirit.

It is He who inspires all holy immolations and all fruitful martyrdoms. He enfolds our poor sorrows in the infinite sorrows of Jesus, mingles our blood with the divine blood, nails us to the Cross with the divine Victim, fuses our hearts with the divine Heart.

Thus the Holy Spirit teaches the mystery of the Cross. He teaches us how to love it, He makes us participate in the sacrifice of Jesus. By revealing the Father to us, He reveals the mystery of the Cross; by our participation in it, He makes us glorify the Father. We have said that devotion to the Holy Spirit is completed in devotion to the Father; and since this devotion is perfected in the Cross, it follows that the Cross is the perfection and crown of devotion to the Spirit. It is the foundation, the center, and the summit of the spiritual life and of Christian perfection.

CHAPTER XIX: SUMMARY AND CONCLUSIONS

THE FOREGOING STUDY HAS treated of a multitude of matters which, though unified into a single idea, may because of their separate presentation have failed to convey a clear impression of the whole. It will be helpful, then, to offer a simple and brief summary of what has been written in the course of these chapters about true devotion to the Holy Spirit.

Our main purpose was to exhort souls to give to the Holy Spirit His proper place in the spiritual life, according to the teachings of the Church.

The Spirit is not an accidental and secondary aid to perfection; He is the Sanctifier of souls, the fount of all graces, the center of the spiritual life. Therefore, devotion to the Spirit is something essential and profound that souls who are seeking perfection must comprehend and practice (Chapter I).

The Holy Spirit is the most sweet Guest of the soul (Chapter II). He is its personal and true Director (Chapter III); the first Gift of God (Chapter IV); the source of all the other gifts and the first link in the royal chain that terminates in perfection (Chapter V). His sanctifying work is to form Jesus in souls, thus producing in them the ideal of the Father (Chapter VI).

In this manner the Holy Spirit enters the portals of the soul and establishes His dwelling there. Active and fruitful, He assumes a more and more complete, living and intimate direction of the soul. He lets Himself be possessed by the soul and He possesses it ever more profoundly; and with Him come all the graces and divine gifts that transform the soul until it is converted into the image of Jesus, so that the Father may find complacency in His Son and be glorified by the soul, through Jesus, with Jesus, and in Jesus.

But the action of the Holy Spirit always requires the co-operation of the soul. Even in those particular operations in which it is moved by a special motion of the Spirit, the soul needs to co-operate. And the more intense its co-operation and the greater its fidelity, the more perfect are the divine operations. This constant and loving co-operation with the action of the Holy Spirit, the faithful correspondence to His love and to His gifts, is the basis of devotion to Him (Chapter VII).

As the Holy Spirit gives Himself to us forever and desires that His action, as far as possible, be constant in our souls, our correspondence, our devotion, must be a total, definitive, and perpetual surrender, a true consecration. The diverse aspects of this consecration can be determined by the different functions the Holy Spirit exercises in our soul, which are only forms or modes discerned by our poor intelligence in the single and most fruitful action of the Spirit. To each of these forms or functions our soul must lovingly correspond.

If the Holy Spirit is the constant and most sweet Guest of the soul, we must give shelter in our heart to eternal love; and as this love wishes to be the unique love of the soul, all earthly affections must be rooted out so that the immense solitude of the heart can be offered to the Paraclete (Chapter VIII).

Faith reveals the Holy Spirit to us. Hope puts us in touch with His divine strength, communicated through His goodness. Charity, the highest Gift of the Spirit, binds us intimately to Him (Chapters IX, X, XI).

Love, known on earth in many varied forms, all of which are found in a rich and simple unity in God, has very special characteristics when the Holy Spirit is its object. It is a love of sweetest docility, of full surrender, of perfect abandonment; it is a love that causes the soul to let itself be possessed and delivered with loving fidelity to the action of the divine Director (Chapter XII).

This docility demands deep silence so that the voice of the Spirit may be heard; exquisite purity so that the profound meaning of His words may be probed; abandonment so that we may be carried along by the divine breath in a perfect spirit of sacrifice, for in His flight the heavenly Dove always tends toward the Cross.

Our love of the Holy Spirit demands more than just letting ourselves be possessed by Him; it requires that we also possess Him, because He is the Gift of God. The Holy Spirit is the intimate Director and first Gift; the soul lets itself be possessed by that divine Director, and strives to possess that unutterable Gift. Thus a concise formula encloses the whole meaning of love for the Holy Spirit: to possess Him and to let oneself be possessed by Him. Certainly these two actions, as forms of the same reality, develop in a parallel manner, so that the more the soul possesses the Holy Spirit, the more it is possessed by Him. But they express divine shades of love leading to formally different states of perfection: by letting itself be possessed, the soul is brought to perfect deification, called by St. John of the Cross the transforming union; by possessing the Holy Spirit, the soul finds its perfection in that intimate and most perfect love which the mystics call "loving with the Holy Spirit" (Chapter XIII), a bold expression but theologically correct.

The loving designs of the Holy Spirit in the sanctification of souls, although most varied — because each soul has its own road and its own mission — have a divine unity. The Holy Spirit is always forming Jesus in each soul; each holy soul is a reflection of Jesus, although the divine Model is copied by each in a different way. Each one goes to the Father and glorifies Him through Jesus, with Jesus, and in Jesus. Consequently, devotion to the Holy Spirit is closely and logically joined with devotion to the Word and to the Father. It is true that through the humanity of Jesus we go to the divinity, according to the divine designs; yet the Holy Spirit also takes us to the Word, to a love more intense and to a union more intimate, and through the Word we go to the Father in whom all is consummated. Therefore, devotion to the Holy Spirit has for natural complement a more intimate devotion to the Word of God (Chapter XIV).

And these two devotions find their crown in devotion to the heavenly Father (Chapter XV). This devotion is characterized by three things: a profound adoration in spirit and in truth, a most tender filial love, and an intense longing to fulfill the Father's will.

As Jesus loved the Father in this way, so also should we love Him (Chapters XV and XVI).

These marks of devotion to the Father lead to one same height, Calvary, because the very essence of the devotion of Jesus to the Father was the Cross (Chapter XVII). It should be the same in regard to our devotion (Chapter XVIII).

Consequently, the Cross, the supreme symbol of love and pain, is the consummation of devotion to the Holy Spirit, and therefore of Christian life and perfection.

PART II
THE GIFTS

CHAPTER I: INTRODUCTORY

OW ARE WE TO KNOW THE HOLY Spirit if, as the Scriptures tell us, He dwells in inaccessible light? To help us understand this we have these words of a Father of the Church: "If that light is inaccessible to our strength, it is accessible to the gifts we have received from God." With the light of faith, with the illuminated eyes of our heart, we can penetrate the shadows of the mystery and contemplate the marvels of God.

We shall not dare to intrude into the august sanctuary of God, nor pretend to display the secrets of His divine life, nor audaciously attempt to explain the infinite and substantial love that binds the Father and the Son in unutterable unity. But, ever mindful of our human limitations, let us endeavor to show the work of the Holy Spirit so that souls may be lifted thereby to as high a degree of the knowledge of God as is possible on earth. Let us study the operation of the Holy Spirit in our souls.

Theologians, with the authority of the Scriptures and Tradition, appropriate to each one of the Persons of the Trinity those operations which, by their nature, resemble the specific character of each Person. Thus, to the Father is attributed the creation, to the Son the redemption, to the Holy Spirit the sanctification of our souls.

If we could only contemplate that marvelous work of sanctification which the Holy Spirit accomplishes in us! One is tempted to say that this work is His masterpiece — but we know that in truth Jesus is His masterpiece. Jesus was conceived by the operation of the Holy Spirit; the Spirit filled

Him with divine plenitude, guided Him in all the steps of His mortal life, to His offering of Himself on the Cross and His immolation on Calvary.

The masterpiece of the Holy Spirit is Jesus. But is not the sanctification of our souls merely the extension and the complement of the Spirit's work in Jesus? To the Apostle Paul, the mystery of Christ is not only the mystery of the Incarnation and the Redemption of the human race; in his profound thought, Christ is not only the second Person of the Most Holy Trinity, united hypostatically to the human nature formed by the Spirit in the womb of the Virgin Mary; no, in Paul's mind, the mystery of Christ is the immense multitude of souls that are members of the Mystical Body. The complete Jesus embraces all of us. To sanctify souls is to complete Jesus; it is to consummate the mystery of Christ. Thus the work of sanctification is the masterpiece of the Holy Spirit when considered as the completion of His work accomplished in Jesus Christ.

The Holy Spirit brings about our sanctification in two ways. The first is, by helping us, moving us, directing us, but in such a way that *we are actually doing our own work.* It is our glory to fulfill our own destiny. God has given us the wonderful and terrible gift of freedom, by which we ourselves are the artisans of our own happiness or our own ruin.

But the Holy Spirit has another way of directing. It is His personal direction of our deeds, when He no longer merely illuminates us with His light, or warms us with His fire to show us the road that we must follow. In this second way, He Himself deigns to move our faculties and to urge us so that *we may perform His work.*

A comparison will help us to understand these two ways. Let us imagine a great artist creating a masterpiece. He arranges for the preparation of the canvas, and the way in which the colors are to be combined. He then calls on his best pupils to share the work. He permits them to do the least important, or least perfect, part of it. But when he comes to the delicate, finest part, where he will reveal his genius, where the inspiration will be crystallized, then the pupils put down their brushes and the master takes over.

So it is with the Holy Spirit. He is going to accomplish a divine work in us; to trace in our hearts the living image of Jesus, that image which we must bear in order to enter into the eternal mansions. The Spirit directs in this work, using us to help; He permits us, His disciples, to trace some lines of the picture, under His guidance, of course, and according to the norms that He indicates for us. But there comes a time when the Spirit no longer wills us to perform the work at our own discretion. He takes charge personally and directly; and with very fine instruments He puts in the delicate characters, the faithful marks of the divine image.

We have our instruments also. They are the virtues that come with grace; and with them, little by little, we destroy the old man with all his concupiscence and trace the image of Jesus in our hearts, thus forming the new man, created according to the will of God in justice and the holiness of truth.

But a time comes when the virtues are no longer sufficient for the accomplishment of the divine work, and our own direction is not enough. Then the Holy Spirit intervenes and Himself carries on the work, using the instruments that the theologians call the gifts of the Holy Ghost.

How often we have heard of these gifts! Holy Church makes frequent allusions to them in hymns to the Holy Spirit: "Thou who art sevenfold in Thy grace," is her address to Him in the Vesper hymn for Pentecost. And in the sequence of the

Mass for that great feast she asks the Holy Spirit to give us His sevenfold gifts:

Thou on us, who evermore
Thee confess and Thee adore,
With Thy sevenfold gifts descend.

Here we might make use of a timely comparison. Science has produced amazing equipment that enables us to pick up invisible waves and to hear what is said or sung in any part of the world; anyone who has a receiving set can pick up these mysterious waves that carry sounds from the most distant places. In somewhat the same way, we may consider the gifts of the Holy Spirit as divine receivers for picking up His inspirations. Just as one who does not possess a radio cannot hear sounds from the other side of the earth, so one who is without the gifts of the Holy Spirit will not be able to pick up divine inspirations. The gifts are supernatural realities that God has willed to put in our souls so that we may be able to "make contact" with the Paraclete.

Naturally, the comparison is incomplete. With this invention of modern science, one can only hear. By these divine receptors, we receive not only the light and teaching of the Holy Spirit, but also His movements in such a way that under their influence we accomplish — in the spiritual order — the best and most perfect acts. The gifts of the Spirit enable us to receive not only His divine illuminations, but also His impulses in such a way that under His influence we move ourselves, as Holy Scripture says very clearly: "For whoever are led by the Spirit of God, they are the sons of God."[1] It is one of the marvelous prerogatives of the children of God to be moved by the Holy Spirit. In truth, many times our acts are

---

1. Rom. 8:14.

our own, but we operate under the motion of a superior force, a divine impulse, a movement of the Holy Spirit.

From these considerations we can reach a very wonderful conclusion: if the Holy Spirit moves us, and our acts are performed under His influence, those acts have a truly divine character. Someone has said very correctly: "The style is the man." Everyone has his own style, a seal and a reflection of his own personality. Thus, when the Holy Spirit works on us, He gives us His divine, unmistakable seal.

How different are the acts which we perform under our own direction, even when they are supernatural, from the acts that we perform when the Holy Spirit works in us! When we work we give our own seal, a seal of imperfections, a fragile seal; when the Holy Spirit acts, He places the divine seal of security, of perfection, of supernatural elevation. Therefore, to repeat, with the Holy Spirit as our Director, we perform acts that have a divine character.

Some examples may illustrate this. The prudent man who prepares to act with only his natural qualities and the supernatural virtue of prudence, succeeds, it is true, but slowly and with much difficulty. The Scriptures tell us about poor human prudence in two great master sketches.[2] We read that the thoughts of man are uncertain, and his dispositions timid.[3] Uncertainty and timidity are our stamp. There is something of these qualities even in our successful deeds.

One who works under the influence of the gift of counsel, which is supernatural prudence, knows — rapidly, surely, firmly — what ought to be done in every case.

Another example: when, guided by the light of faith, we seek to lift ourselves up to the knowledge of divine things, there is the human stamp on our act. We need to analyze,

2. Cf. Luke 12:16-21; Matt. 25:14-30.
3. Cf. Wis. 9:14.

to compare, to reflect; we accumulate ideas, we put them together, we harmonize them. When the saints contemplate divine things under the influence of the gifts of the Holy Spirit, they need only one glance, one profound, rich intuition, which enables them to contemplate in a single luminous instant that which would otherwise have required a long and painful effort.

The acts that proceed from the gifts of the Holy Spirit have a divine stamp, an entirely celestial form, that is the sign of the Spirit. We might even say that the norms of these celestial gifts differ. That is, the norms of the gifts are different from the norms of the virtues. When we work under the influence of the virtues we have a supernatural norm, certainly, but an imperfect one; it is the norm of man illuminated by God. But when we work under the influence of the gifts of the Holy Spirit, the norm is the norm of God communicated to man.

Let us not think that these gifts of the Spirit are proper only to souls that have reached certain heights on the road to perfection; let us not believe that only the saints possess the gifts of the Holy Spirit. All of us possess them. It is sufficient to have the grace of God in our souls in order to receive them. On the day of our baptism we received the gifts of the Holy Spirit together with the virtues and graces.

When we are born we are endowed by God with all we need for our human life, a complete organism, and a soul with the full range of faculties. Of course they are not all developed from birth, but we have them then as the source of everything we are going to need in life. And thus it is also in the spiritual order. When someone is baptized, he receives in all its fullness that supernatural world which the Christian carries within his soul. He receives grace, which is a participation of the nature of God; the theological virtues, which put him in immediate contact with the divine; the moral virtues, which serve to regulate and order all his life; and the gifts of the Holy Spirit, the divine, mysterious receivers for picking up the Spirit's inspirations and movements.

And as long as we possess the grace, we possess also the gifts. They are not something passing; they are permanent, we carry them constantly in our soul. Grace cannot exist without the gifts, and grace and the gifts cannot exist if the Holy Spirit, the divine Director of our spiritual life, is not also present.

St. Thomas Aquinas, whose authority cannot be disputed, teaches that the gifts of the Holy Spirit are indispensable for the salvation of the soul; without them we are not able to accomplish our sanctification. To make clear the necessity of the gifts even in the ordinary life of the Christian, St. Thomas uses what seems to be a very exact comparison. He says that a great doctor by himself can cure a seriously ill person or handle an extraordinary case; whereas an inexperienced doctor, an intern, even though he has many remedies and knows much about medicine for ordinary cases, when a difficult case comes to him, needs the direction of a skilled physician who knows medicine perfectly and therefore understands the sick person's requirements.

We are like the inexperienced intern. We can attend to our own salvation in ordinary cases, but it would be impossible for us to accomplish completely the work of our sanctification without the guidance of the Holy Spirit, who alone knows perfectly what we are and what we should be, and the paths by which we can reach the perfection to which God calls us.

The gifts that the saints receive are not extraordinary divine favors; all of us carry the same gifts within us. At times we do not realize the riches that God has given us; we are not aware that we possess in our souls a most perfect world, more excellent and beautiful than the exterior one, because we have grace which makes us resemble God. We also bear within us the theological virtues, which put us in intimate contact with divinity; the moral virtues, which order and dispose everything in our lives; and the gifts of the Holy Spirit, which keep us in communication with Him and enable us to receive His holy movements.

It is obvious, however, that the gifts do not develop to the same degree and with the same perfection in all souls, any more than do the virtues. Like the virtues, the gifts are vital germs that need to be cultivated. Our work, our effort as Christians, consists in nurturing with exquisite care these precious seeds that God has placed in our soul. And just as the plants have their seasons for blooming — some when fragrant spring is here, others in the heat of summer, others still in the midst of autumn's richness — so each one of the gifts has its special, propitious moment in the spiritual life when it finds its full development.

How do the gifts of the Holy Spirit develop in us? What can and what ought we to do in order to bring them to perfect growth? Three things are necessary.

The first is to increase charity in our hearts, since charity is the root of the gifts. Whenever we love, we are able to receive the inspirations of the Holy Spirit. Even in human love there is a spark of that prodigious privilege that divine love confers. Whenever we love, even with an earthly love, we have intuitions of the thoughts and desires of the beloved that no science can supply. "The heart has its reasons," says Pascal, "that reason does not know." And if poor human love, so imperfect and deficient, has mysterious intuitions; if the one loving sees, hears, surmises, guesses — with how much more reason will the supernatural love the Holy Spirit pours into our hearts, which is called charity, have its intuitions!

In proportion as charity increases, the gifts also increase and develop. We find them in the saints, for the saints have reached a high degree of charity. The first means, then, of developing in ourselves those precious, divine instruments, the gifts of the Spirit, is to develop our charity.

The second means consists in developing the virtues which we receive along with the grace of God. By means of these infused virtues we can go on perfecting one by one all our faculties and setting right everything in our soul. And as the virtues increase, the ground is prepared, so to speak, for the Holy Spirit to come, and with fine and exquisite art, to finish our work.

Thirdly, to develop the gifts of the Spirit, we must be responsive to His inspirations. By our loving and constant attention, by the docility of our heart, we can more clearly hear the mysterious voice of the Spirit of God, we can more perfectly receive His holy inspirations. And the more perfectly we receive them, the more completely will the gifts perfect themselves in us.

Let us practice the Christian virtues with greater care, so that with a submissive spirit and an open heart we may receive the beautiful music of the Paraclete's voice and feel in the depths of our soul His holy inspirations and His divine movements.

CHAPTER II: THE GIFT OF FEAR

E FIND THE NAMES AND the number of the gifts of the Holy Spirit in a classic passage of the prophet Isaias: "There shall come forth a rod out of the root of Jesse, and a flower shall rise up out of his root. And the spirit of the Lord shall rest upon Him: the spirit of wisdom and of understanding, the spirit of counsel and of fortitude, the spirit of knowledge and of godliness [piety]. And He shall be filled with the spirit of the fear of the Lord."[1]

What Isaias calls "spirit," the technical language of theology calls "gifts." The Holy Spirit who dwells in us when we possess the grace of God, this sweet Guest of our soul who masterfully directs our spiritual life, has desired to establish in the different parts of our being those mysterious realities, the gifts by which He communicates with us and influences each and every one of our human faculties.

Let us consider these faculties.

At their summit, like a flash of the very light of God, is the intellect. It makes us resemble the angels and puts a trace of God's image upon our souls. Because of its excellence, the Holy Spirit has placed in it four gifts — wisdom, understanding, knowledge, and counsel — which correspond to the different intellectual habits. The gift of understanding makes us penetrate divine truths. The three others pertain to judgment: wisdom judges divine things, knowledge judges creatures, and counsel directs our acts.

---

1. Isa. 11:1-3.

In the will, the faculty next to the intellect in nobility, is found the gift of piety, which guides and directs our relations with God and men. In the inferior activities of our being, we have two gifts: fortitude to take away the dread of danger, and fear of the Lord to establish the proper relationship between Creator and creature and to moderate the disordered impulses of our concupiscence.

Thus the Holy Spirit has filled our whole being, from the highest to the lowest part, with His gifts, that He may communicate with the complete world we carry within us; that He may be able to inspire and move all our human acts.

At first our attention is called to the fact that in the will, which is of such great importance in our moral life, there is only one gift, piety, having for its object the directing of our relations with others. The reason for this apparent anomaly is, that in our will we have two very lofty virtues, hope and charity. These virtues are superior to the gifts, and consequently can have at the same time the function of virtue and gift.

The Holy Spirit possesses our souls completely by means of these gifts, which are closely related to one another. The prophet Isaias arranges them in pairs: the spirit of wisdom and understanding; the spirit of counsel and fortitude; the spirit of knowledge and piety; the spirit of the fear of the Lord. There is a very close union between the gifts that form each pair, the first in each case being the director of the second: wisdom directs understanding, counsel directs fortitude, knowledge directs piety, and the fear of the Lord is directed by wisdom, which is like a general manager of all the gifts.

In the order of importance, the first is wisdom. Understanding follows, then come knowledge, counsel, piety and fortitude. The lowest is the gift of the fear of the Lord.

Let us now examine them one by one, beginning with the lowest: the gift of fear of God.

How can there be a gift of fear? Is not charity at the root of all the gifts? And do not the Scriptures say that perfect love excludes fear? How is it possible, then, that fear of God can come from the profound and divine root of charity?

In order to understand this we must do a little analyzing. There are various kinds of fear: there is fear of pain and fear of blame; there is also a mundane fear that makes us forget the holy commandments of God and commit sin—fear, that is, of some earthly, temporal evil. How many there are who separate themselves from God through such earthly fear!

There is another fear that keeps us from sin and brings us close to God, but which is imperfect: theologians call it "servile fear," the fear of punishment. There is no doubt that this fear keeps us many times from falling into sin; but the motive is of an inferior order, and without the nobility proper to love. Servile fear is not the gift of fear of God.

There is another fear that is called filial. It consists in the repugnance that the soul feels at the thought of being separated from God. This fear comes from love. It is true that perfect love casts out a certain type of fear, but there is also a fear that is, we might say, the basis of love. Whosoever desires, whosoever loves, experiences a profound fear of being separated from the loved one, of displeasing him. Love cannot be conceived of without this fear. One who loves deeply has a fear that is above all other fears — fear of separation from the beloved. This is the gift of fear which is directed by the Holy Spirit.

The Spirit of God unites us to Himself in such a way that He infuses in us an instinctive, profound, efficacious horror of being separated from God, which makes us say: Everything, except to be parted from Him; everything, except to lose our close union with the Beloved! It is a filial fear, a noble fear, born from the very heart of love. Perfect, loving, filial fear is the gift of the fear of God.

Holy Scripture assures us in many passages that the fear of God is the beginning of wisdom; and this it is in truth, but the expression must be understood properly. The fear of God is not the beginning of wisdom in the sense that the essence of wisdom emanates from it, as conclusions emanate from principles in science; rather, the fear of God is the beginning of wisdom in the sense that this gift produces the first effect in the divine work of wisdom.

Now, in the same way the various kinds of fear are the beginning of wisdom. Servile fear is the beginning of wisdom, but not in the sense of influencing it. Rather, it helps to prepare and dispose the soul so that wisdom can enter. Servile fear is the beginning of wisdom, as the foundation is the beginning of a building. Being hidden, it does not have the beauty of form that the building is going to have, but the building must rest upon it. Thus servile fear, which keeps us away from sin, gives our soul the cleanliness necessary if true love is to enter.

In a more perfect sense filial fear is the beginning of wisdom, because, in order to possess divine wisdom, we need to unite ourselves so closely to God that nothing can separate us from Him. The gift of fear unites us with God in this way. It hinders us from ever separating ourselves from the Beloved, and in that sense it is the beginning of wisdom.

The gift of fear corresponds in a wonderful way to various virtues. It corresponds to humility because that virtue puts us in our proper place, makes us know our true value, and prevents that rebellion against God and that presumption by which we believe ourselves to be better than we are. The gift of the fear of God, by uniting us with God, makes us feel deeply our own deficiency. It corresponds also to that group of virtues related to temperance, since these virtues moderate our concupiscence and the disordered impulses of our hearts. The fear of God, guided by a very high principle, gives us moderation and peace.

Many of the great deeds in the lives of the saints were inspired by the gift of fear. St. Louis Gonzaga wept and scourged himself when he had to confess some little faults that we find it hard to believe were really sins. Why such tears from the saint? Why such grief? Because he examined so closely, under the influence of the gift of fear, the magnitude of those faults which to us seem insignificant; because he saw evil in them, a sign of separation from God. They were certainly very slight, but is anything really insignificant in love? When one loves passionately, does not the slightest danger of being removed from the beloved tear the heart to pieces?

This same gift of fear influenced St. Juliana of Falconieri, who trembled on hearing the word "sin," who would faint when she heard of a crime being committed. This is something higher, something deeper, something much more perfect, than we are able to attain by our natural faculties; it is a supernatural effect which the Holy Spirit produces in souls so that they can look with horror at sin, and thus cling with intensity to God.

Of course there are degrees in the gifts, as there are degrees in the virtues. In the natural order, any faculty can be developed by practice, the acts performed by it becoming all the while stronger, more perfect. The intelligence of a student on the threshold of knowledge is not of the same degree as that of one who has spent his whole life in serious and profound study. The natural faculties grow with exercise, and as they grow we distinguish new degrees of them. The same thing happens in the supernatural order. The virtues have their degrees, and so do the gifts.

The gift of the fear of God, in the first degree, produces horror for sin and strength to overcome temptations. By means of the *virtue* we keep away from sin and conquer temptations, but with many struggles, many failures. We know from sad experience that our spiritual efforts do not always result in victory. How many times we are overcome; and even when we finally come out victorious, how conscious we are of deficiencies, hesitations, effort! With the gift of fear, victory is rapid and perfect. How often have we known this experience in the depths of our souls — the quick, instinctive impulse in the presence of temptation to leave the danger at once! It was the Holy Spirit moving us with His gift of fear.

In the second degree of this gift, the soul not only stays away from sin, but clings to God with profound reverence, avoiding even insignificant acts that are signs of imperfection. The profound respect of the saints for everything sacred — the Church, the Gospel, the priest — is the effect of the gift of fear. Everything divine is reverenced. The soul under the power of this gift does not want to fail in the least detail in respect and veneration for God.

A marvelous effect is produced in the third degree of this gift: total detachment from the things of this earth. That is why theologians say that this gift produces the first of the beatitudes: that of poverty of spirit. When we cling to God and avoid all that could separate us from Him, in such a way that exterior things lose their fascination for us, then the soul knows it is free, and it experiences the divine detachment characteristic of this stage of the spiritual life; it reaches the glorious height of which Jesus Christ spoke when He said: "Blessed are the poor in spirit, for theirs is the kingdom of heaven."[2] The disinterestedness of St. Francis of Assisi, who considered all the things of earth as nothing; the disinterestedness to which Christ counseled the young man of the Gospel — "If thou wilt be perfect, go, sell what thou hast, and give to the poor, ... and come, follow Me":[3] such disinterestedness as this is the fruit of the divine gift of fear.

Is it not true that these considerations open new vistas to our minds, although at first sight they seem so exalted, so difficult, and unsuitable to our ordinary condition? How beautiful are the ways that lead to the heights! We may be down in the valley, or may only have reached the foot of the mountain; still, what a comfort, what a joy, to see the glorious summits and to know we are intended to reach them! What a challenge to our weakness, to our littleness, to realize that the Holy Spirit lives in us, that He has given us precious instruments in our hearts to urge us and lift us up so we may attain the heights!

In each one of these gifts we must contemplate the Holy Spirit, the supreme Director, the ineffable and divine Mover of our souls. For, consoling and comforting knowledge! He is never separated from His gifts. Where He is, there are His gifts, the precious means by which He can influence our whole being.

Let us lift up our eyes to the high places; let us lift up our hearts to heaven — *Sursum corda!* — and penetrate into the infinite bosom of God! Let us contemplate the ineffable, infinite, perfect, and personal Love which unites us in a loving embrace with the Father and the Son; let us invite it, desire it, and beg that it will never abandon us; that it will fill our hearts, and by its gifts will influence, move, and lead us through all the vicissitudes of exile to the blessed heights of the fatherland.

---

2. Matt. 5:3.
3. Matt. 19:21. Cf. Mark 10:21; Luke 18:22.

CHAPTER III: THE GIFT OF FORTITUDE

WHEN IT COMES TO DOING good, we find enormous difficulties in ourselves: the disordered inclination to evil and to the things of this world; the attraction of creatures called in Holy Scripture the "witchery of paltry things."[1] We need the Holy Spirit to moderate our affections, to regulate our lives, and to unite us intimately with God, so that no earthly attraction, no worldly enchantment, can pull us away from His loving embrace. The Holy Spirit accomplishes this, as we have already seen, by means of the gift of fear.

But there is another very important field in which we need the efficacious and decisive influence of the Spirit: the difficulties and dangers of the spiritual life. According to one translation of the Book of Ecclesiastes, Solomon the Wise has said: "All things are hard."[2] Experience teaches us the meaning of his words, and how true they are for human nature. The more noble and generous the undertakings, the greater the difficulties.

How many obstacles have to be overcome before we reach eternal happiness! We may recognize our duty with precision and exactitude; we may have a desire to fulfill it and to take the paths God has marked out for us — but our nature finds it so hard! We need such strength and sacrifice; we fail so many times; and knowing that, we may abandon the right road, we give up the undertaking because it seems too painful.

---

1. Wis. 4:12.
2. Eccles. 1:8 (Douay transl.).

In the spiritual life, there are difficulties and there are also dangers: occasions of sin and obstacles to good. Job said that human life is temptation. St. Peter said that the devil goes about like a roaring lion, looking for a chance to devour us. Dangers come from our associates, from the depths of our own being, and also from the infernal powers that plot against us and keep us from traveling a straight and direct path to perfection and happiness. We need extraordinary strength to help us bear these difficulties, avoid these dangers, strive toward the accomplishment of the will of God, and finally reach the end for which we were made. Heaven belongs to the strong, and for this reason there are relatively few saints: for few have the fortitude to make the efforts and sacrifices required by perfection.

That we may overcome the difficulties and escape the dangers, God has provided us with a set of virtues grouped around the cardinal virtue of fortitude. These are patience, perseverance, fidelity, magnanimity, and a number of others which, like an army in battle array, stand ready to help us. They are very efficacious, yet they are not sufficient; for virtues, as already explained, although they are supernatural, receive in our practice of them our own stamp: the human character, narrow, limited, and very weak.

Therefore does Holy Scripture say that "the deliberations of mortals are timid, and unsure are our plans."[3] Our acts have the seal of weakness and deficiency. If we are to attain salvation, fortitude with its companion virtues is not enough. A gift is needed, the gift of the Holy Spirit that bears the same name as the virtue: the gift of fortitude.

---

3. Wis. 9:14.

The Holy Spirit moves us by this gift so that we are able to overcome difficulties, to avoid dangers, and to have confidence. "I can do all things," exclaimed the Apostle St. Paul, "in Him who strengthens me."[4]

Let us now analyze the reasons why the virtue of fortitude must be completed by the corresponding gift.

The virtues have a norm distinct from the gifts. The virtue of fortitude encourages us in laborious works and fills us with the strength to overcome difficulties; but as it functions according to the measure of our human strength, it cannot encourage us to do anything above that strength. All virtue, theologians say, consists in the middle course; any deviation of our will to the right or to the left removes us from virtue. Fortitude, the virtue, certainly does not permit irrational timidity, but neither can it prompt us to undertake with assurance and boldness anything superior to our human strength. We find this prudent counsel in Holy Scripture: "With what is too much for you, meddle not."[5]

Now, is it not too much for human strength to complete every work and avoid every danger? Where is the man strong, great, persevering enough to finish every labor he undertakes and to escape from every peril he finds in his path? The work which the Christian has to achieve, the sanctification of his soul, the winning of eternal salvation, is the greatest and most arduous work known on earth. Can man, by his own strength — though assisted by divine aids yet still by his own strength—do this tremendous work and avoid all the dangers of a lifetime? Undoubtedly he cannot. He needs some aid that is superior to the virtues; he needs the gift of fortitude.

The measure and norm of the gift of fortitude is infinite strength, the strength of God. By means of this gift the Holy

4. Phil. 4:13.
5. Sirach 3:22.

Spirit prompts us to do all that the strength of God can do. In the supernatural order, under the movement of the Holy Spirit, creatures are actually clothed with the strength of God. St. Paul does not exaggerate when he says: "I can do all things in Him who strengthens me." The words may seem boastful and proud: *I can do everything.* How can St. Paul say this when the ability to do everything is proper to God alone? What he means is: *I can do everything because I depend on God, because I possess His strength, because I am clothed in His divine fortitude.*

Such is the norm of the gift of fortitude, the infinite strength of God. With this strength we can conquer every difficulty; in fact, we often observe how obstacles become a means to some good end in the all-powerful hands of God. And with this same strength we can overcome all dangers, for none is so grave as to withstand the power of the Most High.

Not only does the gift of fortitude help us overcome difficulties and avoid dangers, but it also gives us a confidence like that which the Apostle Paul describes in the passage just cited; a confidence, a security, that produces peace in our souls in the midst of dangers, in struggles, in all our tribulations.

There is nothing so glorious as the spectacle offered by the lives of the saints: in the midst of difficulties, in their struggles against the powers of earth and hell, they preserved peace and happiness, for they were ruled by the Holy Spirit and worked under the efficacious and omnipotent force of the gift of fortitude. Let us take a few examples.

By means of the gift of fortitude the saints have attained the incredible perfection that makes them *take joy in suffering.* It is hardly possible for us to understand how happiness can spring from the very depths of pain, but it is true.

St. Francis of Assisi and his companion, on a certain journey, stopped that the saint might explain in what perfect happiness consists. I shall not dwell on the well-known story except to remind you of the conclusion which the Seraph of Assisi gave to it: "O Brother Leo, perfect happiness consists in suffering for Christ, who willed to suffer so much for us." These are not the words of a scholar trying to impress his audience: they spring from one who had the sincerity of a child. Francis truly means that the greatest happiness, the most perfect happiness, is the celestial happiness of suffering. This he could only say under the influence of the gift of fortitude.

St. Ignatius, the Bishop of Antioch, while being taken to Rome to his martyrdom, gave another example of what the gift of fortitude does for the soul. He addressed an amazing letter to the Roman Christians, the purpose of which was to entreat them, in the heart of Christ, not to prevent his martyrdom: "... If the wild beasts do not throw themselves upon me, as has happened with some martyrs, I shall incite them to do so. Forgive me, my children, but I know what is good for me; for I am the wheat of Christ and I must be crushed by the teeth of wild beasts so that I may be converted into immaculate bread." These are the words and the attitude of a very wise man, a man under the influence of the Holy Spirit, who enjoys the efficacious strength of the gift of fortitude.

In other saints we find the gift of fortitude having an influence on acts that are not so extraordinary and heroic. Pope Gregory VII is an example of it in his gigantic struggle against the enemies of the Church. The superhuman strength shown by St. Teresa in the reform of the Carmelite Order likewise manifests the working of the gift of fortitude. She endured enormous difficulties in her contacts with all kinds of people while at the same time suffering a tremendous desolation of soul. Could she have accomplished her work without the gift of fortitude?

It is necessary even in ordinary life. Every Christian finds himself at some time or other in a difficult situation in which he needs the prompting of the Holy Spirit. Fortitude is also indispensable to perseverance in virtue, to the efforts that must be made to attain heaven. Without it, the heart is wanting in peace and confidence.

Thanks be to God, we received the gift of fortitude on the day of our baptism. We keep it as long as we have grace in our soul. The Holy Spirit is within us, and we can receive His efficacious aid whenever it is needed.

There are degrees of the gift of fortitude. In the first degree we can do all that is absolutely necessary for the salvation of our soul; all that God commands us, even extraordinary and heroic things. In the second degree our spirit acquires a superior strength, not only that we may accomplish what is absolutely necessary, what is of precept, but also that we may do the things of counsel, according to the duties and the spirit of each soul in the state in which God has placed it. In the third degree the gift of fortitude elevates us above every created good; it makes us conquer ourselves, and places us in the very heart of God, where boundless confidence and unchanging peace reign.

If only we knew the gift of God; if only we knew what a marvelous world we carry within our soul! If only we realized the incomparable and divine beauty of the supernatural world!

In the exterior world there are marvelous things. Who is not delighted with the perfume of spring? Who has not experienced the mysterious charm of the dewy woods? Who does not feel the grandeur of the ocean when he hears its mighty voice, when he sees the surge and beat of its great waves? Who does not experience a delicious peace while contemplating on a tranquil night the stars that sparkle so mysteriously in the heavens? Yet all this is nothing in comparison with the supernatural world.

Or if we pass to the realm of science and art, to all the marvelous works that man has produced, this is still nothing in comparison with our interior world, because there we have God. His graces and gifts are found in the sanctuary of our soul, and so we carry a divine world within us.

Come, Holy Spirit, Light of souls! Open our eyes that we may perceive the wonders in our heart! Enlighten us, move us, quicken us, prompt us, that we may forget this poor exterior world, so deficient and imperfect, and may live in that other, interior world where Thou art and where, like a splendid Sovereign, Thou dost give us Thy gifts of infinite power.

CHAPTER IV: THE GIFT OF PIETY

THERE IS NO PART OF OUR BEING that the movement of the Spirit does not reach; there is no occasion in all our spiritual life that He does not attend with His divine influence, by means of some of His gifts. He communicates to us the vigor, courage and superhuman strength to accomplish all our undertakings and to overcome all dangers for the glory of God.

But our spiritual life is not intended to keep us closed up within some interior castle, remote from everything and everyone. All life demands relationship with others, and this is especially true of the spiritual life. We have duties to fulfill toward God and neighbor; we cannot live in selfish isolation. The Christian spirit is a spirit of charity, and charity requires communication — and not only charity, but justice and many other virtues as well.

A group of virtues has been provided for us, with justice at the center, by which all our relations with God and our neighbor will be ordered and disposed. For those to whom we owe some heavy debt, there is justice; for our obligations to God, there is religion; for our parents, our family, and our country, there is piety; for our benefactors, there is gratitude; and so on for all our relations with other people.

But, as already noted, virtue is always limited by the human stamp of imperfection. The Holy Spirit will have to act upon our relationship with others by means of a gift. The gift of piety it is that unifies in an admirable way all these relationships, guides them, makes them more profound, more perfect.

In the first place, it unifies them. Observe that in the field of the virtues there is a whole multitude provided for the

142

ordering of our relations with others, while in the domain of the gifts, there is only one. This is because the higher and the greater a thing is, the nearer to God, the simpler it is. The Apostole St. Paul speaks, in words we have already noted, of this very lofty principle, this norm of our relationships: "You have received a Spirit of adoption as sons, by virtue of which we cry, 'Abba! Father!' "[1]

Because God is our Father, we have very intimate and holy filial relations with Him; and from this Spirit of adoption who makes us look upon God as our Father comes the order and union that the gift of piety establishes in our relationship with our fellow man. Let us analyze this doctrine. By means of justice and the moral virtues our relations with others are regulated, each of our neighbors being given his due. Now, there are debts we can pay with mathematical exactness, and others we can never take care of ourselves. How could we pay God for the benefits we have received from Him? "How shall I make a return to the Lord for all the good He has done for me?"[2] No matter how sincerely and completely we offer our life to Him, we can never repay, for He has given us everything; even though we gave it all back to Him, there would still remain an unpaid debt. To enable us to make a return for this debt in our small way, we have the virtue of religion.

The *virtue* of piety demands that we repay our parents for the benefits received from them (benefits which in fact can never be fully repaid; for how can we fittingly repay them for the life they have given us?) And, like justice, religion, and piety, there are other virtues of the same group ordering our relations with others, and having a motive and a norm proper to their particular work. But the *gift* of piety has no limited norm such as a debt or a benefit; for the sacred norm of this gift is the Father Himself.

---

1. Rom. 8:15.
2. Ps. 115:12.

The virtue of religion produces in us gratitude to God for numberless benefits received in the natural and the supernatural order, and honor and devotion to Him who has sovereignty over our being. It prompts us to respond to His beneficence, and to fulfill our duties toward Him as our Sovereign, by means of the acts of religion.

But the gift of piety is not concerned with what is *owed* to God; it does not measure the honor due to Him for the benefits that have been received from Him. The gift of piety is inspired by the Spirit of adoption by which we call upon God as our Father. Since He is our Father, we should have a deep filial affection for Him in our hearts, because it is proper that children love their Father. The gift of piety, or rather, the Holy Spirit through the gift of piety, develops in us this filial affection; and thus we are concerned about the honor and glory of our Father because we are His children.

The virtue of religion beholds God as Sovereign; the gift of piety sees Him as Father. The virtue of religion is mindful of benefits received, the gift of piety leads the soul to say: "He is my Father; therefore I must bear in mind His honor, His glory, and His greatness."

The sentiments of the soul under the direction of the gift of piety are often expressed in the Scriptures. "We give Thee thanks, O Lord God almighty, who art, and who wast, because Thou hast taken Thy great power and hast begun Thy reign."[3] Here thanks are not rendered for His benefits, nor because He has received us into His kingdom, nor because He has made us: thanks are given for the power of His virtue, for the glory of His triumph.

Everyday in holy Mass the Church voices these same sentiments: "We give Thee thanks for Thy great glory." Do we really understand these words? We give thanks to God, not

---

3. Apoc. 11:17.

because of what He has given us, but because He is great, because of His glory. It is natural for a son who truly and worthily loves his father, to take immense care of that father's honor and glory, not regarding the benefits that may come to him from it.

The gift of piety is clearly distinguished from the virtue of charity: the virtue of charity has for its object God Himself, while the gift of piety looks to God's honor. Undoubtedly it does so by means of charity, for charity is the root of that adoptive affiliation that the Holy Spirit makes us feel in the depths of our soul. But while charity makes us love God for Himself, the gift of piety makes us watchful of His honor, makes us give Him all our actions so that He may be honored and His glory increased.

When St. Ignatius of Loyola chose for His motto "For the greater glory of God," he was without doubt inspired by the gift of piety. This gift helps us to fulfill all the duties we have toward God in a delicate, attentive, filial manner. Also, as a logical consequence of the Spirit of adoption which the Holy Spirit infuses into our souls, it makes us feel a singular and affectionate interest in all our fellow men.

Piety, in the natural order and in the order of the virtues, refers principally to our parents and, as a logical consequence, to the fulfillment of our duties toward all our relatives, toward all who make up our family, even to love of country. Piety, as the gift of the Holy Spirit, leads us to knowledge of God the Father, and to a sense of our fraternity with all men; for all men are our brothers if God is our Father; and all the glory and grandeur of God, to which we are drawn because of the gift of piety, logically makes us honor all who share in this glory. And every Christian, indeed everyone not reprobate, has a participation in that divine greatness, or at least is intended to have it.

When Francis of Assisi had not yet found his true path — when, according to the fashion of his time, he was still dreaming of glory as a knight errant — a leper came to him, and Francis felt a supernatural movement in his soul. He responded to it, and in that very moment he received a revelation: the revelation of human fraternity. When Francis understood and knew that all men are brothers, he received the marvelous effect of the gift of piety. This gift enables us to perform our obligations toward others, not by the measure of strict justice, but in accord with the great affection we bear them in our souls. Rightly has St. Thomas said: "Love has no measure." And when it is love, not duty, that inspires our actions, we pass all limits, we abandon all measures, and generously pour out the love of our hearts. This is the gift of piety. With it the soul can give itself to God and to others without reserve, with all the generosity, with all the expansiveness, of a supernatural and divine love.

To complete our understanding of the gift of piety, we should notice some of the principal effects it produces in the soul.

With respect to God, the gift of piety inspires us with sentiments of confidence, and prompts us to give ourselves to Him. A child trusts its father, and gives him its heart; a soul under the influence of the gift of piety has complete confidence in God and gives itself wholly to Him. For more than nineteen centuries we have had this sublime thought from the Gospel: "Unless you . . . become like little children, you will not enter the kingdom of heaven."[4] Yet no one before St. Thérèse of Lisieux so perfectly understood, expressed, and practiced the way of spiritual childhood.

Many virtues and gifts contributed to her formation; but her "little way" is particularly marked by the gift of piety.

---

4. Matt. 18:3

To become as a little child is to sense deeply our divine filiation. The saint said that because she was living in a modern world of discoveries, she also wanted great discoveries in the spiritual order; that she wanted to go up to God and to reach her perfection in an elevator. No doubt she would have used the word "airplane" if she had lived a few years later. The arms of Jesus were her spiritual elevator. She was like a child in the embrace of its father. How often she repeated that comparison! The unlimited confidence that Thérèse of Lisieux had in God was filial confidence. The absolute surrender by which she put all that she had, all that she was, into the hands of God was the result of the gift of piety.

In the high degrees of this gift, the Holy Spirit infuses into souls the desire to be united with Jesus Christ the Victim, in order to expiate the sins of the world and to promote the glory of God.

We believe that all who worthily receive Communion — not only the ministers at the altar, but also the faithful — participate in the sacrifice of Jesus. Because of this participation, and with the help of the gift of piety, we should experience, in a divine, deep, and efficacious manner, the sentiments Jesus had in His heart when He offered the sacrifice of the Cenacle and the sacrifice of Calvary. We should desire to unite our sufferings with the sufferings of Jesus, and to offer them together with His; to carry within our hearts an echo of the desire, immense and divine, that Jesus had within Him when He offered Himself as a Victim for the sins of the world.

With regard to our brethren, in the first degree of this gift the soul gives itself generously to others, in the way proper to the gift. The second degree is no longer an overflow of generosity whereby the soul gives what is superfluous: it now gives what it needs itself. Let us recall what St. Paul said: "I

could wish to be anathema . . . for the sake of my brethren."[5]
How did the Apostle come to desire the loss of the divine gifts
so as to give them to others? A strange generosity! A generosity without limits that proceeds from the gift of piety.

The last degree of this gift, particularly in those dedicated
to the apostolic life, consists in giving oneself without reserve,
in giving everything for others. "But I will most gladly spend
and be spent myself for your souls, even though, loving you
more, I be loved less."[6]

Thus the gift of piety, springing from charity like an effusion from the Spirit of adoption, has no measure; it lacks the
narrow, rigid norm of the virtues; it rather breaks through
measures and limits, and in an impulse of holy generosity
makes the souls that possess it in its fullness give everything,
and even themselves, for the good of others.

Each one of the gifts opens up a new vista for souls, a view
of an unknown and mysterious world, a world beautiful, holy,
divine. The more knowledge we have of the works of God,
the greater is our astonishment. There are things we hardly
suspect in the supernatural world. When we succeed in getting
a glimpse of them, we feel that we rise a little from the earth,
that our startled eyes see, though still imperfectly. In reality
the truths pertaining to the gifts of the Holy Spirit are very
lofty; but those gifts are truly ours.

A faint parallel might be this: If a physiologist should
speak to us of the marvelous and mysterious things that happen
in the physical order, things unknown to those who are not
initiated into the science, we could not deny those facts merely
because we are not trained to grasp them. Perhaps it would be
difficult to understand them, but because they are verified in
our lives, they have a consequent intense interest for us.

5. Rom. 9:3.
6. 2 Cor. 12:15.

Likewise, we must accept as a fact that we have all the gifts of the Spirit. Even the repentant sinner regains them by receiving absolution, for he cannot have grace without the gifts, nor without the Spirit: the Spirit never separates Himself from His gifts.

These marvels are truly present in our soul, even though they may be prevented from reaching their perfect development because of our fault or our deficiency. Let us be more attentive to the divine inspirations. Let us enter more fully into the spiritual life, and yield to the beauty of that mysterious world. Wonders would then be accomplished in our hearts, wonders such as those manifested in the hearts of the saints.

May the divine Spirit pour His light into our souls, touch our hearts, reveal to us the world of sanctity and grace, so that we may love Him more and more. May He lead us with His holy movements, and guide us into the world of light and love, of generosity and elevation; the world that is neither bought nor sold; the eternal and exceedingly delightful world where we hope to be happy forever in the Heart of God.

CHAPTER V: THE INTELLECTUAL GIFTS IN GENERAL

E HAVE SEEN THAT THE first three gifts of the Holy Spirit pertain to our affective life: fear and fortitude direct our sensibility, piety directs our will, so that we may have worthy and holy relations with others. The next four gifts are intellectual: they perfect our intelligence and lead us to the knowledge of supernatural things.

The intellect is the highest faculty, the one that rules over all the others. The will itself, so supremely important in the moral order, is subject to the intelligence. Hence this noble ruling faculty must be attuned and perfected by the movements of the Spirit of God. Its object is to know, both in the natural and in the supernatural order. Supernatural knowledge is of capital importance in the Christian life, for Jesus has said: "This is everlasting life, that they may know Thee, the only true God, and Him whom Thou hast sent, Jesus Christ."[1] The supernatural knowledge of God, of Jesus Christ, of the mysteries of heaven, is the proper object of faith. But the theological virtue of faith, even though superior in dignity to the intellectual gifts, is obscure and imperfect and has to be bolstered and clarified by them.

Before treating of each gift in particular, we will indicate their general characteristics.

The four intellectual gifts correspond perfectly to the natural habits of our intelligence, for "grace is founded on

---

1. John 17:3.

nature," as St. Thomas tells us. There is a marvelous parallelism between the intellectual and the divine, since nature and
grace have the same source and emanate from the same
principle, God, who formed our nature and is also the Author
of grace.

In our intellect we find: the *first principles,* which are the
basis of understanding; *knowledge,* which is a perception of
the nature of things through their causes; *wisdom,* which is
the capacity to relate all things to their ultimate end; *prudence,*
which is the art of applying speculative principles to practical
purposes. Now there is a wonderful correspondence of the
four intellectual gifts of the Holy Spirit with these four habits
that exist in the natural order. The intellectual gifts of the
Holy Spirit are: *understanding, knowledge, wisdom,* and
counsel.

A common characteristic of these four gifts is that they
are all founded on faith. Faith is a virtue by which we trust
in God's divine authority and believe all that He has revealed
to us. It is the light on the way of our exile, like the little
lamp that shines in a dark place, as the Apostle St. Peter says,
a sign of our expectation of the day of glory, of our hope for
the rising of the morning star in our hearts.[2] Faith is the guide,
even though the truths of faith are made more brilliant by the
illumination of the gifts.

A comparison comes to mind. Science can apply the rays
of the sun to many uses; it can concentrate them, combine them,
separate the different elements that compose them. It can do
marvelous things with those rays, but back of all of them there
is one single reality, the light of the sun. In a similar way
the gifts of the Holy Spirit multiply, refine and transform the
spiritual light of faith, but it is always the same light that
irradiates all supernatural knowledge. It is always the little

---

2. Cf. 2 Pet. 1:19.

lamp of faith that enlightens us while we await the arrival of the splendid day of eternity.

In some extraordinary circumstances, God illumines certain chosen souls with the light of prophecy, but the usual light of the spiritual life is faith, and this light is the basis of the intellectual gifts. By faith we know all the truths that Jesus wished to reveal to us. We know the mysteries of the kingdom of heaven, we know all we need to know for our salvation; and we know it on the authority of God, on the authority of the Church established by Jesus Christ. However, when by means of the gifts of the Holy Spirit we penetrate those truths of faith, then we discover their depth and appreciate the harmony that exists among them. We have an intimate, profound knowledge of them, although we may never have objective evidence in this life: faith never loses its mysterious darkness. In heaven, the gifts of the Holy Spirit will continue, although their foundation will not be faith any longer, but the Beatific Vision, the splendid vision of the fatherland.

What a difference between the knowledge we have by simple faith and the knowledge obtained under the direction of the intellectual gifts! St. Francis of Assisi spent entire nights repeating: "My God and my All!" These few words do not keep the majority of us attentive for five minutes. Why were they enough to furnish Francis with whole nights of prayer? Because he said them with the light of God; because the gifts of the Holy Spirit revealed to him the supernatural riches the words contained.

St. Thomas teaches that there are two ways of knowing: one by discourse in its various forms, the other by intimate experience. The first is purely intellectual; the second springs from the very depths of love. We can have the first by reading books on the mysteries of faith, by listening to sermons about them; it can be more or less broad, more or less perfect, yet it is a knowledge of pure understanding. The other is granted to loving souls united with God: in the very close union of love, these souls know divine things by sweet and intimate experience. That knowledge is obtained through the gifts of the Holy Spirit.

A Franciscan lay Brother said to St. Bonaventure, the Seraphic Doctor: "Ah, fortunate are you learned men who can love God so much more than we ignorant ones!" St. Bonaventure replied: "No, no, it is not learning, not knowledge acquired from books, that measures love. An ignorant little old woman, if she is united to God, can love Him more than a great theologian can." The lay Brother understood the lesson and went through the streets shouting enthusiastically: "Ignorant little old woman, you can love God more than Fray Bonaventure!"

And thus it is truth; there is a knowledge that is measured by love. In the natural order it is proper and logical that love should come from knowledge; but in the supernatural order, even when this rule of natural psychology is observed in a certain way, light and knowledge also follow love. He who loves more, knows more; and all that we read about the saints proves it.

Even in the natural order, love is a powerful spur to knowledge. When we love some science very much, love sets all our faculties in motion and fixes our attention so that our efforts become more intense and fruitful. In the natural order, too, as has been said earlier, a mother has intuitive and marvelous knowledge about her children; it seems that she guesses their thoughts and looks into their hearts. This is because love establishes such harmony and proportion between those who love each other that they seem to form one single being. And in virtue of this admirable harmony of love, it is sufficient to penetrate our own heart in order to understand the heart of the one we love.

In the supernatural order this is still more perfect. Charity, that queen virtue which unites and gives life to all virtues, binds us to God to such a degree that we can say He makes us one with Him. "He who cleaves to the Lord," says the Apostle St. Paul, "is one spirit with Him."[3] The expression is bold, but well founded. The same Apostle also says: "It is now no longer I that live, but Christ lives in me."[4]

Love accomplishes the most perfect union. When charity unites us with God so that we are one single spirit with Him, we recognize divine things by a sweet experience in the same intimate way in which we are conscious of the depths of our own heart. Souls intimately united to God by charity seem to find the elements of the knowledge of God in the depths of their own being. This is the basic explanation of why the intellectual gifts give us a new, intimate, and at times very sweet knowledge of divine things.

We have seen that when St. Francis of Assisi spent whole nights saying "My God and my All," it was because from the depths of his seraphic love came the splendid light of the gifts, throwing a brilliant effulgence upon the secrets of God. How many examples like this do we not have in the lives of the saints! There have been some who were not able to leave the sanctuary: with their spirit fixed on the Tabernacle where Jesus dwells, they were entranced in contemplation of celestial things. It was because they loved, and from deep in their hearts flashed the glorious light of the gifts, particularly (as I shall explain later) the gift of wisdom, the highest, deepest, and most divine. But all the intellectual gifts share in this character: all make us know. Why? Because we love. The light of the gifts is a light that comes from love.

---

3. 1 Cor. 6:17.
4. Gal. 2:20.

But let us not think that the gifts of the Holy Spirit make us know God in a perfect manner, as we are to know Him in heaven. Here on earth, as already explained, they have their foundation in faith, and in spite of the fact that they penetrate truths and illuminate them in a heavenly manner, they always leave a certain obscurity that will never disappear in this our exile. In our heavenly home, the intellectual gifts, enlightened by the light of glory, will leave no obscurity, and will complete our happiness.

In mortal life, the knowledge that the gifts give us of divine things, especially of God Himself, may be called negative; we do not know what God is; we know what He is not. St. Thomas Aquinas says that the greatest knowledge we can have of God in this world is to understand that He is above all our thoughts and words; to know that our poor strength cannot perfectly capture Him, that He is something greater than we can express, than our intelligence can conceive. Therefore, the highest knowledge of God attained by the mystics is called by them the "divine darkness." It is truly darkness, but a darkness more splendid, more luminous, than all the forms of earthly wisdom.

One can hardly find human comparisons to express this character of the knowledge conferred by the gifts: but perhaps there is an analogy between this darkness and some of the experiences of human life. When we see something grand, something sublime, is it not true that we cannot define our feelings, our thoughts — and that, precisely because they are indefinable, they are deeper, more intense? When we ponder the immensity of the sea, are we not deeply impressed just because neither our eyes nor our imagination can comprehend it? When on a starry night we look up to the great heavens where at enormous, fantastic distances colossal stars revolve, we are struck with agreeable amazement. What we see is too great for us, and for this very reason it enchants us. If it were not so great, if we could measure what we see, we would not have such a magnificent impression.

The same thing happens when we contemplate a heroic deed in the moral order. We are filled with astonishment, and are not able to define our impression. They have something negative about them; and just because they do, they fill us, they satisfy us, they seem to correspond to that desire for the infinite which we carry in the depths of our soul.

In the knowledge that the intellectual gifts of the Spirit produce in our spirit, there is no reasoning: there is only intuition. Reason is something human; intuition is something angelic or divine. However, there is a trace of it even in the natural order. We say of a man who has probed deeply into some field of knowledge that he is familiar with it, that he has the watchful, observant, artistic eye. What else is this but that, in the natural order, he has arrived at the lofty heights of intuition? One who has reached this state does not analyze, does not reason. He sees; he has a direct apprehension which makes him understand more than reason can. Let us turn to St. Thomas, who assures us that in the natural order there are movements of God similar to the movements of the Holy Spirit in the supernatural; the truly inspired artist, in the moment of his inspiration, is moved by God and receives some wonderful intuitions.

Even more do the gifts of the Holy Spirit make these profound intuitions possible in the supernatural order. The soul that is under the power of the gifts does not analyze or reason, but *sees*. In a flash, in one single vision, it beholds marvelous things. What reason and the reading of erudite works cannot teach it, it can understand by the profound movement of the Spirit.

The spiritual world, then, is truly a world of marvels. We hardly touch its threshold, we barely get a glimpse of its wonders; but each time we draw near to it and observe it with attentive eyes, we know that it is a world of inexpressible grandeur.

Would that we could behold that world, that we could leave this poor earth, so full of troubles, where at each step we stumble and come upon sorrow and pain. Would that we had the powerful wings needed to lift ourselves up from the things of earth, from its miseries and its dullness, to reach the heights, the high peaks where we behold the sun, and our poor spirit is bathed in the splendid light of God!

CHAPTER VI: THE GIFT OF COUNSEL

IN THE LAST CHAPTER WE SPOKE IN A general way of the intellectual gifts as a preparation for treating of the one that is nearest to the affective gifts; the one that directs the gifts of fear, fortitude, and piety. This is the gift of counsel.

There is a profoundly practical form of activity in our intelligence. Before performing any deliberate action, we go through a mental process with the purpose of examining carefully, not only the lawfulness of what we intend to do, but also its convenience, its timeliness. Ordinarily we are not aware of this process, just as we are not aware of what happens when our food goes through the digestive tract to be assimilated by the entire organism. Precisely because we are accustomed to use our intelligence to regulate our actions, the procedure goes by unnoticed. But on certain occasions, in more difficult and complicated activities, when we do not see our way clearly and immediately, then, because of our greater concentration on the matter, we are aware of our deliberation.

It is no easy thing to determine what should be done in difficult matters, and to know what should be known about the lawfulness, the appropriateness, and the opportuneness of an act. We analyze, reflect, and recall the past to guide us in the present and to foresee the future — and how many times, after we have reflected and analyzed at great length, we still do not know what to do in a given circumstance, but have to go to a wiser, more experienced person for advice.

To help us determine what should be done in a particular case, we have prudence in the natural order, and the infused virtue which bears the same name in the supernatural.

Prudence is not the speculative knowledge of ordinary spiritual things; it is the application of this knowledge and these general principles to concrete cases with their special circumstances of time, place, manner, etc. Prudence is a difficult virtue to practice — not only the prudence needed to direct others, but even that prudence which is indispensable in governing ourselves. It is difficult because, while we must look upward in order to work according to higher principles and rules, we must look downward and remain in touch with this prosaic earth in order to be aware of each one of the circumstances that surround the contemplated act.

We may think of prudence as the director of a great chorus of many voices, each carrying its own melody. The director must mark with his baton precisely the moment when every voice must enter, and the tones for every melody. In a word, he must harmonize all those voices to produce a unified whole. This is the work of prudence. Prudence directs, in a certain manner, the other virtues; it marks for each one of them its opportunity, its degree, and tells how and when it should be exercised. Prudence, the profoundly esthetic virtue, gives wonderful harmony to our life.

But in this matter as in all others in the spiritual life, the virtue is not enough. Timidity and uncertainty, as we have already seen, are the usual characteristics of prudence the virtue. How difficult to unite prudence and boldness! There are bold men who are unmindful of prudence, and there are men who seem prudent yet who do not dare to do the bold things they should. Thus goes human work: timid, as is proper to an imperfect being who cannot see the future, and is unable to examine the present, or to apply the knowledge gained from the past to assure the present and the future.

At the same time, our decisions are uncertain. In any matter whatsoever, and especially in spiritual things, how difficult it is to arrive at stability and security! We plan and arrange things without having the assurance that they will attain the desired result; our procedures are unsure and do not always bring about what we have intended.

Therefore human prudence would not be enough, supernatural prudence itself, prudence the virtue, would not be enough, to lead us to the heights of glory. Human life is so complicated, so difficult, the ways by which we reach perfection are so painful, we find so many troubles, so many contradictions in our life, that if we had no other direction, we would never attain our end.

But God, who never fails us in our needs, has given us a gift by which the Holy Spirit becomes our guide. As the archangel Raphael led Tobias on his journey, so the Spirit who lives in our souls guides us along the winding and troublesome paths of this life, until we reach our perfection in the inexpressibly loving embrace of God.

That superior prudence, that divine prudence which is the fruit of a movement of the Holy Spirit, is the gift of counsel. It does not have the same name as the virtue, because the prudence we receive from the gift of counsel does not spring from the depths of our intelligence; it comes to us from above, from a superior Being: it is communicated to us by the Spirit. Just as, in a particular case of doubt, we seek someone more informed than ourselves to advise us, so does the Spirit counsel us by means of this gift. But His counsel is not a passing thing, like the advice of human beings; no, it is a light that we receive, it is a gift. Through it, the Spirit moves and guides us in a definite way along the difficult paths that lead to Divinity.

Prudence, ruled by reason, gives a human mode to our actions: uncertainty and timidity; whereas the Holy Spirit puts a divine character on the acts that proceed from the gift of counsel. The virtue and the gift have different norms. That of the virtue is right reason, enlightened by faith, which helps us to judge whether we should perform such and such an action at a certain time. The norm of the gift is higher; it is divine, it is eternal reason, the norm of God.

At times the saints have been able to do things that fill us with amazement. For example, St. Catherine of Siena spent entire Lenten periods without any other food than Holy Communion. In the light of human prudence, there is no justification for this. Right reason demands that we give our bodies the necessary food; it prohibits such excesses, though at the same time it does not tolerate neglect of mortification, for the middle way must always prevail in the practice of virtue. But St. Catherine accomplished this amazing thing because of a superior instinct, a divine norm. She did not see the usual rule of reason; she saw the exalted rule of the will of God.

Let us imagine that we could look into the divine mind in order to discover in that infinite mirror of light the proper thing to do in every circumstance; as we might look, on earth, into the brilliant mind of a learned man to find the correct answer to a problem. This is the way of the gift of counsel. When we work under its direction our decisions will be quick, sure and audacious. With what boldness do the saints proceed, with what security, and with what rapidity! They do not follow the counsels of men, nor the dictates of their own reason. They have a higher norm: eternal reason, the mind of God, that illuminates their spirit and lays before them the road they should follow.

In numerous instances we can discover the influence, the effect, of this gift upon the saints. For example, how could St. Vincent Ferrer have performed miracles with such naturalness if he had not been guided by the gift of counsel? The saint would speak a few words from the Gospel, then add: "In the name of Jesus Christ, you are now healed"; and he worked these miracles just in passing, as any ordinary act of his life. Now, if one of us should try to imitate St. Vincent and perform miracles, he would commit a gravely imprudent act. St. Vincent could perform them because the Holy Spirit moved him; because he was in a singular manner under the direction of the Spirit.

In this gift, as in all the others, there are degrees. In the first, the soul succeeds rapidly in doing the will of God as regards what is immediately necessary in the spiritual life. It is no simple thing to have this security. While the known will of God is by no means always easy to fulfill, yet it is often more difficult to know God's will than to fulfill it. Have we not all found ourselves in situations in which we could not exactly say what our obligation was? What did God want us to do in such cases? The gift of counsel helps us to answer that question in a quick and certain manner.

The gifts work in us simultaneously, or rather, the Holy Spirit makes us work and advance under the influence of His gifts, and on some occasions several of them co-operate in the work of our spiritual life, just as many organs co-operate in our body, and many faculties in our soul. But in this world of the gifts, the actions that proceed from them have to be ruled by the gift of counsel.

Now this gift also influences the actions of our everyday life, those actions that are ruled by the ordinary virtue of prudence. As in a battle the general who has the responsibility of a special division works with freedom in it, but receives orders from a higher chief, so the virtue of prudence rules our actions, but receives directives from another, more excellent supernatural arbiter, the gift of counsel.

In the second degree, the gift of counsel shows us the will of God, our designated way, not only in the necessary things of our spiritual life, but also in the things of counsel; in the things that, while not absolutely obligatory, are very beneficial and useful for helping us to reach God.

In the third degree, the soul seems to rise from the earth and to live in another, higher world. The hand of God guides it with security, without mishap, and without timidity. The soul goes along the path that our Lord indicates, until it arrives at that height of perfection to which it has been called by God.

Happy the souls that yield to the Holy Spirit's guidance! What peace, what security, and what tranquillity are theirs! They do not experience the uncertainties of human life — those uncertainties which are among our greatest miseries. At each step we find a difficulty. As the Wise Man has said: "All things are hard." And they are especially so in the spiritual order. How are we to get out of these troubles that we find everywhere we turn? What ought we to do about them?

The Holy Scriptures tell us that there is a time for speaking and a time for keeping still — are we to speak or remain quiet in this moment of vexation? There is a time for rejoicing and a time for suffering — how can we know exactly what to do at some precise juncture? How many uncertainties in this life, how many hesitations, especially when our spirit and intention are right and we do not wish to stray from the paths marked out for us by God! Happy the souls that are led by the Holy Spirit in the midst of life's vicissitudes, among the winding pathways of earth! The hand of God guides them in a sure manner, they have tranquillity and peace because they have light; because the Holy Spirit moves them; because they go under the shadow of His wings, traveling triumphantly along the paths of life that are to take them to eternal joy.

CHAPTER VII: THE GIFT OF KNOWLEDGE

IF THE NATURAL ORDER IS SO BEAUTIFUL, so magnificent, we cannot doubt that the supernatural is even more so; just as the statue surpasses in beauty the pedestal on which it rests, just as the jewel is richer than its setting. If in the natural order there is a great wealth of intellectual gifts which integrate, so to say, the riches of our human knowledge, in the supernatural order, and above all, in that very lofty region where the gifts hold sway, there are also multiple and exceedingly rich gifts of the Spirit which enable us to have profound and perfect knowledge in the divine order.

In the natural order we have the habits of the *first principles,* of *knowledge,* of *wisdom,* and of *prudence;* and there are gifts of the Spirit that correspond to each one of these intellectual habits. The previous chapter treated of the gift of counsel, which is a higher prudence. Let us speak now of the gift of knowledge.

Among the most precious of the treasures that make up our intellectual wealth is the capacity to know. Knowledge scrutinizes the world, probes into the depths of all phenomena, of all beings, and, recognizing the wonders God has wrought in the natural order, leads, as notably in our own times, to astonishing discoveries.

In the supernatural order, there is a very profound science that also makes wonderful discoveries: it is what the Scriptures call "the science of the saints." We read in the Book of Wisdom: "She guided him [the just man] in direct ways, . . . and gave him knowledge of holy things."[1] This knowledge of the saints is divine knowledge, it is the gift of the Holy Spirit.

There is another science in the supernatural order: theology, in which are found the great principles of faith, supported by the solid arguments of reason. But this is not the science of the saints, for even a sinner can be a theologian. The knowledge of the saints is the knowledge of those who possess the grace of God, and therefore bear the Holy Spirit in their souls; who are moved, led, and guided by Him to a divine mode of understanding.

The gift of knowledge has some points in common with human knowledge and with the gift of wisdom, but it also possesses entirely distinctive marks. Human knowledge is that which makes things known through their immediate causes. To say this more simply, it is a man's natural understanding of creatures. The gift of wisdom, as we shall see, looks deep into the very bosom of the divine, and from that high vantage point contemplates creatures. The gift of knowledge follows a different course: it gives us an understanding of creatures after the divine manner so that we may be able to lift ourselves from them to God.

Human knowledge is discursive. It passes from one truth to another, and thus covers the whole field of learning. Our intelligence naturally proceeds in a slow and laborious manner. By reasoning, it assembles all available truths until it arrives at a systematic and more or less complete whole. The gift of knowledge is not discursive: It is intuitive; it has the divine character proper to the action of the Holy Spirit; it gives us an insight into the mysterious relationships between creatures,

1. Wis. 10:10.

and particularly into the great, the transcendental, relationship that creatures have with God.

Under the influence of this gift, we do not have the same knowledge as acquired through human science. Human science gives all things their proper name; it exposes their behavior, their properties, and the laws that govern them. The divine gift does not teach us the properties of creatures, but considers them in a broader, more profound manner as ordained to God. Someone has happily said that before creatures had their present names, they had a common name: they were called "reflections of the divine bounty, resplendent stairs by which we mount to God." The gift of knowledge also gives creatures this common name; in the light of the gift, all are reflections of divine goodness, heavenly beauty; at the same time, they are adequate means of helping us to God, luminous ladders by which we ascend to heaven.

Creatures, considered thus, in their intimate relationship with God, have two distinct characteristics: their own nothingness, and the stamp of divinity upon them. A deep insight into this double aspect is a necessary condition of any understanding of them, and such insight is had through the gift of knowledge.

What is created is vain. Solomon said in the Book of Ecclesiastes, in a transcendent and profound phrase, "Vanity of vanities, . . . all things are vanity."[2] God had endowed him with deep wisdom, and covered him with glory that had no equal in those times. He himself tells us that his heart was denied nothing it desired. And when he had contemplated everything, experienced everything, tasted of all earth's fountains of delight, he came to this heartbreaking conclusion: All things are vanity.

_____
2. Eccles. 1:2.

In reality this is true, for no creature can satisfy the immense capacity of our heart, its infinite thirst: God made it for Himself alone. No matter how much we strive to fill our heart with creatures, this will never be. They are vain; they are not for us: we were born for greater, higher satisfactions.

But how difficult it is for us to comprehend the vanity of things! They dazzle us with their brilliance. They attract and ensnare us with their charms. How frequently they take us away from God! Therefore does the psalm ask, "How long will you be dull of heart? Why do you love what is vain and seek after falsehood?"[3] How many times creatures seduce us and entice us away from our path, the straight and sure path that leads to heaven! We look for vanity and we love the lie, the pleasure that debases us, the honor that inebriates us, the material goods that enchain us. It is vanity that makes us prisoners; it is the creature that gets possession of our heart, that attracts our soul, and separates us from God, who alone can give us peace and happiness.

Vainly are we warned against the vanity of creatures; vainly do we read learned treatises on the same subject. Many times not even a sad and unfortunate experience is enough to tear the blindfold from our eyes. We let ourselves be carried away by the bewitchment of vanity, we fasten our heart on some creature.

Sooner or later we find emptiness and bitterness, and the experience should be sufficient to send us back to God. But no; very shortly the brilliance and the charm of creatures seduces us again, and we fall once more into the old entanglement. How many of these lapses and how much of God's grace do we need to understand at last the vanity of created things?

---

3. Ps. 4:3.

A keen sense of that truth has been characteristic of all outstanding conversions. It was St. Francis Borgia who exclaimed when contemplating his dead sovereign: "Never again will I serve a master who can die!" St. Sylvester was also turned from all created things by the sight of a corpse. How often a word or a deed has revealed the truth to men! Then is accomplished in them that complete transformation known in Christian language as "conversion." That sudden and profound conviction of the vanity of things is the fruit of the gift of knowledge.

Merely to consider these things is not enough. We read the pages of Scripture that treat of the vanity of things. We read the immortal words of the Gospel: "If thou wilt be perfect, go, sell what thou hast, and give to the poor, . . . and come, follow Me." It is the divine lesson on the vanity of things of earth: sell all you have, for everything is vain. We believe in the Scriptures and in the word of God. Yet our belief remains ineffective; it does not cause a profound transformation. But one day, a word, an incident, a light from God, reveals the truth to us, and then our conversion takes place. The first action of the gift of knowledge is to reveal in a profoundly intuitive manner, and with irresistible conviction, the vanity of things. After this vision, we turn earnestly to God and begin to walk the road of Christian perfection.

Spiritual writers speak at times of a second conversion, in addition to that first one by which we leave sin and enter upon the way of grace. In the second conversion, when the soul takes a new route in the spiritual life, when God calls it to a higher perfection, the gift of knowledge produces an even deeper and more perfect conviction that the things of the earth are vain. At times this effect is bitter, painful, even terrible. Virtue is not always sweet: sometimes it seems cruel.

There are virtues that tear the heart to pieces, that disconcert us, that disillusion us; but that is the way the gift of knowledge fills us with complete scorn for the things of earth. Here is the "night of the senses" of which St. John of the Cross speaks, the long and tremendous purification to which God subjects a soul when He wishes to lift it up to great heights.

To such a soul, all creatures have suddenly lost their charm; their former allure is gone. No longer does the soul find rest in the old delights. It is night, a dark night in which shines not a single star — a blessed night, for the soul has been preserved from the charm of creatures, to find itself on the straight and sure way that leads to God.

But if it is true that there is vanity in creatures, it is also certain that there is in them a certain divine spark. Each creature might seem the crude wrapping that encloses a heavenly pearl. The created thing is vain because it is deficient, because it is limited, because it will never be able to fill our heart. But there is also in every creature, from the highest of the seraphim to the lowest atom of matter, a flash of divinity. In a magnificent poetic figure already quoted, St. John of the Cross describes God as He passes through the universe, showering graces, and covering all created things with His light as His divine countenance is reflected in them.

All things have upon them the mark of God; they are made to His likeness. The Book of Genesis says that when God beheld His creation, He saw that it was good. Yes, all things are good because they all have something from God, they all bear a reflection of His goodness, in all of them the beauty of the Creator is portrayed in a manner more or less distinct.

Ordinarily we do not see that beauty in its true light; what it holds of physical beauty dazzles us. But when the gift of knowledge has made us see the vanity of earthly things and has purified our souls, then we contemplate the things of earth in a new way.

Francis of Assisi was the saint who possessed in magnificent abundance the gift of knowledge. Let us recall the stages of his extraordinarily beautiful life. First, there was his dissipation in creatures. He dreamed, like most men of his time, of attaining great glory as a knight. When God revealed to him the vanity of earthly things, he felt the necessity of getting rid of everything. He threw his rich clothing into the hands of his father, saying: "Now I can say more truly, 'Our Father who art in heaven.'" Then, clad in coarse sacking, he set off to Portiuncula to wed the Lady Poverty. The first stage in the life of Francis ended in scorn for the things of earth. The gift of knowledge made him get rid of everything and fall in love with poverty, because poverty is truth, because it is the ladder that leads to God, and because he knew, in consequence, that poverty is the greatest wealth.

Henceforth his gaze was transformed and he saw creatures in a new manner. With what depth of love did Francis look at all the things of earth! The flowers, the birds, the water, the sun — all had a divine meaning for him; all spoke to him of God, and he felt a deep, immense and rare fraternity with all.

Do you recall how he referred to creatures? — sister water, brother fire, brother sun, brother wolf? With what tenderness he protected the little worms that crawled along the road so that travelers would not step on them? How he objected to the putting of narrow enclosures around trees by which their growth would be limited?

And with that profound knowledge of nature, with that divine way of looking at creatures, he did things that, to ordinary men, seemed like madness. Do you remember the occasion on which he spoke to the birds — how, when he started to preach to them, the little creatures gathered around him to listen? Madness, they will say, those who judge only by human standards. Divine sublimity, we must say, who are initiated in the mysteries of the kingdom of heaven. He looked at creatures with different eyes, not with the poor human vision that sees only the transitory and superficial; he looked at them profoundly and saw in each one a reflection of God; each was like a very clear crystal in which he contemplated the Creator.

It is possible to find this fruit of the gift of knowledge in the life of many other saints. We remember that St. Francis de Sales made use of anything whatsoever that he observed in nature in order to lift himself up to God. When he looked at the fields and the flowers, he said to them: "Quiet, quiet — don't tell me that I may love, for I am dying of love!" For him, creatures had a mysterious language. All spoke to him of God, just as a picture, a flower, a perfume, can be for us a reminder of one we love. That is why he told the flowers to be quiet, for it seemed to him that all creatures were inviting him to love God, and he could no longer support the ardor of his soul.

In the high degree of the gift of knowledge, we enjoy a vision similar to the beautiful and profound one Adam and Eve must have had in paradise before the fall. The Scriptures tell us that Adam gave each thing its proper name, which indicates that he had a deep and perfect knowledge of everything around him. When his virgin nature had just come forth, fresh and beautiful, from the omnipotent hands of the Creator, when his spirit was clothed in grace, when the Holy Spirit, by means of His gifts, moved him, with what insight Adam must have looked upon all creatures; with what penetration he must have contemplated the universe; with what appreciation he must have beheld the splendid verdure of paradise!

In the perfection of the gift of knowledge is found complete detachment. Souls that are not subject to the thrall of creatures discover the holy liberty of the children of God, the joy of freedom, the deep happiness of perfection. At the same time their outlook becomes celestial and they behold the world differently — with a divine glance.

Let us not end these considerations without indicating another excellent and apparently strange effect of the gift of knowledge in its higher degrees. Souls that possess it look at suffering and humiliation differently than others. This unusual and, at first sight, inexplicable love of suffering is noticeable in the lives of the saints. We have spoken of St. Teresa's alternatives — pain or death: both things from which we ordinarily flee, but for Teresa of Jesus, the only two things worth having. St. Mary Magdalene of Pazzi modified the expression of St. Teresa thus: "Not to die, but to suffer." St. John of the Cross, when Jesus asked him, "What recompense do you desire for all that you have done for Me?" replied, "To suffer and be despised for You."

Does it not seem strange to ask for sacrifice and humiliation as a reward? Yet, in the light of the gift of knowledge, sacrifice and humiliation have a supernatural significance. We, imperfect as we are, recognize nothing but the superficial; the saints, with the light of God, look into the depths of things. Sacrifice and humiliation are precious; they are the opposite of the "witchery of paltry things." By suffering and humiliation we resemble Jesus Christ, and nothing is so divine as that which pertains to Jesus Christ and makes us like unto Him.

Talking of these things, it seems as if one were standing in a deep valley and looking up at a very lofty peak, immaculately white with snow, a glorious height that it may seem impossible to reach. On the other hand is it not sweet and beautiful to contemplate from the depths of our misery those great summits of sanctity to which our brothers have attained—the dwelling place of God?

What must the life of a saint be like — that looking at things in the light of truth, that penetrating into the depths of them, that experiencing of new desires and impressions together with peace of soul and joy of spirit: a feast of light, a feast of love, a feast of peace!

Even if we do not have the strength to scale these soaring heights, the celestial vision can enkindle in us the desire of living a more perfect Christian life. When we contemplate a splendid mansion, the desire comes to us to make our own poor house more beautiful and comfortable; and when we hear a sublime musical composition, even though we do not pretend to produce anything like it, we feel a greater love for music and, according to our talent, we try to become more proficient in it. Even so, contemplating the marvels which the Holy Spirit produces in souls, our heart is thrilled, our spirit encouraged, although we ourselves journey with such slow steps toward Him who is Light, who is Love, who is Happiness; toward Him who bathes all loving souls in splendid light, in most sweet love, in infinite peace.

CHAPTER VIII: THE GIFT OF UNDERSTANDING

SOME WORDS EXPRESS OUR THOUGHTS with admirable accuracy. Though they may not be precise definitions, they are exact expressions of the object signified. Such is the Latin word *intelligere* (*intus-legere:* "to read interiorly, to penetrate").

In the natural order, intelligence is the ability to perceive the abstract, the immaterial truth. In the supernatural order, intelligence penetrates higher truths. As the natural light of reason makes us understand sensible things, the light of the gift of understanding, of which we shall speak in this chapter, serves to penetrate supernatural truths and to reveal their intimate depths.

St. Ignatius Loyola, in his Spiritual Exercises, points out that it is not great knowledge which profits the soul but the penetration and savoring of spiritual things. To find spiritual profit, we do not have to multiply readings and meditations: we should rather go to the heart of some few truths, understand them as much as we can, and delight in them. When the Spiritual Exercises are made, or during a day of retreat, or simply whenever we meditate attentively on some supernatural truth, it seems that our soul is transformed, that we become another being. With the new light given us, our soul has a changed attitude toward spiritual things.

To attain perfection, we need to ponder in this way the exalted truths of faith. But faith alone, which is based on the authority of God who revealed these truths, is not enough to make us penetrate them: we need the additional power of the gift of understanding.

The other intellectual gifts are not intended for this specific purpose of penetration. The gift of counsel, as already explained, helps us to apply the great Christian principles to our actions; knowledge is the means by which we find the Creator through creatures, and wisdom (as we shall see later) makes us look at all things from the lofty viewpoint of God.

The gift of penetration, the gift of intuition, is the gift of understanding. By means of it we go deep into the meaning of supernatural truths, of the Christian mysteries, of the dogmas of our faith. And the more developed is this gift in our soul, the more profound is our vision, the more penetrating our intuition.

Why and how does the gift of understanding penetrate into supernatural truths? Let us try to understand this by applying the general principles already described with regard to the gifts. The intellectual gifts give us a profound knowledge of divine things because through them we are united to God in a sweet, intimate experience produced by love. This happens in the gift of understanding as it does in the other gifts. It is necessary to have charity, the profound root from which spring forth like divine shoots all the gifts of the Spirit. By charity we are united to God, we cling to Him; and from this intimate union and firm cleaving there results an experimental knowledge.

We have a particular power of penetration for understanding the people we love. We do not need to talk in order to know their intimate thoughts or to share our own with them. In the same way, when the soul is united to God, it sees Him and knows Him by a direct and sweet experience.

Each one of the gifts unites us to the Holy Spirit as to the Director, the Mover of our souls; but, at the same time, it unites us to Him as to the object of our love. For, as we have seen, the Holy Spirit is also the Gift, the highest Gift, of God.

St. Thomas Aquinas tells us admirable things on this point. Before a gift is given, it belongs only to the giver; but when it is given, it is his to whom it is given. The Holy Spirit is from God, He is God; but when given to us, He is ours. He is ours, says the holy Doctor, as much as anything we have the liberty to dispose of can be ours. Thus we are free to dispose of this Spirit who has come to us. That is to say, we can enjoy Him when we wish, because we possess Him, because He belongs to us, because He is at our disposal.

And being thus united to Divinity, we have, in a certain way, the sense possessed by the Divine. The enlightened eyes of our heart have a penetrating and profound power, and we can read the depths of supernatural truths.

In a special way, the gift of understanding supposes the knowledge, the perfect comprehension, of our end.

St. Ignatius in his Exercises establishes the end of man as the beginning and foundation of all the marvelous considerations he brings forth in order to lead the soul to God. It is the first truth that he examines thoroughly, and the method has become traditional. Whenever the Exercises are practiced or missions are given, they begin by the presentation, in one way or another, of this transcendent doctrine of our last end.

And rightly so, for in actuality the end, which is last to come about, is first in the order of thought. From the beginnings logically emanate conjunctions; thus, in the practical order, everything is related to the end that we propose for ourselves.

In order that a lecture be clearly understood it is indispensable for the speaker to announce the topic he intends to develop, the end which he proposes; if we do not know that, it will be difficult to follow him. The same thing is true with regard to the appreciation of the great masterpieces of art. If we know the purpose the artist had in mind, we understand his work better. If we do not know it, how can we grasp adequately the meaning which the artist wished to impart to the picture?[1]

Likewise, when we have a perfect knowledge of our end, our will is bound to it, for essentially we already possess that ultimate end by possessing God in our heart. This is the work of the gift of understanding; by it the Holy Spirit moves us so that we can penetrate the depths of all supernatural truths and thus attain our eternal salvation.

Not that by this gift we contemplate supernatural truth in all its splendor and fullness. Only in heaven shall we be able to have a clear and unshadowed vision of divine things; only in heaven, when with the light of glory we see God face to face and know in our own hearts His beatific love, will our vision of divine things be positive, radiant, and full. On earth, even under the direction of the gifts, we live always in the semi-darkness of exile. To repeat what has already been said, the gifts of the Holy Spirit are founded on faith, and faith is always obscure.

But in spite of the fact that the gift of understanding gives us a negative vision, we can penetrate deeply and efficaciously into supernatural truths. We are enabled to distinguish the true from the false in the supernatural order; even more, to comprehend that divine things are above human things.

An observation here will help us to understand this clearly. In order to speak of supernatural things we must always make use of symbols, of figures; it is the law of our limited reason. St. Paul says: "For since the creation of the world His invisible

---

1. The author seems to say this, but whether it is true from an aesthetic and philosophical point of view is a matter for the philosophers to decide.

attributes are clearly seen — His everlasting power also and divinity—being understood through the things that are made."[2] Therefore, when treating of the supernatural order we find symbols everywhere because there are mysteries everywhere. We cannot speak of divine things except by comparing them with the things of this world, making use of images, symbols, and figures. Thus we say that baptism is a new birth, that man is born again, as Jesus Christ explained to Nicodemus. Nicodemus did not understand, so Jesus said to him: "Thou art a teacher in Israel and dost not know these things? . . . If I have spoken of earthly things to you, and you do not believe, how will you believe if I speak to you of heavenly things?"[3] Jesus said also, to His Apostles: "I am the Vine, you are the branches,"[4] in order to explain the close union that exists between Him and us. And these were His words when preaching abnegation: "If anyone wishes to come after Me, let him deny himself, and take up his cross, and follow Me."[5] On every page of the Gospel we find symbols such as these.

But there is danger of taking these figures and symbols too literally, because by using them we minimize divine things and reduce them to the lowest proportions. Now, the gift of understanding makes us penetrate forms and symbols in such a way that we know that the thing symbolized or signified is very superior to the symbol or the sign; that the symbol is nothing more than a rock on which we place our foot for support in order to spring forward into the infinite. Thus the gift of understanding penetrates all the wealth of supernatural truths and gives us a vivid, intimate knowledge of divine things.

---

2. Rom. 1:20.
3. John 3:10, 12.
4. Ibid. 15:5.
5. Matt. 16:24; Mark 8:34. Cf. Luke 9:23.

Understanding is one of the gifts of contemplation. By means of it and by its influence, the Holy Spirit elevates souls to a singular and profound vision of God and the things of God. One might say that contemplation is the very beautiful light of those who love, and that it has for its essential principle the gift of understanding.

But it is not only intellectual; it also has a great influence on our practical life. Holy Scripture says that faith works through charity; and the gift of understanding, while enabling us to penetrate the meaning of the truths of faith, must also lead to an understanding of matters related to action, to the works of love and charity required for the gaining of eternal life.

So the gift of understanding, indispensable to the attainment of everlasting happiness, also has its influence on the practical matters of life. There is an exact and comprehensive rule for discovering the field of work that is proper to this gift: it helps us to discover what is concealed, all that is hidden from us which we need to know for our eternal salvation. Wherever there is mystery, the gift of understanding enables us to comprehend and penetrate — if, to repeat, it is something necessary for our salvation.

Do you recall from the holy Gospel how Jesus always answered the questions of His Apostles, even when they were importunate? How many times they asked Him about matters that now seem very simple to us, and our Lord, with heroic patience, explained the most obvious things because they were related to the salvation of souls and to the mysteries of the kingdom of heaven. He did not answer what they asked out of mere curiosity — for instance, on the day of His Ascension: "Lord, wilt Thou at this time restore the kingdom to Israel?" Then His reply was: "It is not for you to know the times or dates which the Father has fixed by His own authority."[6] Likewise when St. Peter asked about St. John, "Lord, and what of this man?" the answer was: " . . . what is it to thee? Do thou follow Me."[7] Jesus never answered the idle questions; but those that pertained to the salvation of our souls, no matter how importunate they were, He always answered.

Let us now examine the principal cases in which the gift of understanding reveals hidden things to us.

The substance may be hidden under the accidents, as in the Holy Eucharist. The gift of understanding makes us pierce through the accidents to the substance of Jesus Christ hidden there. There have been saints, endowed, as it were, with an understanding of the Eucharist, for they discerned the Presence of Jesus wherever He was. Undoubtedly this was an effect, a fruit, of the gift of understanding. Under the accidents, they could discover the substance.

Concepts and *truths* also lie hidden under words. How many difficult expressions there are in the Scriptures! And because they contain mysteries, the gift of understanding makes us penetrate the words that we may discover their secret sense. *Realities* are hidden under figures and symbols; St. Paul tells us that all that happened to the Israelites in the Old Testament was a figure and symbol of the New. Does he not say that the rock from which came forth refreshing water was Christ, and the manna, a symbol of the Eucharist? And does he not teach us the symbolism of many of the ceremonies of the Old Law? Behind the figure is the thing signified or prefigured, and the gift of understanding discovers it.

Under the visible is hidden the invisible and the divine. We have an example of this in the material world. The Scriptures tell us that the heavens sing the glory of God; that the

---

6. Acts 1:6-7.
7. John 21:21-22.

earth shows forth His majesty. Indeed, all creation is filled with the divine. But in order to discover this divine hidden under the visible, we need the gift of understanding.

Under the causes are hidden the effects. The sacraments, the causes of grace, are exteriorly only visible things. A priest pours water on the head of a child while saying mysterious words; the minister of God extends his consecrated hand over the repentant sinner and says: "I absolve thee in the name of the Father, and of the Son, and of the Holy Spirit." But underneath these things, underneath these causes, true prodigies are performed. St. Thomas does not hesitate to say that the justification of a single sinner is a greater work than the creation of the world.

The providential designs of God are hidden in human events. On one day, the last day of the world, and eternally in heaven, we shall contemplate the profound meaning of human history. Now we see things in a fragmentary and imperfect manner: the reason for war, for catastrophes, for all the tremendous vicissitudes of history. Now, with hesitant tongue, we can hardly say anything about them because we know they are under the control of the wise providence of God. In heaven we shall comprehend their profound meaning; we shall know, with the exactitude of an accountant balancing his books, the reasons for all these human affairs. And then we shall praise God for both peace and war, both sorrow and happiness; for everything is planned with admirable wisdom.

By means of the gift of understanding we begin to contemplate hidden things while we are still on earth, for this gift penetrates all supernatural truths and reveals their secrets under any veil. Every Christian has this gift, together with the other gifts of the Holy Spirit. They are not extraordinary favors conceded to a few; everyone who is in grace possesses them. And if he always has them, it is because he needs them at every step.

At certain times in our life we have seen with greater clarity one or many of the truths the Gospel teaches. At a great liturgical solemnity, perhaps, or in the course of a spiritual retreat, or while receiving the Holy Eucharist, has there not passed through our mind a flash of celestial light? Have we not seen clearly in a moment certain things we could not understand before?

It is the gift of understanding given to every Christian which makes him apprehend supernatural truths when this is necessary for the attainment of his salvation. And as it increases, this gift produces things even more wonderful in our soul; it make us penetrate into the very mysteries of religion; by it we understand the beautiful harmonies in spiritual things.

Just as we contemplate from the summit of a mountain some marvelous sight — range after range of peaks, smiling valleys covered with flowers, and dim horizons that are lost in immensity — so by the gift of understanding, when it has reached its highest degree, we are led to contemplate magnificent panoramas: those infinite horizons of the supernatural order that reveal, as far as is possible on earth, the perfections of God: His justice, His mercy, His love. By this gift we also understand, to the extent that it can be understood in this our exile, the submerging, the annihilation, if we may so speak, of the Word Incarnate in the mystery of the Incarnation, in His most sacred Passion, in His descent to the tomb.

The light of the gift of understanding even helps us to know ourselves deeply and to discover the profundity of our misery. Sometimes the humility of the saints seems excessive as when St. Francis of Assisi wished to be trodden on and called the outcast of the people. How can saints, we say, whose life is admirable, men and women actually canonized by the Church, have had such a low idea of themselves? It is because they were filled with the light of God.

When a room is in semidarkness we may have the illusion that it is clean; but when there is a very bright light, we perceive even the tiniest speck of dirt. That is what happens to us when we have the light of God. Then we feel our smallness and our misery; before God we are all very small.

To the gift of understanding corresponds the beatitude: "Blessed are the clean of heart, for they shall see God."[8] Cleanness of heart and the peace which emanates therefrom are its fruit and its reward. Sometimes that cleansing is terrible, because the spirit is purified only through pain. The dark night of the soul of which St. John of the Cross speaks, is, in great part, the work of the gift of understanding. It leaves the soul in profound desolation in order to transform its comprehension, to cleanse its vision; so that it may one day be able to see God.

As Jesus drew near to Jericho, a blind man called out to Him. The Apostles did not wish the Lord to be bothered by this suppliant, but the more they tried to keep him away, the more the blind man cried out. Jesus went up to him and said: "What wouldst thou have Me do for thee?" And the answer came: "Rabboni, that I may see!"[9]

In these words, the blind man expressed his greatest desire, the pressing need of his soul. Is it not true that this is one of the great necessities of our heart and that it should be one of our great desires? So sad and painful is blindness — so rich and beautiful is light! Every day let us say to the Lord, as did Bartimeus, the blind man of the Gospel: Lord, that I may see!

8. Matt. 5:8.
9. Cf. Mark 10:51-52.

CHAPTER IX: THE GIFT OF WISDOM

T HE PREVIOUS CHAPTERS HAVE brought to our attention the admirable parallelism that exists between the natural and the supernatural order. With regard to the first, our intellectual wealth does not consist in isolated knowledge, but rather in a co-ordination of knowledge, a system, a unity; each science co-ordinates the knowledge that belongs to it and unifies it in the causes and principles that it studies. But our mind tends toward a still superior type of co-ordination, that of wisdom, unifying and co-ordinating in the highest and deepest things all the vast field of human knowledge.

With even greater reason must these co-ordinations be made in the supernatural order. The piecemeal unification of truths through the gift of understanding would not be sufficient to bring to perfection the supernatural science. All the supernatural knowledge we possess must be co-ordinated, systematized, and unified. The gift of knowledge establishes a certain co-ordination; but the supreme co-ordinator, which contains, so to speak, in perfect unity all supernatural knowledge, is the gift of wisdom. It has a similarity to that concept of wisdom in the natural order which is also in its proper field the co-ordinator of all our knowledge of cause and effect.

In the supernatural order of the gifts, wisdom comprises all supernatural knowledge, co-ordinates it in the Supreme Cause, the highest Principle: God. This most exalted of all gifts has an incalculable wealth, for St. Paul affirms that the spiritual man judges all things, because he has received the Holy Spirit, who examines the utmost depths of God: "For

the Spirit searches all things, even the deep things of God."[1]
We do not speak, he says, with the words of human wisdom,
but with the wisdom of Him whom we have received. The
gift of wisdom covers all things, but in the vast stretch of
knowledge that it opens up there is a perfect unity, because
the soul looks at all things from a great height and through the
Supreme Cause: God.

The knowledge obtained from the gifts of the Holy Spirit
is born of an intimate experience, of a connaturality and proportion with its objects. This intimacy comes from our union
with God in the holy virtue of charity. As indicated earlier,
even in the natural order, love is a source of knowledge. We
understand very well what we love. The artist who loves
beauty comprehends all things related to beauty. There is connaturality, there is proportion, between artistic beauty and the
artist, for the spirit of the artist is formed to recognize beautiful things. The archeologist has a deep feeling for whatever
is ancient; his love makes him better understand all the things
related to his field of learning. And when we love one another, with what facility we comprehend the intimate sentiments of the beloved, whose thoughts we seem to guess; and
the more intimate the relation, the more perfectly in exact
degree is the loved one known.

Jesus Christ Himself tells us with respect to His love: "He
who eats My flesh and drinks My blood, abides in Me and I
in him";[2] and, in truth, the one who loves is in the beloved.
He projects his heart, his intelligence, his being into the one
he loves, and carries that beloved in the intimacy of his own
soul, in the depths of his own heart. Thus did St. Paul speak
to the faithful: "I have you in my heart."[3]

---

1. 1 Cor. 2:10.
2. John 6:57.
3. Phil. 1:7.

But even this power we receive from love, this power to understand what we love and to apply all our faculties to the profound knowledge of the beloved — is it enough to explain the intimate experience we have of divine things by means of the gift of the Holy Spirit? No, there is something more: there is charity by which we are intimately united to God Himself. No effort of ours will ever measure the closeness of that union.

Jesus, particularly on the night of the Last Supper, spoke about this union: "As the branch cannot bear fruit of itself unless it remain on the vine, so neither can you unless you abide in Me. I am the Vine, you are the branches. . . . Without Me you can do nothing."[4] And as if that comparison were not sufficient to express the very close union that exists between Him and us, He went so far as to compare it to the ineffable union between the three divine Persons of the Trinity. And later on this night of His sacred Passion He prayed to the Father "that they may be one even as We are one: I in them and Thou in Me; that they may be perfected in unity."[5]

And because we are so united with God through charity, and this union is closer than any earthly union, it makes us penetrate, with an experience sweet and intimate, the things that are divine.

Let us consider a simple comparison which will undoubtedly help our understanding. When we eat of any fruit, we appreciate its flavor much more than by reading about it in a botanical treatise. What description could equal the pleasure of actual taste? When we are united to God, when we enjoy Him by an intimate experience, we have a much better knowledge of divine things than through the description of scholars or through the books of the wisest of men. The knowledge of

4. John 15:4-5.
5. Ibid. 17:22-23.

the gifts is acquired by connaturality and by intimate experience through the close union we have with God. This is true of all the gifts, but particularly of the gift of wisdom. Dionysius, when speaking of a certain mystic, said: "Hierotheus is perfect in divine things, because he not only learns them, he experiences them." The gift of wisdom gives to our souls this power to experience divine things, to taste them in the depths of our being, and, by that pleasure and experience, to judge all things.

Now let us explain how this doctrine of connaturality and of experience is applied especially to the gift of wisdom.

Through charity — that queen virtue, the form and soul of all the others, the richest gift, after grace, that we have received — we are united to God as to the Mover and Director of our souls, as to the ultimate end of our actions, as to the object of our experience and our delectation.

We have seen that each gift has its own individual manner of bringing us near to God. The gift of understanding looks at Him as the supreme end of man, and because of its consideration of that end, it penetrates into the supernatural truths. But do we know how the gift of wisdom makes us draw near to Him? It reveals Him as infinite goodness, tasted and experienced. There is a remarkable analogy between the object of charity and the object of the gift of wisdom. The object of charity is God Himself, in His infinite goodness; the object of wisdom is that same goodness, but as an experience, as something savored. Through charity we love God in Himself; through the gift of wisdom we *know* His infinite goodness because we taste and experience it.

The gift of wisdom is closely related to charity, for it stems from charity and leads back to it. It comes from charity, for the one who possesses the gift of wisdom knows why he loves. To quote the words of a mystic, through the gift of wisdom "we see with the eyes of the Beloved"; with the eyes of God. The expression is bold, but it expresses the reality. If we could, so to say, enter into God and look through His eyes, we would see things in a divine manner. And so it is with things that are seen with the gift of wisdom: they are seen in God, they are seen from the heights.

But we *can* penetrate into God and see through His eyes and consider with His mind because charity has united us closely with Him; because we have clung to Him and formed with Him one single spirit.

The gift of wisdom which comes forth from charity also leads back to it. The light of this gift is not cold and lifeless like the light of human wisdom. It is glowing and life-giving like the rays of the sun, which of its essence pours forth light, warmth, and energy. The light of the gift of wisdom sets the heart on fire with love and in that way returns to the principle from which it emanated, completing the divine circle.

It might seem strange that the gift of wisdom, which, like all the other intellectual gifts, has its foundation in faith, should go beyond it. The knowledge we have through the gift of wisdom, while remaining within the sphere of faith, exceeds in an incredible manner the knowledge that comes from faith. How is this possible?

If we penetrate into the nature of intelligence and will, we find the secret of this apparent anomaly. St. Thomas teaches that it is better to know than to love things inferior to us, but that it is better to love than to know things superior to us. With respect to God, it is better to love Him than to know Him; for knowledge causes things to come to us and to adapt themselves to our manner of being, but love, which is charity, makes us go out of ourselves and throw ourselves upon the beloved object. He who knows, adapts the thing known to his own manner of being; he who loves, resembles the thing loved. When we treat of inferior things, we lift them up by knowing them, for we give them our own mode of being; but when we love inferior things, we debase ourselves. On the other hand, when we know superior things we belittle them by adapting them to our intelligence; but when we love them, we lift ourselves up to them.

Therefore, in this life it is better to love God than to know Him, and it is better to love Him through charity than to know Him through faith; for in this world knowledge always has its deficiencies, while love, being a gift of the Holy Spirit, has greater perfection. Charity on earth does not differ essentially from charity in heaven, while faith stops at the threshold of heaven, so that vision may replace it. Therefore it is not without reason that charity surpasses its foundation, and that by means of it we enjoy a broader, more profound, and, we may say, more divine knowledge than we have through faith.

Truly, the field of the gift of wisdom is wide, very wide. It encloses all the objects of faith, divine and human: "The spiritual man judges all things."[6] Nothing escapes the eye of supernatural wisdom. But its proper object, its primary object, is God; the eyes of wisdom view the depths of Divinity through contemplation. And because they contemplate the divine, as already said, they see "through the eyes of the Beloved," and from that vantage point discover all the things that must be known in the supernatural order.

This gift of wisdom is above all the other gifts and directs them all. It is the gift supreme. Even the gift of understanding is ruled by it. It is the first in the enumeration of Isaias already quoted: "There shall come forth a rod out of the root of Jesse, and a flower shall rise up out of his root. And the spirit of the Lord shall rest upon Him: the spirit of wisdom

---

6. Cf. 1 Cor. 2:15.

and of understanding, the spirit of counsel and of fortitude, the spirit of knowledge and of Godliness. And He shall be filled with the spirit of the fear of the Lord."

The gift of wisdom is of capital importance in super-natural contemplation. Certainly the gift of understanding purifies the soul for contemplating divine things and pene-trates the truths of faith. By these two operations it prepares the soul, so to speak, for wisdom. This latter, theologians teach us, is characteristic of the highest degrees of the spiritual life. It is, we might say, the gift of the saints. Not that they alone enjoy it. Thanks be to God, from the day of our bap-tism we possess all the gifts. In us, however, they do not always attain their perfect development, either through our fault or, at least, through our neglect.

All men have the same faculties, but many are poor and unlearned, many have never cultivated their intellectual powers. They may have developed their muscles and possess great physical strength; but they have neglected to develop their minds. In the same way, there are souls who neglect the de-velopment of the magnificent gifts they have received from the bountiful and sanctifying hand of God. The saints, who have reached the heights of perfection, possess all the gifts most perfectly; but, in a singular manner, they possess the gift of wisdom.

This gift produces in us the most faithful resemblance to Jesus Christ. Recall the mysterious words of the Apostle St. Paul: "But we all, with faces unveiled, reflecting as in a mirror the glory of the Lord, are being transformed into His very image from glory to glory, as through the Spirit of the Lord."[7] This series of lights and of glories through which the soul is transformed into Jesus is the work of the gift of wis-dom. When wisdom has reached its perfect development in

---

7. 2 Cor. 3:18.

the soul, then the soul has the image of Jesus, it has the reflection of infinite Wisdom, as charity is the reflection of the Holy Spirit.

Therefore the seventh beatitude is the fruit of the gift of wisdom: "Blessed are the peacemakers, for they shall be called children of God."[8] The gift of wisdom produces this peace, which the Apostle called "the peace of God which surpasses all understanding":[9] peace that surpasses all that we can perceive through our senses, that is above all human peace. The divine glance produces a profound, unshakable peace in us. Souls that possess the gift of wisdom in its perfection are the peaceful ones; they are the children of God. They have the perfect adoption, the perfect filiation, because wisdom has engraved on their souls the most perfect image that one can have on earth, the image of the Son of God.

It is natural that in this gift, as in all the others, there should be degrees. The first degree, which the soul possesses from the moment it possesses the gift, makes us cling to God; and because we cling to Him we have a right judgment, a supernatural rectitude for judging divine things, and the power to use divine norms in the regulation of our activities.

In the second degree, we feel a special delight in divine things. Let us recall the words of St. Paul which Holy Church repeats to us during the paschal season: "If you have risen with Christ, seek the things that are above, where Christ is seated at the right hand of God. Mind the things that are above, not the things that are on earth."[10] Mind the things that are above! It is the function of the gift of wisdom to give us a taste for these divine things. Through the sweetness and pleasure we experience in them, we begin to scorn mere

---

8. Matt. 5:9.
9. Phil. 4:7.
10. Col. 3:1-2.

human satisfactions. We have seen this change take place in the saints. St. Thérèse of the Child Jesus asked God to put a drop of bitterness for her in all earthly delights. Such a petition seems incredible to us, for it is the opposite of what we would ask. Yet the young saint of Lisieux wished never to relish human pleasures, for having tasted divine happiness, she could not be satisfied with anything less. As delicate palates accustomed to choice foods can no longer enjoy ordinary dishes, so the things of earth cannot be appreciated and enjoyed when one has had an intimate experience of things divine.

There is another effect proper to the gift of wisdom: it makes us know what a treasure pain is and gives us a lively desire for it. We have already said that the gift of knowledge enables us to know and love pain, but this knowledge and this keen desire are greatly deepened by the gift of wisdom. All the saints who have loved suffering and been impatient for their hour of martyrdom have been under the influence of this gift. Remember their words: Ignatius of Antioch — "I am the wheat of Christ, and must be crushed by the teeth of wild beasts to be converted into immaculate bread!" Teresa of Avila — "To suffer or to die!" Mary Magdalene de Pazzi — "Not to die, but to suffer!"

When the profound reason back of all these desires is not understood, they seem strange, morbid, even mad. But in the light of the gift of wisdom, the Cross is beautiful, pain is sweet, for it has in it something divine, something of Jesus; it is the straight and luminous ladder by which we mount to heaven. Where pain is, there is the Cross, impregnated with love; from the depths of pain blossoms forth the perfect happiness so marvelously described for us by St. Francis of Assisi.

In order to understand these things we need the gift of wisdom. As St. Paul tells us, the carnal man does not perceive divine things, while the spiritual man judges all things. When the gift of wisdom has developed in us, the Holy Spirit enables us to penetrate into the riches of the Cross, into the marvels of pain, so that we desire them with all our heart, with all the power of our soul.

In the highest degree of the gift of wisdom, souls live as if in heaven; they begin to taste the delights of the Beloved and no longer seek the things of earth, for now they see everything in relation to the heavenly kingdom. This is what St. Bernard has to say about it: "Whatever you may write, it cannot delight me unless I read in it the name of Jesus. However you may argue or converse, your words cannot give me pleasure unless I hear in them the name Jesus. For Jesus is sweetness to the taste, music to the ear, joy to the heart." Such souls begin to contemplate in this life something of God; they see all things with the eyes of the Beloved and their vision of the universe comes from the lofty throne of Divinity.

We have now reached the end of our exposition of the gifts of the Holy Spirit. These marvels of God are beyond all human words; the fullness of their light can never be expressed. Yet, even though our efforts cannot lead to the perfect comprehension of such an inexhaustible subject, at least our souls have been opened to its marvels. We feel a spirit of unrest, for who can sleep when he has had a glimpse of paradise?

There is an unknown world, a divine world, filled with immense riches, with a sweetness beyond all dreams, and for this world we were created. We were not meant to find our happiness in time, to have our treasures stolen by thieves or destroyed by rust: we were made for a superior world, a secret world, a world proportioned to the infinite desire of our soul. We are now aware of its reality. We can say: "There is a greater beauty than our eyes can see, a more radiant glory than we can conceive, a happiness beyond all measure, beyond all imagination, beyond all thought."

May the Holy Spirit, whose movements are the teachers of all things, complete our humble efforts. May He shed His light in our souls. May He enkindle in our hearts the holy fire of love, so that we sigh for nothing but the infinite, the eternal, the divine.

PART III
THE FRUITS

CHAPTER I: THE CONSOLATIONS OF THE SPIRIT

I N HOLY SCRIPTURE AND IN THE LITURGY, earthly joy is most fittingly called consolation. Consolation is the happiness that carries pain with it. It springs from the very heart of grief; therefore the Holy Spirit is called "the Paraclete," the "Consoler," because He gives souls in exile a happiness which is not incompatible with grief, but rather supposes it. Therefore in the Sequence of the Mass of Pentecost the Holy Spirit is called *"Consolator optime* — Best Consoler"; and in the Collect we ask God to grant us the joy of the divine consolations of the Holy Spirit.

It is these consolations that we shall now consider. Let us begin by asking why the Holy Spirit is the Consoler and by describing the principal characteristics of His divine consolations.

When Jesus Christ our Lord came into this world, when He consummated His work and transformed all existence, He did not eliminate pain. We might say, rather, that He increased it, made it more profound and universal. Did He not say, "I have come to bring a sword, not peace"?[1] This is the sword that separates us from the things we love, that penetrates to the depths of our heart and rends it, the sword of pain.

The Christian life, to repeat, does not suppress suffering. That life implies the purification of our hearts, and the heart is not purified completely except by suffering and sacrifice.

---

1. Matt. 10:34.

To live the Christian life fully is to take up the Cross and follow Christ to Calvary, as He Himself taught us.

But if Jesus did not suppress pain, He did something greater and finer. He enclosed it in joy and arranged it so that perfect joy would blossom from its depths. The joy that enfolds grief, that is the blossoming flower of pain, is called in Holy Scripture and in the liturgy, consolation, the consolation poured into our heart by the Paraclete.

May we not say that the consolations of human life are as a reflection of the deep, ineffable happiness that Jesus carried within Him? In this regard we must marvel at the wondrous soul of Christ; therein, during His mortal life, pain and happiness existed together, bound by the golden ring of His unspeakable love.

The Christian life is a reflection of the life of Jesus. The heart of the Christian is the image of the divine Heart; and it can contain, if it is faithful to Jesus, both deep pain and celestial consolations.

Happiness enfolding pain — happiness that is born of pain — is the consolation that the Holy Spirit gives to souls.

And if the Holy Spirit is the Consoler, it is because He is infinite Love. Even in human life, if we consider attentively, we shall understand that the only thing that can console us is love. Knowledge is precious, but it does not console; art delights us, but its object is not to console; the only thing that consoles is love. When our heart is torn to pieces, when great bitterness fills our soul, nothing but a divine reality can assuage our pain — love: love that knows how to bind divinely both pain and grief; love that alone possesses the heavenly secret of drawing forth happiness from profound sorrow and pain.

Because the Holy Spirit is Love, He is the Paraclete. Let us enter into this mystery with deep affection and respect. How does the Holy Spirit enfold our pain in happiness? How is it possible for Him to permit us to suffer, intensely at times, while He inundates our souls with divine consolations?

The first consolation, or perhaps it is better to say the first trace of consolation, that the Holy Spirit bestows on souls is the *joy of freedom*. If we are not happy, it is because we are not free; because we carry chains we may be unaware of, or may even love. These chains are our attachments, the wealth that turns our heart to material things, the pleasures that weaken our will, the pride that carries us above ourselves.

We often think we shall find consolation in the things that attract us and excite our passions. We deceive ourselves. These things impede our true happiness; they make us slaves, and a slave cannot be happy. When those chains are broken, when our soul is purified and our heart detached from earthly things, we begin to know the inexpressible consolation and heavenly joy of our freedom.

St. Francis was the saint of happiness because he was the saint of detachment. When he had given everything he owned into the hands of the bishop, and had been wedded to Lady Poverty in the church of St. Mary of the Angels, he felt divine happiness welling up in his heart, and so full was his joy that he spent the rest of his life singing. He had the ineffable consolation of freedom.

The Holy Spirit frees us. He detaches us from the things of earth, and breaks our chains. How often we have heard these words from the Canticle of Canticles: "Love is strong as death."[2] This means that love is like death in separating us from everything. Death separates us from the riches we have accumulated with so much care, from the social position we have achieved with so much anxiety. Death snatches us from our loved ones, and even disintegrates our body into its elements, stripping from our soul its material cover. And love is

---

2. 8:6 (Douay transl.).

as strong as death. It too detaches us from all things; therefore it liberates us.

The Holy Spirit detaches our heart from earthly things, infuses into our soul divine poverty, and makes us free. This is the first consolation of the Spirit, *the consolation of freedom.*

When the heart is free of affection for earthly things, heavenly love triumphantly enters. We possess God in the precise measure in which we abandon creatures. When the heart is empty, when the soul is detached and the chains that bind us to earth are broken, we find the Beloved in our soul; God our Saviour fills us with His majesty, with His beauty, with His goodness, with His unutterable riches.

The function of love is to unite those who love each other. Two beings become one, and this fusion is never accomplished so perfectly as in divine love. To repeat again what Holy Scripture says: "He who cleaves to the Lord is one spirit with Him."[3] The marvelous union of divine love gives us God to possess and carry in our heart, as our own, our treasure. And who can doubt that we are consoled, that we vibrate with happiness, when we are bearing infinite Love within us? The troubles of this earth, the shadows of life, and the pains in our body do not matter if we have God in our soul.

Remember the words of Donoso Cortés: "When love calls me I do not ask questions; I follow, because wherever it takes me there will we be, the Beloved, myself, and our love, and that is heaven." Not heaven in all its fullness, in all its splendor, not the ineffable and eternal felicity of the fatherland; but a very solid, intimate consolation, a consolation that makes us forget the troubles of life, or at least enfolds them in the splendor of celestial happiness: *the consolation of union.*

Yet even though we possess God on earth, even though our heart is a divine temple and we bear the celestial treasure

---

3. 1 Cor. 6:17.

within, the possession of God is always imperfect. While we are on earth, we can lose Him; and even if we do not lose Him, yet He is not revealed to us in the full splendor of His beauty; the narrowness of our spirit cannot hold the marvels of Divinity. But the Comforter gives us *the consolation of hope.*

Holy Scripture teaches this most clearly. St. Paul has a profound expression of it: "You . . . were sealed with the Holy Spirit of the promise, who is the pledge of our inheritance."[4] What is a pledge? When a man has made a promise, in order to guarantee that he will keep it he gives something valuable so that the one to whom he has made the promise will be assured of its fulfillment.

If we live the Christian life, we have in our heart "the substance of things to be hoped for."[5] The Holy Spirit has given Himself to us; our soul is His temple; we possess Him in the intimacy of our being. And the Holy Spirit is in heaven. Although we do not yet possess Him in all His fullness, in all His splendor, we have in substance what we are to receive in the future life. He is the pledge of our inheritance. And we rejoice in our hope, not only because we trust in the promise of God, but also because we carry within us the guarantee of its fulfillment.

How marvelous is God — how generous! His word is infallible, His promise certain. Did not Abraham rejoice because of the promises he had received from God, promises that were to be realized only after many centuries? Such faith did the great patriarch have in the divine assurance that the secret word which God spoke to him on one mysterious night was enough to fill his soul with the joy of hope. We are more favored still. Not only do we have the divine promises, we have also the Holy Spirit, the pledge of our inheritance.

----

4. Eph. 1:13-14.
5. Hebr. 11:1.

There is still another consolation which the Spirit pours into our heart. It is the *joy of pain*. It might seem absurd to combine two things so apparently incompatible and contrary. What heavenly bond can join them? Only love. As it wondrously united them in the soul of Christ, so does it bring them together in our poor hearts. Such love is hymned for us by the author of the Imitation of Christ in one of his most beautiful chapters:

"A great thing is love — a great good every way; which alone lighteneth all that is burdensome, and beareth equally all that is unequal. For it carrieth a burden without being burdened, and maketh all else that is bitter, sweet and savory.... Nothing is sweeter than love, nothing stronger, nothing higher.... When weary, it is not tired; when straitened, it is not constrained, when frightened, it is not disturbed."

Is love not a marvelous thing? It alone can find joy in suffering for the beloved. Is it not sweet to the mother's heart to suffer on behalf of her children, to endure pain for those dear little pieces of her own heart? Whoever has genuine love feels a wonderful joy in pain endured for the loved one. Pain is the most perfect giving of ourselves. The most perfect love on this earth must be able to say: "I love you enough to suffer for you; I love you enough to die for you."

And the Holy Spirit, infinite Love, who gives Himself to us, who lives and abides in our soul, illumines our spirit, and warms our heart with a celestial tenderness, teaches this ineffable secret of joy in suffering. Once again we might quote, in illustration of this, St. Paul, St. Ignatius of Antioch, St. Teresa of Jesus, St. Thérèse of Lisieux.

Recall again what St. Francis of Assisi once told Brother Leo: Perfect happiness does not consist in speaking all languages, nor in accomplishing great deeds, nor even in converting infidels to the Faith and bringing sinners to the feet of God; perfect happiness consists in suffering much for the blessed Christ who willed to suffer so much for us. Perhaps we may not understand this sublime doctrine. If we do not, let us remember these greatest witnesses of all, the saints, who show us that it is possible to find happiness in pain; and not just any kind of happiness — *perfect happiness.*

These are, in broad outline, the consolations of the Holy Spirit. The Father has sent Him to us, and He is called the Paraclete because He is Love. He is the only One who can enfold grief in happiness, the only One who can bring forth happiness from pain. He is our Consoler because He gives us the consolation of freedom, the consolation of union, the consolation of hope, and the consolation of pain.

To receive these, our heart must be dilated, our spirit purified, our soul must glow with love. The consolations of the Spirit are within our reach; but we are not always disposed to perceive their exquisite flavor. Just as in the natural order there are delicious foods that not every palate can appreciate, so in the spiritual order, the more our soul is perfected, the more we advance along the paths of virtue, the more our heart and our spirit can perceive the divine taste of the consolations of the Spirit.

However, in all the stages of our spiritual life the Paraclete consoles us in some measure, because He knows how to adapt Himself to our smallness, He knows what each one of us requires and what each has to suffer. Sweetly He answers our needs; He softens our pain with celestial joys so that, filled with fortitude, we can carry in our heart an image of the Heart of Christ, and joy and pain can exist together within us, united by the golden ring of love.

CHAPTER II: CHARACTERISTICS OF THE CONSOLATIONS

E KNOW FROM OUR OWN experience that life is a matter of lights and shadows. It is impossible to find anyone who is without sorrows; impossible also to find anyone in whose life there is not, if only for a few brief instants, a spark of happiness. Our Lord, who wished to build the magnificent edifice of the spiritual upon the human, and who designed nature to be the pedestal of grace, has arranged that the spiritual life also should have its consolations and joys.

Undoubtedly there are more sorrows in our spiritual life than in our material, but there are also more consolations. A verse from the Psalms expresses it thus: "When cares abound within me, Your comfort gladdens my soul."[1] These two things, solace and desolation or sorrow, are indispensable. They have their respective purposes to accomplish and their fruits to bring forth. The life of the spirit demands solace for solace expands the heart, and when the heart is expanded it runs in the way of the Lord. As the Psalmist says in another place, "I have run in the way of Thy commandments when Thou didst enlarge my heart."[2] Consolations nourish us, fortify us, and make us capable of performing all the sacrifices necessary to fulfill the holy will of God. As in the natural order God willed to put delight and comfort in the most essential things of life in order that we should do them not only for

1. Ps. 93:19.
2. Ps. 118:32 (Douay transl.).

duty's sake but also with pleasure and facility, so in the super-natural order He willed to give a ray of happiness, a drop of comfort, that we might fulfill our duties with greater ease.

God's knowledge of how to proportion and time our con-solations and our desolations is marvelous. He measures out for our soul the precise quantity of each, at the moment when it is needed. We can trust His understanding and His care for the health of our soul, because He is infinite Wisdom, infinite Love. He seeks only our good. He knows the con-solation or the sorrow that is needed. For desolation is as indispensable as solace, and sorrows contribute forcefully to the development of our spiritual life. At times we feel re-pugnance for these trials of the spirit, but they are pains that purify us, detach us, make our love more disinterested, open our eyes to the divine light and our heart to the ineffable love of God.

The spiritual life requires joy and stress just as the fields need sunny and cloudy days to produce their harvest, just as the earth needs warm rain at times, and at other times sharp frost, to be prepared for a new sowing. There is no doubt that God holds the key to the mystery of spiritual consolations and desolations; and we can trust Him who does all things well. There is nothing capricious about Him. All His works bear the stamp of deliberation and harmony.

By reading the Sacred Scriptures we can, so to speak, get a glimpse into the secrets of God. We can discover, even though remotely and imperfectly, the meaning of spiritual tribulation and comfort. It is a wonderful thing to penetrate into these secrets; for not only is the spiritual world useful, not only has it a divine fruitfulness, but it is also beautiful. It is a work of art, one of the most marvelous to come from the hands of the divine Artisan. However, it is not only the aesthetic contemplation of these truths that ought to attract us.

By penetrating into this world, so beautiful and ordinarily so unknown, we can find precious resources to aid us in traveling more swiftly along the ways of God so that we may attain that spiritual life which is the true life and the foundation of life eternal.

Writing to the Galatians about the work of the Holy Spirit, St. Paul uses an expression which is enough to tell us the nature of the divine consolations: "the fruit of the Spirit."[3] The phrase is enlightening because the comparison it establishes between the phenomena of our spiritual life and the harvests of our fields is a very adequate one. The plants, when they have reached maturity, produce their fruits, whose characteristics are mildness, sweetness, and delicious taste. The word "fruit" expresses two principal ideas: perfection and sweetness, or, in other words, maturity and delectability. These are the two marks of the consolations which the Holy Spirit pours into our souls.

In the Sacred Scriptures the soul is often compared to an orchard. "I have come into My garden, . . . I gather My myrrh and My spices."[4] The soul is a garden into which the Holy Spirit has poured precious, divine seed — the name given by the Apostle St. John to grace. Grace, with its royal retinue of virtues and gifts, is the seed which the Spirit has planted in our souls.

We hardly have an idea of these riches within us. Grace is so wonderful, so excellent a gift that St. Thomas calls a single degree of it superior to all the work of creation. Let us meditate for a moment on these words. This marvelous earth of ours, with the splendor of its visible beauties and the richness of its hidden wealth, with its immense oceans, its mysterious forests, its flowering fields, is inferior to one degree of grace!

---

3. 5:22.
4. Cant. 5:1.

And, as we know well, our world is a speck lost in the immensity of space. Thousands of other worlds revolve there which are greater, much greater, than the one we inhabit. And all these worlds, like a harmonious concert, pursue in established rhythm the path which the hand of God has traced for them. Yet all that admirable unison which forms the visible universe is worth less than one degree of grace!

And if to the visible universe we add the invisible, the angelic world, which is immense, noble, beautiful beyond all thought: the myriads of angels, excellent and superior to all other created things, each with its own privileged intelligence and admirable heart; if we unite these two worlds, they are together less than one single degree of grace!

The holy Doctor even assures us that greater than the creation of the world is the work of God when He justifies one sinner. A sinner confesses his fault, the priest extends his consecrated hand and pronounces the sacramental words. It is a common thing among us, yet in that soul is accomplished a wonder greater than when God made the world from nothing.

Grace is so excellent, so beautiful, because it makes us resemble God. By grace we belong to the divine order, to the divine family. St. Paul dared to say it thus: "We are also His offspring."[5] There is an admirable and very rich cortege that accompanies grace, namely, the infused virtues and the gifts of the Holy Spirit. Having these, we have everything necessary to live the Christian life on this earth and to be eternally happy in heaven.

The seed that the divine Sower planted in the fertile field of our heart, when developed under His gentle operation, reaches a certain maturity and then produces its fruit, mild and delicious: the consolation of the Holy Spirit. These two

---

5. Acts 17:28.

things, maturity and delectability, we have previously called the proper characteristics of the fruits of the Spirit. Let us consider them.

Philosophy teaches us that pleasure is proper to function. When we perform our tasks in a right manner, in accord with the capacity of our intellectual life, we experience pleasure. Pleasure, then, is the result of a perfect work — a teaching which even ordinary observation enables us to understand. The man who has accumulated treasures of knowledge does not enjoy that knowledge fully by having it habitually in his soul; but only when he puts it into practice, when he works, when he does something with it. The artist who has amassed treasures of beauty in his heart does not enjoy them fully by having them stored there; but only when he works, when he opens the eyes of his soul, when he experiences the profound intuitions of art. Enjoyment is found in activity; and so we enjoy the consolations of the Holy Spirit because His fruits are, not habits, but acts.

The gifts of the Spirit are habits, active principles in our souls which can operate at the proper moment. The fruits of the Holy Spirit are these spiritual operations: acts of virtue, acts of love, communications with God. They come enclosed in sweetness, they delight our heart and fill our soul with their fragrance. How many times these divine consolations, rapid and fleeting as our own works, leave in our soul a trace of something divine, an exquisite perfume that delights us long afterward.

Not every operation of ours is pleasurable, as we see even in the natural order. Our wise man, who reviews, so to speak, his knowledge, and who through some necessity has to give attention to a truth of little importance, does not experience joy, because that truth is too trivial for his intellectual capacity. The musician who listens to a melody that lacks the grandeur or the beauty to which he is accustomed, does not find aesthetic joy, for that music is too simple for his understanding.

Nor do the wise man and the artist find pleasure when they try to lift themselves to a level beyond their capacity. When, without having enough preparation, we attempt to comprehend a profound truth, we do not enjoy the experience, we only suffer. We do not find joy and delight in that truth because it is not suited to our intellectual power. Similarly, when we listen to a great symphony without preliminary study we glean little pleasure, because what we hear is beyond our musical knowledge. Pleasure accompanies work that is proportioned to the ability of the worker, that is neither greater nor less than his talent.

This is also true in the spiritual order. The fruits are spiritual joys that accompany our works when these have attained a degree of maturity. When our works are beneath our capacity, or above it, there is in them neither joy nor consolation. On the other hand, when our spiritual faculties have reached a certain development, a certain perfection, there is consolation, the fruit of the Holy Spirit. Celestial joy comes from the achievement of perfection, even of a relative perfection.

The fruits are distinct from the beatitudes — though these latter are also fruits, and the most exquisite, most perfect fruits that the Spirit produces in souls. But they suppose a divine perfection; they are something of the heights, something very exalted, that develops only in lofty places. They truly resemble heavenly joys and delights.

The fruits are found in all the stages of the spiritual life because they suppose not an absolute but a relative perfection. We might say that each time a soul accomplishes a stage in the spiritual life, it finds a divine delight. Each level of the spiritual life has its corresponding fruits.

The work of the Spirit in us is a work of order because the spiritual life consists in the perfect ordering of our being.

In the beginning of time, a marvelous order existed. When our first parents were in paradise, when human nature in its integrity, not yet stained by sin, showed vigorous, splendid, and beautiful under the foliage of Eden, everything in man was in harmony. The struggles we now experience in our hearts did not exist — those struggles of which the Apostle said: "I see another law in my members, warring against the law of my mind and making me prisoner to the law of sin that is in my members."[6] All man's being was in consonance, his lower part marvelously subordinated to his superior part, and the whole completely subjected to God. His nature was a lyre in perfect tune that sang unceasing praises to the divine glory. Then sin appeared and the harmony was broken. We inherit from our parents a damaged nature, a nature despoiled of its primitive harmony, a nature in constant combat.

The work of grace is to re-establish in us, as far as the economy of the redemption demands it, something of the concord of paradise; to subject the inferior part of our soul to the higher part; to order our heart with all its affections, and to place our whole being under the dominion of God.

This is an admirable work of order and harmony, but it is a slow work. God is not accustomed to transform us in an instant. Little by little our souls put aside their defects and develop virtues. Step by step they become detached from creatures and united to God and He gradually penetrates them like a celestial perfume, until that intimate union is reached in which the soul can say with the spouse in the Canticle: "My Lover belongs to me and I to Him."[7]

---

6. Rom. 7:23.
7. 6:3.

In each one of the various degrees of grace there are special objectives. When our sensibilities are ordered and our lower faculties subjected to the higher, then come the fruits of the Spirit, the first heavenly consolations that are the splendor of the divine order. When our relations with other men conform to justice and charity and order, then, as a fruit of that order, greater divine comforts appear. When, reaching even loftier heights, we have succeeded in unifying our affections, purifying our heart, and ordering the superior part of our soul, then the most exquisite and wonderful consolations come to delight us.

Just as all flowers do not open their calyxes in every season, nor all plants produce their fruits at the same time, so each consolation of the Holy Spirit has its special moment for appearing in our spiritual life. But we may be certain that if we are generous, if we are strong, if we follow the paths Christ has marked out for us, if we are docile to the Spirit's inspirations, we shall find all along our road not only thorns that torture us, but flowers that breathe forth sweet perfumes, and fruits that are delicious to our spiritual palate.

For God, the immeasurably wise, infinitely good God, loves us. With wonderful power, but exquisite gentleness, He leads us through the winding, painful paths of this world until we reach our home. Then there will be an end of trouble, our tears will be dried, and we shall no longer need consolations, for the heavenly Sun of celestial happiness will shine forever in all its fullness.

CHAPTER III: SOLACE AND DESOLATION

I N THE SUPERNATURAL GARDEN THERE IS a choicer, more opulent variety of fruits than we find in the gardens of earth. Indeed, we might say, with St. John of the Cross, that there is hardly one fruit which resembles another in taste. God, who is admirable in all His works, puts traces of the divine in them, especially in those of the supernatural order. Some fruits of the Spirit are perceptible even by our lower faculties; the inner sweetness overflows, as it were, and touches even the inferior part of our soul. At other times the consolations are only spiritual; the lower faculties sense nothing, but the intelligence and the heart know a divine sweetness, a light that fills them with peace, an affection that satisfies even though the senses do not experience it.

Some consolations are momentary, others leave an exquisite and long-lasting perfume. At times they are very light, and again they deeply move the soul with their power and vigor. We recall that certain saints have begged the Lord to cease pouring His delights into their souls, for they could not support the force of the divine torrent. Has there ever been anyone on earth who threw away delight? But the pleasures and transports of heaven are so intense they almost overwhelm the soul.

Spiritual consolations are not constant in the supernatural life; ordinarily, they are intermittent. As was said in the last chapter, there are seasons of joy and seasons of suffering; times of consolation and times of desolation. The reason for these variations is not that God is limited or restricted in His gifts, but that we have need of the sterner experiences. If consolations expand the heart, if they fortify and give courage, desolations, on the other hand, produce precious fruits, fruits that are perhaps even richer and more abundant. God has put a divine efficacy into pain. Desolations purify us, elevate us, illuminate us. They prepare our soul for union with God. We see, therefore, that it is His wisdom and goodness which intertwine consolations and desolations in our life; now He bathes us in solace, now He leaves us uncomforted. Both states are tokens of His divine munificence, proofs of His love, for both are most advantageous to our spiritual progress.

It is very common in the beginning of the spiritual life, when a soul has turned to God and wishes to essay the painful but holy path leading to perfection, that our Lord should fill her with consolations so as to attract her, to steal her heart away. When she has given her heart completely, then, with inimitable mastery, He begins to draw away His consolations, in order that suffering and pain may come and accomplish their rich and solid work.

If we had greater serenity of soul, more intense faith, we would receive with equal gratitude from the hand of God delight and anguish. We would comprehend perfectly that everything God does to us He does for our good; that sorrow and happiness are both messengers of His eternal love, instruments He uses with ineffable tenderness to accomplish His divine work in our soul. Joy is more agreeable to our poor nature than sorrow: with difficulty do we appreciate the value of sufferings and the knowledge that perfect happiness springs from them. But consolations and desolations alike come from love, to do the work of God within us.

The nature of the development of our spiritual life logically demands this alternation. It has already been said that the fruits proceed from a certain perfection; when the soul

attains that relative perfection, the Holy Spirit pours into it
His fruits. But the soul is not allowed to rest in that perfection. For love is never satisfied, and in the spiritual life there
is no terminal except when we enter, finally and triumphantly,
into the glory of God.

So, when the soul has reached a certain perfection and
experienced the consolations of that stage, our Lord prepares
a new stage. The soul must travel still other paths, in which
it is again a beginner lacking the perfection proper to them.
It is necessary then that joy be withdrawn until the soul succeeds, by its efforts, and above all by the grace of God, in
attaining a new level of perfection, to which corresponds a
new kind of delight.

But also at times, our Lord, through some loving motive
or because of some profound providential design, withholds
His consolations completely. The last days in the life of
St. Thérèse of the Child Jesus were a period of terrible desolation, of unspeakable sufferings. By reason of the perfection
she had attained, that unique soul should have died in peace
and in joy, for peace and joy belong to the heights of the
spiritual life, and certainly St. Thérèse had established her
dwelling on the heights. But God willed to submerge her soul
in desolation. He wanted her to suffer for other souls. We
may call this desolation of St. Thérèse *co-redemptive;* the union
of her very intense suffering with the profound sorrow of the
Heart of Jesus was effected to obtain singular graces for other
souls. The Little Flower herself gives us an understanding
of this secret of God in her delightful autobiography. She
tells us that she sat at the table of the incredulous in order to
suffer with them and to secure special graces for them in
that way.

We cannot come to a conclusion about the state of our
soul from its suffering or its rejoicing. The spiritual novice

will say: "When I feel fervor and consolation, everything is very well with me; when I do not, things are going wrong." This reasoning is incorrect. Consolations and desolations cannot be taken as a measure of spiritual condition. Both are necessary to health and progress. Consolation indicates, certainly, that the soul has taken a step in the spiritual life; but desolation may be a sign that it is even nearer to the summit.

In reality, we should neither look for consolation nor refuse desolation. What we must seek, is God; what we must cling to, is His holy will. All other goods are secondary. He will send them to us in His own good time.

In our ordinary, everyday affairs we know that it is not a balanced attitude to demand that everything be agreeable. The pleasures that accompany our deeds are given us by God to help us accomplish His designs. For example, food has pleasing flavor and variety because God wants us to nourish ourselves properly. But anyone who seeks above all else the pleasure to be found in food, forgetting its rational purpose, falls into the disorder of gluttony. The glutton does not look on food as a means of sustenance: he sees in it only a source of sensual satisfaction.

The same thing is true in the spiritual order. God gives His consolations to us in our supernatural activities to facilitate these and to enable us to do what we must for our salvation. We should not disturb the proper order by subordinating perfection to pleasure; rather should we subordinate pleasure to perfection. It is not delight as such, in the natural or in the supernatural order, that we should be concerned about, but rather the substantial things themselves. We should advance in the way that God has planned for us and remember that the good things He sends us from time to time are to help us obey His sovereign will. They are not the end of the spiritual

life, which is to become perfect, to become like Christ, to produce a solid and divine work that will some day lead us to
eternal beatitude.

God detaches us even from the consolations He sends us,
by means of the terrible desolations with which He often wills
to afflict our souls. He does not want us to be separated from
Him by spiritual consolations. He is our All. It is He whom
we must cling to with all our heart, with all our soul. His
gifts are something secondary. As a bride-to-be would be very
foolish to forget her betrothed while becoming fascinated by
his gifts, so we should not set our heart on the gifts of God,
even when they are spiritual. He wills that our eyes and our
heart should be always directed to Him.

Nevertheless, it is proper to desire spiritual consolations.
Holy Church teaches us this, for example, in the liturgical
prayer for the feast of Pentecost: "Grant that by the gift of
Thy Spirit right judgment may be ours, and that we may ever
find joy in His comfort." The Church shows us how to ask
for consolations rightly: they should come when God wills
and as God wills; they should be useful and holy; they should
lead us to God.

Yes, we may desire the consolations of God, we may look
for them with moderation, and we may prepare ourselves to
receive them. The first means for obtaining them, as for
obtaining any other grace, is prayer. Prayer, as we have been
told so often, is the key that opens divine treasures, both in
the natural and in the supernatural order. God has promised
to listen to our prayers. Jesus Christ told us this time after
time; and on the night of the great mysteries, the eve of His
passion, He said: "If you ask the Father anything in My name,
He will give it to you."[1]

---

1. John 16:23.

Every right prayer has its own singular efficacy, as we know very well. If sometimes we do not obtain what we ask, it is because we do not ask in the name of Jesus — we cannot ask in His name for what is opposed to the sanctification of our soul. But besides a possible failure on our part to ask with the proper conditions, our prayer may seemingly go unanswered because it is not the proper moment for God to give us that particular grace, and He is waiting for another time that will be more profitable for our soul.

To obtain the fruits of the Holy Spirit we should pray for them, and the liturgical prayer just quoted furnishes, as we have said, a brief but exact petition. We ought to pray that the consolations of the Spirit be ours at all times. And praying for the fruits of the Spirit, which bring them, is the first step toward obtaining them.

The second step is to take away the obstacles opposed to the reception of heavenly consolations. Our daily experience tells us that certain actions or conditions disturb us, and others hinder us. For example, infirmities of body hinder the appreciation of many things. The same thing is true in the spiritual order: there are circumstances that prevent us from enjoying the consolations of God. When we are too attached to the things of earth, when vices, especially of the gross, base kind, find their way into our heart, we cannot perceive spiritual things. "The sensual man does not perceive the things that are of the Spirit of God."[2]

Man is a complex being. The ancients called him "microcosm," a small universe. He has affinities with heaven and earth: with inanimate matter, because of the chemistry of his body; with plants, because he lives; with animals, because he feels; with angels, because he understands and loves. God made man to be a summary of all creation; He made him to be

2. 1. Cor. 2:14.

a harmonious unity. But since the fall, instead of harmony there is often disorder. At times it is as if the animal nature in man had conquered the angelic. This is the "sensual man" St. Paul speaks of — the man who sees only the earth, who looks only for gross pleasure, who goes about like the prodigal son feeding on the husks of swine.

The sensual man does not perceive the things of God, not only because his intelligence is darkened to divine things, but also, if one may so express it, because his spiritual palate cannot perceive the sweetness of celestial delight. It is difficult for the joys of heaven and earth to be united in the same heart. To make ourselves worthy of the consolations of the Holy Spirit, we must root out from our heart and our life all those pleasures that keep us from tasting the delights of heaven.

Yet this negative work, though very useful and necessary, is not enough. The fruit is a work of perfection; not absolute perfection, but perfection relative to the stage through which the soul is passing and in conformity with God's designs for it. This certain necessary perfection is not attained without efforts, sacrifices, and struggles.

We can go further. Because each fruit of the Spirit supposes us to have reached a certain degree of perfection, the divine process in the work of our sanctification is a process of order. By means of the spiritual life we approach that admirable order that Adam and Eve enjoyed in paradise before sin stained their souls. To live spiritually is to have our affections and our actions in order. St. Augustine defined virtue by saying that it is order in love. Order in our love produces order in our actions, in our thoughts, and in our faculties.

We may say that each one of the stages of the spiritual life gives order to a portion of our being. First, the inferior part of our soul is affected in this process, being subjected to reason and to faith. Then our relations with others are ordered, so that they are based on justice and charity. Next, our heart is ordered most perfectly when all our affections stem from a divine affection. Finally, our intelligence is purified so that it can see heavenly things, and our will adheres marvelously and perfectly to God, who is our last end.

Each step of that orderly process is marked by the appearance of some fruit of the Spirit. Whatever part of our soul is perfected, it receives an effusion of heavenly consolations. Therefore, if we desire to obtain the fruits of the Spirit, we need to work, to try to purify our souls little by little, to advance little by little on the road to perfection.

The plants that produce the fruits of the Holy Spirit are the virtues, and especially the gifts of the Holy Spirit. When we practice the virtues, when we prepare our souls to receive the influence of the Spirit by means of the gifts, then we arrive at a certain maturity that brings divine consolations with it. Accordingly, there are three things that we must do to possess those celestial delights. We must pray; we must purify our soul, eliminating all that hinders us from perceiving the sweetness and mildness of the heavenly fruits; then, by also working ceaselessly and struggling against our interior and exterior enemies, we can be assured that the precious fruits will fill our souls with sweetness.

However brief and superficial these considerations may be, is it not true that they open new horizons for us in the spiritual life? The divine world in which our souls must live is a world that has its tempests, its days of stress, but also its days of splendor. It is a world in which we suffer, but in which we also rejoice. It is a world of thorns, but it has, as well, flowers and delicious fruits.

How clearly God's wisdom, love, goodness, munificence, can be seen in the supernatural life! Someone who had advanced very far on its path spoke these words to Jesus. At first they may seem disrespectful, but in reality they are a delicate expression of praise: "O Lord, You have deceived me with a divine and most sweet deception. You invited me to suffer, and You said to me: 'If you wish to come after Me, deny yourself, take up your cross and follow Me.' You did not mention happiness or consolation to me. You have deceived me. I carry a Cross upon my shoulders and bitterness in my heart, it is true, but Your divine Spirit has inundated me with exceedingly sweet and delicious consolations. Oh, be eternally blessed, You who not only desire that I carry the Cross with You, but also desire that I carry in my heart a spark of the ineffable consolation You bear in Your own soul!"

CHAPTER IV: CHARITY, JOY, AND PEACE

S T. PAUL THE APOSTLE, IN HIS EPISTLE to the Galatians,[1] enumerates the fruits of the Holy Spirit. They include charity, joy, peace, patience, goodness, benignity, longanimity mildness, faith, modesty, continency, and chastity: we say "include" because there is such a rich variety of heavenly consolations that it is impossible to name them all. We might refer again to the statement of St. John of the Cross that there is hardly one heavenly consolation that resembles another. But in spite of this abundance and variety, they can be grouped by reason of analogies that unite them into types. In this sense, all the consolations of the Spirit can be reduced to the twelve enumerated above.

Attention should be called to the fact that, even though some of the fruits have the same names as virtues, in reality they are not the same. The name is based on certain likenesses existing between the virtue and the fruit. Thus, charity, patience, modesty, faith, chastity, etc., can signify either a fruit or a virtue, but these are, nevertheless, two different realities.

The Angelic Doctor makes a profound and subtle analysis of the fruits of the Spirit. St. Thomas' key for the above classification of the fruits is the diverse operations of the Spirit in our souls. These operations are varied, but they have nevertheless a principle of unity: *order*. The Spirit produces

---

1. Cf. Gal. 5:22-23 (Douay transl.).

in us a total ordination, a perfect ordination, of all our faculties, of our whole being. This is perfection, this is sanctity.

The fruits suppose maturity and perfection; and when there are maturity and perfection in the soul, there is order. Therefore, to understand the classification of the fruits, we must study the various kinds of order the Holy Spirit produces in souls.

St. Thomas points out three: the order of the soul itself, and the order of the soul with respect to exterior things — both with respect to other men and with respect to things inferior to man. This might be formulated in another way. There are in man two lives, or rather two forms, two aspects, of the same life: the contemplative life, entirely accomplished in the depths of our soul, which puts us in communication with God; and the active life, which establishes contact with other men and all things inferior to man. To each of these ordinations a group of fruits corresponds.

The root of this intimate process of ordering is love. Our heart is the center of our life. At the back of all our problems there is always the problem of our heart, for love, that noble and kingly sentiment, is the first and fundamental affection in the soul. All the other affections we know are related to love: hope is love that longs for union with the beloved; sadness is separation from the beloved; anger is the energetic reaction, at times disordered, to attain what is desired.

All our restlessness and all our joy come from our heart. From it also come all our iniquities and all our virtues; all our miseries and all our glories. Truly, the heart is the key of our whole life. Thus Jesus said to His Apostles: "For out of the heart come evil thoughts, murders, adulteries, immorality, thefts, false witness, blasphemies. These are the things that defile a man."[2] But heroic acts come from the heart as

---

2. Matt. 15:19-20.

well: purity and all the virtues. For in the spiritual order also, God has willed the heart to be the center of our life. We have quoted St. Augustine's excellent definition of virtue: "Order in love." From the same saint we have the bold expression: "Love, and do what you will." We know that the essential elements of the spiritual life are two forms of love, for Jesus said: " 'Thou shalt love the Lord thy God with thy whole heart, and with thy whole soul, and with thy whole mind.' This is the greatest and the first commandment. And the second is like it, 'Thou shalt love thy neighbor as thyself.' On these two commandments depend the whole Law and the Prophets."[3]

The doctrine of Jesus is one of love. The spiritual life is love, divine love: charity. When love has thoroughly prepared our hearts, then appears the precious fruit of charity. It is different from the virtue; it is a sublime emanation from it; it is joy; it is the delight of loving.

The supreme happiness of heaven consists in submerging ourselves forever in the love of God; the supreme misfortune of hell consists in this, that the last spark of love departs from the heart. In hell no one loves; St. Teresa defines the devil as " the one who does not love." On earth at times love fills the depths of our soul and it seems that we carry within us a little portion of heaven; at other times we feel that love is gone, as if the desolate winds of hell were piercing us through and through.

The Scripture tells us that "the charity of God is poured forth in our hearts by the Holy Spirit who has been given to us."[4] This gift of the Holy Spirit, charity, is the supreme order, the greatest prerogative we have received from God. Charity is the queen virtue, the flower of all the others. And

---

3. Matt. 22:37-40.
4. Rom. 5:5.

if, as St. John tells us, God is charity, that name applies in a particular manner to the third Person of the august Trinity. For He is infinite Love, the personal Love of the Father and the Son; He is Charity; and the charity He diffuses in our hearts is the image of Himself.

Imagine a very beautiful person bending over a pool of limpid water, and the water's shining surface reflecting that person's likeness. Thus may we think of the Holy Spirit when He pours Himself out, when He gives Himself to us. He is reflected in our soul and produces there the heavenly image of His beauty, which is charity.

The love of charity is not like any other: it is a perfect love, a love with divine character. By this gift of heaven, we love God disinterestedly and not for the rewards we hope to receive from His bountiful hands. When charity reaches a certain degree of maturity, we come to experience the first fruit of the Holy Spirit: the joy of loving.

In the natural order, whoever bears in his heart a real and profound love knows the first signs of this joy, even when he does not yet possess the beloved, even while he still struggles to conquer the fair prize. The simple fact of carrying in the heart a love for someone is a joy; it is already a consolation that fortifies, that purifies, that ennobles. With much greater reason, in the supernatural order, does the charity we bear in our hearts produce exquisite pleasure. But in order that its sweetness be perceived, charity must reach a certain maturity.

Every soul in grace has charity. We received it at baptism, together with its accompanying virtues and gifts; and when we recover grace in the confessional, we recover charity also. However, as in the natural order we do not derive satisfaction and joy from our various talents and aptitudes if we do not exercise and develop them, even so, when the charity which we have in our hearts has not yet reached its maturity, when it has not been exercised, we do not have the celestial delights that fill the souls of the saints. He who has charity has already the capacity for loving God, and possesses the root of those consolations and of that infinite sweetness that this virtue produces in souls; but he needs to develop it, to bring it to a certain degree of ripeness.

Therefore, let us not forget that the fruits of the Holy Spirit have two characteristics: they suppose perfection, and they produce sweetness when the roots from which they emanate have reached their maturity, their perfection.

Such is the first fruit of the Holy Spirit, charity, which, intimately bound to the virtue of charity, is the consolation, the sweetness, that charity fostered to full growth produces in the soul.

Next to the fruit of charity, St. Paul places joy. And it is logical that joy should follow upon love. Every lover rejoices to find the beloved. Recall the words of the spouse in the Canticle: "I found Him whom my heart loves. I took hold of Him and would not let Him go...."⁵ This is a cry of triumph, a song of joy. In the spiritual order, as in the natural, when love attains union it produces joy — but a joy as superior to that of natural affections as charity is more excellent than all the natural affections.

Nor is this joy found only on the loftiest heights of love, though it is true that full, complete union, perfect sanctity, is realized only on those heights. But it is also certain that from the very beginning of our spiritual life we possess the Beloved of our heart. For charity is love without absence, love always possessed; and charity is inseparable from the one who has the Holy Spirit as his Guest. "If anyone love Me," our Lord has said, "he will keep My word, and My Father will

---

5. 3:4.

love him, and We will come to him and make Our abode with him."[6]

On earth, at times, the poor human heart feels the pain of unrequited love. Such a sad condition of things is unknown to the love of charity, where there is always correspondence: "He who abides in love abides in God, and God in him."[7] Charity, to repeat, is love without absence, love that is sure of possession, joyful love.

But if this is so, if I bear love in my heart, why am I not constantly happy? What is lacking to my happiness?

We are too often unhappy because we too often keep charity in an obscure corner of our soul, so to speak, and are not aware of our joy. We do not exercise the heavenly virtue that the Spirit pours into us; we do not realize the treasure that we possess. However, when union has reached a degree of maturity, then we do begin to have knowledge of our happiness. When we experience the divine presence of the Beloved in our heart, then is produced that fruit of the Holy Spirit that is called joy.

It is the nature of human love to grow slowly, to develop by degrees — not like the love of God, which is a divine and infinite conflagration. Our love is a fire that increases little by little until it is converted into an immense blaze. But at each stage, the union between God and our heart becomes closer; at each step we intone the triumphant Canticle of the spouse: "I found Him whom my heart loves. I took hold of Him and would not let Him go."

Therefore, in each degree of love, when the soul has arrived at the relative maturity proper to that state of the spiritual life, it knows the joy of possessing God, the exquisite, ineffable joy that is the second fruit of the Holy Spirit.

---

6. John 14:23.
7. 1 John 4:16.

Third among the fruits of the Holy Spirit is peace, which is logically connected with joy. St. Thomas teaches that peace is the perfection of joy. A joy which cannot be experienced because of exterior or interior obstacles is frustrated, imperfect. Jesus Christ spoke of this to His Apostles on the eve of His passion: "These things I have spoken to you that My joy may be in you, and that your joy may be full."[8] This full joy cannot be disturbed or snatched away; it is possessed in absolute and complete serenity. Some joys that we know in our human life do not fulfill all that we seek in them; they seem to diminish, to disappear, just when we expect to benefit from them. Life is full of things that hinder us from relishing such joys.

On the other hand, peace is the singular pleasure that we experience when we taste the joys of our soul in their fullness. When those things are removed which hinder the sweetness of our joy, then we have tranquillity, peace, that celestial gift that refreshes all our faculties, that full purification of the heart that makes us see the vanity of exterior things.

The Martyrology is full of examples of saints who, in the midst of the troubles, persecutions, and vicissitudes of life preserved their peace intact and enjoyed without hindrance or diminution the good things within their souls. We have already quoted St. Paul: "I am sure that neither death, nor life, nor angels, nor principalities, nor things present, nor things to come, nor powers, nor height, nor depth, nor any other creature will be able to separate us from the love of God, which is in Christ Jesus our Lord."[9]

St. Ignatius of Loyola said on a certain occasion that he could think of no one capable of disturbing his peace. The only thing that might upset him a little, continued the saint,

8. John 15:11.
9. Rom. 8:38-39.

would be the suppression of the Society of Jesus; and even if that should occur, a few moments of recollection would serve to tranquillize him again. The divine fruit of the Holy Spirit called peace filled the soul of this great saint.

However, to experience complete peace, it is not enough to prevent exterior things from disquieting us. The most profound causes of our disturbances are not without, they are within; they do not come from other creatures, but from ourselves. How often, having attained something that we think will give us the contentment we have been craving, we suddenly feel disappointment. What we have does not satisfy our heart, so it goes fluttering about distractedly, seeking something that will fill the immense void. Though we have the love of God in our heart, though we feel that divine joy, our heart, restless and inconstant, goes searching everywhere for something to satisfy it, as if the tremendous happiness within it were not enough. What is lacking? Peace.

Peace is the complement and perfection of joy. It not only delivers the soul from the fretful trouble of exterior things, but calms the inner fluctuations of its desires and marvelously disposes and unifies its affections. Thus it makes our heart single in its triumphant love, which then has complete mastery over our being.

Here, then, are the three fruits of the Holy Spirit which, by ordering the soul, give it a true experience of heaven: the delight of loving, the joy of union, the tranquillity of peace. Without doubt, in order to possess these three completely it is necessary to attain the heights. But God has willed that we shall find, all along the road of the spiritual life, some measure of these precious things that satisfy the longing for happiness we have in our soul. Thanks be to Him, at every stage of the journey toward Him there are charity, joy, and peace, even though they may not be in their fullest perfection.

May these considerations reveal celestial horizons to our hearts, thirsting for light, love, and happiness. May they help us to recognize the divine gift we carry within, to enjoy its sweetness, and thereby to experience in this our exile a reflection of heavenly beatitude!

CHAPTER V: PATIENCE AND LONGANIMITY

WHO DOES NOT KNOW THAT in this world are things both good and bad? If there were nothing but good, love with its train of joy and peace would be enough to put our soul in order. But as we know very well, there are also evils about us. And if love is for the purpose of putting our soul in order with respect to good things, sorrow has been given us to order our souls with respect to evil. For sorrow has been sanctified and divinized by its contact with Jesus.

In the eternal, glorious life of heaven there are no evils, only an unspeakable array of good things. The blessed fear nothing because in heaven there are no tears, no bitterness, no grief, no struggle. They hope for nothing because they possess everything. They bear in their hearts an indescribable, full, imperishable, and eternal happiness; in God, to whom they are intimately and ineffably united, they possess all good things, so that their desires are complete and their fears forever ended. Therefore in heaven love is sufficient: love victorious, mastering all souls, showering its light, its perfume, and its delights over the hearts of the elect.

But such is not the case on earth. God has placed many good things in life, both in the natural order and in the supernatural and divine; but there are always some evils present with the good. Evils are inevitable in human life; God did not wish to remove them from the earth, and Christ did not will to make our life completely free of them.

St. Augustine, in his masterful way, gives us the clue for understanding this plan, which at first sight seems incomprehensible. He says that God preferred to bring good out of evil rather than to prevent evil. And indeed it is worthy of divine wisdom, love, and power to be able to draw out of those dark depths some magnificent good. Jesus Christ, who came to transform all things, who elevated, sanctified, and divinized them, did not wish to suppress evil, but gave us the divine secret of getting good out of it. Together with love that orders our heart and our soul with respect to what is good, Jesus has left us, as a precious inheritance on earth, pain: Christian, supernatural, divine pain, the inseparable companion of love and the cause of many of its wonders.

How beautiful, how rich, are the designs of God concerning pain! Truly, a great part of our treasures, our prerogatives, and our happiness comes from it. Pain marvelously cleanses; the Scriptures say that just as gold is purified in the crucible, so are souls purified in temptation and pain. Pain enlightens; there are things we do not comprehend unless we have suffered, because grief sheds some special celestial light over our spirit. Pain is the sap of all the virtues; without it they cannot grow and reach their full maturity. Pain makes love pure and disinterested, makes us one with the beloved; there are no bonds comparable to the holy bonds of pain. It encircles our head with an aureole of glory and pours into our soul divine and exquisite drops of happiness.

Echoing St. Augustine, who says that virtue is order in love, we might say that virtue and perfection are order in pain.

It is so difficult to put order in our souls, to attain harmony, in the face of evils. To see this, it is enough to analyze carefully the divers manners in which souls react to the afflictions they must endure. Some are so oppressed when they see themselves surrounded by evils that they plunge into the depths of despair, at times even into the madness of suicide. Others, without going so far, suffer to the limit of their capacity, dragging along the cross of their griefs without any consolation. There are still others who begin to understand what pain is and at least fortify themselves by resignation to bear it. And last of all, those brilliant with God's light go deep into the very bosom of grief and find in the fullness of bitterness an exquisite drop of honey, a heavenly sweetness, that makes them love pain and look for it with eagerness and embrace it for all the good it will bring.

Even in the spiritual life there are struggles. There are periods when the sky seems to grow dark on the road to perfection, and the earth to give way beneath our feet. There are hours of sorrow and desolation when bleakness surrounds the poor, afflicted soul and the heart is like a cold, heavy stone. There are times of bitterness when the Beloved apparently draws away and forgets, while the soul cries out everywhere in vain, not finding Him. For voices are lost in those empty spaces, and that crying seems to rouse no echo in the divine Heart.

On the very heights of the spiritual life, indeed, we feel that our desires are not satisfied — not because God is not enough, but because we do not yet possess Him fully; because we have not yet captured Him in a final and perfect way. For this reason those most intimately united with God, the saints, have suffered the unspeakable torment of desire. That martyrdom, according to St. Teresa who endured so much of it, is the greatest anguish that can be felt on earth; and it is also the principal suffering of the souls in purgatory. It consists in desiring, with all the ardor possible to one's being, to possess God, to possess Him fully; and in seeing, at the same time, that the period of exile still stretches out before the soul and the blessed hour of peace and liberty still does not come.

As the Holy Spirit by means of the fruits of charity, joy and peace puts order into our soul with respect to good, so He has some exquisite, exceedingly fine fruits that enable us to find rest and even delight in our constant struggle against the evils that surround us. He puts order in our soul with respect to afflictions, with a Christian suffering, a sanctified suffering, a divinized suffering.

There are two classes of afflictions that we must bear on earth: one comprises all that goes contrary to our wishes, our inclinations; the other consists in the desire for the good things that we lack. How painful is the time of waiting for some necessity or benefit ardently wished for! How the soul is tortured when we have set our desire on this thing and the delay persists! The moments seem like centuries and the pain of waiting begins to fill our heart with bitterness.

But the Holy Spirit aids us. There are two prerogatives which He places in our soul in order to strengthen us in the struggle: *fortitude in suffering* and *the heavenly science of hope.* Both are divine forms of approach to one same reality: pain.

We have practical examples of this work of the Holy Spirit in the lives of the saints. Let us recall, for example, St. Lidwina, stretched on her bed of pain, covered with wounds and sores, yet tranquil and smiling, as if she were on a bed of flowers. Let us think of St. Paul, who tells us he had fears within and struggles without; St. Paul exhausted by his travels, meeting dangers on the sea, on land, among his enemies, and among his friends; beaten, stoned, betrayed; bearing in his heart such depths of pain and desire that he yearned to be delivered from this life; yet showing a daily solicitous care about all the churches.[1] We could continue thus through a

---

1. Cf. 2 Cor. 11:23-28; Rom. 7:24.

long series of saints, each one of whom had that fortitude in suffering and that divine science of hope.

At the same time that the Holy Spirit gives us fortitude and hope to help us bear afflictions, He pours into our soul the heavenly delight of his consolations, as He does whenever He perfects any portion of our being. While teaching us to suffer, He fills us with joy. Not only does He strengthen us against pain and support us with divine hope: this, which is already so much, is not yet enough, for the works of God are perfect, the Holy Spirit is always the Paraclete. To fortitude and hope are added the two fruits, patience and longanimity, the personal consolations that are given to us so that we may find happiness in suffering and in expectation, or hope deferred.

At first it seems strange to us to find pleasure in suffering and in unrealized hope. But with God's light we can penetrate the secret of pain, and succeed in glimpsing the profound and divine reason for these consolations.

Pain, when we see it thus, is a marvelous thing. Pain gives us joy, it consoles us; and why?

First, because it purifies us. We might imagine that gold, if it had intelligence, would feel a certain deep joy while burning in the crucible, knowing that it would come out purified. We have intelligence and we have received divine light in order to comprehend the mystery of pain. Therefore we feel the satisfaction of suffering, because we know that from that crucible we will come forth more beautiful, more pure, more worthy of God.

But this is not the only consolation that pain bestows upon our soul. There are no bonds comparable to the bonds of pain for uniting us with God. Why? Because Jesus Christ sanctified pain by His contact with it; because He desired to make use of pain to redeem the human race; because as often as we suffer, we complete — as St. Paul says — the passion of Christ.[2]

He whom we love is a God nailed to a Cross. Pain makes us resemble Him. It is characteristic of love to have a tremendous desire to resemble the beloved; it is characteristic, too, for those who love to resemble each other; and if we have set our desire on a crucified God, our flesh must be torn, our heart filled with suffering, our body must bear the marks of the body of Jesus. The desire to become like Jesus fortifies, and the satisfaction of reproducing in ourselves the image of Jesus Crucified is a deep and very sweet consolation.

But there is something more: pain is giving. To suffer for love is to give ourself in a very perfect way. To the one we love, we can give our smiles, our glances, our words, and the works of our hands; but when we suffer, we give something more, we give our blood — if not that of our veins, then the more noble blood of our heart.

Pain signifies a magnificent donation of our very selves, and therefore when we suffer there vibrates in our heart a very profound love. And if we suffer for love, the suffering turns into delectable joy.

We have quoted the saying of St. Thérèse of the Child Jesus: "I found happiness and joy in the world, but only in pain." The words are not a mere literal paradox — was the ingenuous soul of St. Thérèse of Lisieux capable of such a thing? No, this is the expression of a profound mystery. What she said is the truth, and St. Francis of Assisi, in his wonderful parable about perfect happiness, had expressed it in his own way. Happiness that comes from pain is perfect because it is purified. It is a happiness that nothing, that no one, can take away from us. It indicates the complete giving of ourselves, and is the mark of triumphant love.

---

2. Cf. Col. 1:24.

Do we get a glimpse now of how the Holy Spirit, while preparing and putting our souls in order in regard to afflictions, while giving us fortitude to suffer, pours also into our souls the delights of His consolation? Patience is serenity in pain. Patience is love that suffers. And that virtue, or if you wish, that sum of virtues which makes us capable of facing evils and of enduring anguish, is converted for us into a fountain of consolations; it is something delightful, something sublime, to suffer for love.

Thus the Holy Spirit bestows upon us a divine fruit, patience, in the midst of our ordinary struggles. But, as has already been noted, we not only have to endure afflictions, we have to suffer the deferred expectation of good things needed and desired. If we had no other pain than this, it would be enough to make our life a vale of tears.

Every person on earth is forced to wait. The farmer patiently waits for the germination of the seed, for shoots to come forth. At first they are small, weak, and tender, and he waits for them to grow little by little, to produce leaves and flowers and fruit. Then he waits for the slow maturing of the fruit until the happy moment of harvesting arrives. No matter what we seek, we go slowly to the attainment of it. Slowly is the spirit formed in wisdom; slowly is the perfection of art achieved; slowly does man become rich; and slowly are hearts conquered.

In this world, everything is done slowly. Time figures necessarily in our life, and God, who in the spiritual order and in the economy of His graces has wished to adapt Himself to the norms of our life, takes account also of time.

God is very slow, because He has all eternity; because He knows perfectly the part that time plays in human life. God is very slow: thousands of years passed in order that Jesus, the Desired of the Nations, might appear in the world. Souls are sanctified slowly. Our human impatience sometimes does not tolerate this slowness; we would like our soul to be purified rapidly, our mind to be quickly illuminated with the light of God, a volcano of love to burst forth in our heart. But no, the law of life — of all life, the natural and the spiritual — is slowness. Time ripens the fruits in the field, and time ripens the fruits in the soul.

It is necessary to wait, but the waiting is painful because the desire is so keen. This is the reason why the saints, in the last stages of their spiritual journey, felt an unspeakable martyrdom: the martyrdom of desire. St. Teresa of Jesus expresses it in immortal words: "Come on quietly, death, so that I do not hear you coming, for the joy of dying might return life to me." St. Paul, in one of his profound and clear-cut phrases, speaks of "desiring to depart and to be with Christ."[3]

It is so painful, it is so sad, to wait! Nevertheless, the Holy Spirit gives us the divine science of hope. The patriarchs possessed it. They lived on hope. In those long years that they were on earth, their souls were at peace, and their eyes peered into the obscurities of the future, and they were happy because one night in the silence of their tents they had received a promise from God. They knew that the promise would be converted into reality; therefore they lived on hope.

The prophets lived on hope, for they had a glimpse of the future, they contemplated the marvels that would later be accomplished on earth. And although centuries had to go by before those marvels would come to pass, they were full of joy and their hearts expanded with hope.

The Holy Spirit teaches us to hope for the good things that we desire, and when the poignancy of hope is not yet extinguished in the soul, He pours upon it His divine consolations

---

3. Cf. Phil. 1:23.

The fruit of hope is longanimity. This consists in knowing how to hope and even to find an intimate satisfaction, a secret delight, in the slowness of God. Souls so favored know that God will give them what He has promised. They know that He loves them, that in His own opportune time He will shower His gifts upon them. They understand that the action of God is slow because of the impatience of their desires, and despite that impatience they cleave steadfastly to His will. Therefore they find a secret joy in waiting and hoping, because God wants it so; because He gives the necessary time for the precious fruits of the soul to ripen.

This is a brief and perhaps too informal account of those two fruits of pain that the Holy Spirit gives to our souls: *patience* and *longanimity.*

By the first three fruits — charity, joy, peace — He shows us how to make use of good things, to enjoy them, to find an exquisite delight in them. By these other two just explained, He teaches us how to conduct ourselves with regard to afflictions, and helps us to find in pain choice and heavenly consolations.

If only we understood that life which the Holy Spirit gives to our souls! Everything in it is harmony; everything is order. And if there are obscurities, those obscurities are luminous. And if there are secrets, those secrets contain true rays of light, of love, and of hope.

CHAPTER VI: GOODNESS, BENIGNITY, MILDNESS, FAITH

NOT ALL IN THE SPIRITUAL LIFE IS contemplation and love. There is a very important part which is called the active life. In this there are special difficulties, and a particular ordering of the Holy Spirit is required for them.

St. Thomas teaches that full enjoyment of heavenly consolation in the contemplative life is impeded whenever our active life is not yet perfectly disposed and ordered. Because the active life is so complicated and difficult, it is the source of much disquietude, of many impediments that deprive us of the fullness of divine joys. Therefore the Spirit must give order to the ways of that life also; and when He performs this work, it is to be expected that He will produce some special fruits for its completion. We have already seen that the fruits always correspond to each phase of the process of ordering that takes place in our soul. Where there is order, there is sweetness; wherever the Holy Spirit accomplishes His work, His heavenly fruits are to be found.

There are, as pointed out in a previous chapter, two fields, two parts, in our active life: one comprising our relations with other men, the other, our relations with inferior things. In this chapter we will treat of the first.

Of necessity we must live with our brethren. We cannot remove ourselves from them. Suppose that the life of the hermit were accessible to all — that life which was in vogue early in the history of the Church, when men desiring to sanctify themselves went off to the solitude of the desert and there, in contact only with nature and God, progressed from virtue to virtue until they reached the heights of sanctity. Suppose, I say, that this were still possible: it would not be best. St. Thomas teaches us that we attain sanctity more efficaciously by living with others than by withdrawing ourselves from them.

Human life is not a life of isolation; it is a life of association, of companionship. By the will of God we were born in a family, which is part of a larger society. It is impossible for us to avoid relationships with others, and at times these relationships are very difficult.

It is easy and pleasant to have dealings with people who are kind to us and with whom we have some bond of liking. But to deal with everyone, the good and the bad, those who are sympathetic to us and those who repel us, those who wish us well and those who wish us ill, requires a balance very hard for our soul to attain. Our relations with men must conform not only to the rules of reason, but to the divine norms left us by Jesus Christ. And we know from experience how hard this can be.

Men struggle with one another, they fight, they bring harm to each other. How easily do we all fail in charity even with those who are nearest to us, with whom we are united by blood and affection. How great are the evils that arise because we do not preserve Christian norms in our dealings with others. The late Pontiff Pius XII, speaking of the terrible threat of war, told us that wars come precisely from the fact that men forget the divine principles of Jesus Christ.

Our relations with others, then, are both very important and very difficult. It is necessary for the Holy Spirit with His light, His fire, and His action to come and dispose our heart, our soul, and our life so that our association with others may be harmonious and holy.

For the purpose of regulating our life, we possess various virtues which we received on the day of our baptism. Justice, with its conjoined virtues, governs our relations with our neighbor. Then there is a special gift of the Holy Spirit which disposes our relations with others, the gift of piety. The virtues of justice and the gift of piety prepare and regulate our active life so that we may exemplify the words which Christ pronounced on the eve of His passion: "Father, . . . that they may be one, even as We are."[1]

How do the virtue of justice and the gift of piety, under the influence of charity, queen and model of all virtues, put order in our relations with others?

Order in this important matter can be reduced to two things. First, the Holy Spirit gives us a benevolent will toward others; that is, He gives us a desire to do good to all. Our relations with other men are summarized in the precept of fraternal charity that Jesus preached with so much earnestness during His whole life but especially on the eve of His passion: "A new commandment I give you, that you love one another; that as I have loved you, you also love one another."[2] To make us understand the importance of this precept, He said on that same blessed night: "By this will all men know that you are My disciples, if you have love for one another."[3] The authentic sign of the Christian, then, is fraternal charity. Do we understand the full meaning of the divine precept, of the new commandment of Jesus, "Love one another"?

To repeat: we Christians have to love, without exception, the persons for whom we feel sympathy and those for whom we feel a natural repugnance; we have to love the good and the bad, friends and enemies. Charity does not admit exceptions. We must pray for those who persecute us, and do good

---

1. John 17:11.
2. John 13:34.
3. Ibid. 35.

to those who harm us. A hard, a very hard thing for our poor human nature — but how great, how noble and holy is this doctrine of charity!

If we have to love our neighbor, every neighbor without exception, then naturally we must also have the will to do good to him. For the love of charity is not a speculative love, it is not a love of simple affection; it is an efficacious love, active and operative. To love thus is to desire to do good to others; to all. Right order in our relations with others consists in this disposition.

Moreover, the will to do this good, is not enough, however sincere it may be; love asks for more. The Apostle St. John, the master of love, who received his divine knowledge listening to the heartbeats of Jesus on the night of the Last Supper, gives this simple and profound rule of love: "My dear children, let us not love in word, neither with the tongue, but in deed and in truth."[4] It is not enough to wish to do good, it is necessary actually to do it.

Clearly, our works are always inferior to our desires, because the will to do good can be unbounded, whereas the execution of that will is not. We are very limited creatures; our spiritual and material resources are so meager that we cannot do good to all men, nor even to all those who are very close to us. But Christian order demands that we try to do good to all according to the measure of our strength, according to the opportunities that present themselves to us, and as discretion guides us.

Consequently our relations with our neighbor can be reduced to two points: to have the will to do good to others, and actually to do good to as many as possible. That is the disposition which the Holy Spirit forms in our souls; but it is very slow in its development and we must engage in numerous

4. 1 John 3:18.

struggles to achieve victory. Little by little that charitable and generous will is forged in the depths of our being; little by little we accomplish the intentions of our heart. And when the two things, our will and its execution, reach a certain maturity, then God grants us the divine consolations, the fruits of the Holy Spirit.

Two fruits correspond to these two dispositions that the Holy Spirit accomplishes in our soul: goodness and benignity. Goodness is the desire to do good to all. Benignity is the generous execution of that interior intention.

At first we may not understand how joy and consolation can be found in these arduous works of charity. It is so hard for us to come out of our own egoism and truly love others that we conceive the fulfillment of the divine precept of charity only in terms of stern efforts and great sacrifices. Undoubtedly these are needed to fulfill the commandment of Jesus. But the things that God ordains, even when they are very difficult, always contain a drop of heavenly sweetness.

In the wish to do good and in the accomplishment of this wish, there is a profound consolation, a very noble satisfaction, even in the natural order. Generous hearts find deep rewards. Meanness is at variance with happiness; hatred does not produce it. It is goodness that brings joy, even in the natural order. It is the good people who are happy: those who extend their hand to everyone, who do all the good they can round about them.

In the supernatural order this joy is more intense and more perfect because the principle of our good actions is a ray of light sent by the Paraclete upon our spirit; a heavenly sentiment which moves our heart. In the eyes of the Christian, every man is Christ, for Christ Himself said to us: "As long as you did it for one of these, the least of My brethren, you did it for Me."[5] All men are members of the Mystical Body; all are incorporated in Christ and bear within themselves something of Him. As St. Augustine says, we have been "transformed into Christ."

Our neighbor, then, is Jesus. This poor, ignorant, and, if you will, perverse neighbor is Jesus. He has something divine in him; even when he has fallen into the bog and become soiled, he is a jewel, and a jewel does not lose its value because it has been dropped into the mud. Each one of our fellow men is Jesus; and when, with God's help, we understand this, our heart grows larger and larger and we want to do good to all men, because all men are Jesus.

Are we beginning to get a glimpse of this fruit of the Holy Spirit? It is the joy of willing to do good. It is the joy of personal love toward all men, a love that is not of the earth but of heaven; a love that is an image of the immense love borne in the Heart of Jesus, who died for all, who desires that all be saved.

After willing to do good to our neighbor we have actually to do it, in every way that we can. To this second disposition of our relations corresponds a new fruit of the Holy Spirit, benignity. It causes us to experience an intense delight when we put our beneficent will into operation.

We can easily understand the pleasure of doing good, even — as we have already said — humanly speaking. Is it not satisfying to dry a tear, to draw a smile from lips livid with hunger or illness? Could we do anything more enjoyable than give happiness to someone, help someone with our counsel, pour a drop of the balm of consolation into some sorrowing heart? Exceedingly sweet satisfactions, even in human terms, come to us in this way. But when we lift ourselves a little above the things of earth, when the light of heaven

---

5. Matt. 25:40.

illumines us, then this joy becomes truly divine. Do we think, at times, that being happy consists in drawing to ourselves all the good things of earth; that we have to be the center in a palace of happiness? This is to deceive ourselves. Happiness is not found in selfishness, it is found in generosity. In order to be happy we need to go out of ourselves, to forget ourselves a little, to give away our heart and all the good things we have. Giving is intimately related to loving, and giving and loving are things of God.

God loves; God gives. He is always giving. He opens His hand, the Scriptures tell us, and fills every living creature with blessings. God does good to all creatures, pouring His graces and gifts everywhere.

By coming out of ourselves, by giving our heart through goodness and our goods through benignity, we resemble God. It is a divine pleasure to give, and giving themselves is the pleasure of all apostles. When we read the lives of the great ones, like St. Paul and St. Francis Xavier, they seem strange to us at first. What joy, what happiness, could St. Paul find in those difficult and dangerous journeys? He was stoned and beaten, he was the object of scorn. Still he went on, tirelessly, ardently, preaching the Gospel everywhere. We wonder how it is possible to forget oneself to such a point. St. Paul had a cultivated mind, a great heart. He would have been able to succeed in science, art, commerce, or any other of the ordinary activities of life. How could he leave all in order to seek and serve those who many times did not thank him? How could he say, "I overflow with joy in all our troubles"?[6]

These joys are the fruits of the active life, goodness and benignity. Jesus Christ enjoyed these exquisite fruits of the

---

6. 2 Cor. 7:4.

Spirit and He continues to enjoy them in heaven. What must be His joy to know that all men have gained through Him the possibility of salvation! What satisfaction, what truly divine delight, must be His as He reflects that millions of souls are happy because of Him, because He died for them, because He gave them grace and marked out for them the road of sanctification! Next to the essential felicity of the Beatific Vision, the soul of Jesus must rejoice most in the happiness of having done good to all souls.

And we can participate in these celestial joys of Jesus and the Apostles. We also can do good; in a small way, perhaps, but we can do it. And we can be certain that whatever good we do for Jesus Christ, whatever benefit we confer on our neighbor, we will not go unrewarded. For Jesus said: "Whoever gives to one of these little ones but a cup of cold water to drink because he is a disciple, amen I say to you, he shall not lose his reward."[7] There will be an assured reward in eternal life; but even on earth, there will be heavenly consolations, the delicious fruits of goodness and benignity.

Special fruits of the Holy Spirit are also needed to correspond to the difficulties and the troubles we encounter in our dealings with our neighbor.

No matter how real our own goodness, no matter how great our generosity, we will assuredly come across men who oppose our plans, who wound us, who bring evil upon us; as long as the world is the world there will be good and bad in it, and it is impossible for us to remove ourselves from what is bad and communicate only with those who are good.

In our dealings with men there is necessarily much to make us suffer, and if we did not have the gifts of God we would react angrily to those who oppose us. Anger is a passion by

---

7. Matt. 10:42.

which we respond to the evils and injustices inflicted by others. Someone wants to keep from us that which is lawfully ours, and anger comes to our aid. Someone wants to oppose a good work we have undertaken, and anger makes us sufficiently strong to resist the effort to interfere with our design.

But Jesus Christ has taught us about mildness, or meekness. At first the idea of this virtue seems difficult to us. Why take away the right to anger? Why preach its opposite? Mildness seems to place us in a position of inferiority; the world believes that sweet and gentle people are ignored by others. But in the Sermon on the Mount Jesus said: "Blessed are the meek, for they shall possess the earth."[8]

Do we know what it is to possess the earth? It is to win hearts and souls. Mildness has this divine efficacy. Anger removes us from others; it may have easy victories, but they are superficial. By means of anger we believe that we fortify our possessions and our personality; but in reality, anger sows in the hearts of our fellow men a seed of hatred that will one day produce its fruit. On the other hand, mildness sways hearts and souls. It is not anger or violence that truly wins the earth, it is gentleness, the divine sweetness taught by Jesus Christ. And there is history to prove it; the whole record of humanity is a commentary on the beatitude of the Mount, "Blessed are the meek, for they shall possess the earth."

From these words of our Saviour we know that the virtue of mildness, which seems so difficult, has its exquisite joys: the sweetness of being gentle, of gaining the earth, not by the noise of arms, not by the impact of violence, but by the power of meekness.

And thus the Apostle enumerates it among the fruits of the Holy Spirit. Its work is to accomplish the ordering of our soul with respect to the evils that other men bring upon us.

8. Ibid. 5:4.

It takes away difficulties and gives us pleasant, peaceful relations with others. And last of all, it gives us deep satisfactions by helping us to win souls.

There is a final fruit of the active life which St. Paul calls faith. The Latin *fides,* and even the word "faith" in our language, has two meanings: it signifies the acquiescence that we give to a truth on the authority of the one who teaches it to us, and it also denotes the fidelity and the sincerity with which we treat others, the rectitude, the loyalty, and the whole sum of marvelous virtues that exalt man. It puts the last touch to our relationship with men. To desire to do them good, to pour out our gifts into their hands and into their hearts, to be gentle with them and loyal besides, that is perfect order in human relations.

A special consolation of the Holy Spirit corresponds to this loyalty: the joy of being loyal, the joy of knowing that truth is the norm of our conduct, that we are sincere with others, that we are faithful to our word and our affections.

Here we have the four fruits of the Holy Spirit intimately connected with our active life, or rather, with that phase of it represented by our relations with other men.

Wherever there is order, there is consolation; wherever there is a work of love of the Spirit, there are His divine fruits. How splendid is God in His gifts! How easy He makes virtue! He leads us lovingly by the hand through the difficult, winding pathways that ascend to the summit of perfection.

Therefore in reality virtue is not difficult. It demands strenuous efforts, but we have graces. It requires sacrifices, but we have consolations. We have already noted a verse in the Psalms that tells us in an admirable way what the Christian life means: "When cares abound within me, Your comfort gladdens my soul." The cloth of Christian life is woven with the golden threads of joys and sorrows, but in divine proportions. Our Lord has imposed some austere duties upon us, but He has also given us some heavenly comforts. Let us, then, heed the invitation of Jesus Christ: "If anyone wishes to come after Me, let him deny himself, and take up his cross and follow Me."[9] Let us take the cross upon our shoulders and remember that it offers not only a deep pain but also a wondrous consolation, a heavenly delight.

9. Ibid. 16:24; Mark 8:34.

CHAPTER VII: MODESTY, CONTINENCY, CHASTITY

HE APOSTLE ST. PAUL, WITH HIS clear vision, his concise and energetic language, with the celestial light that impregnated his spirit, expressed briefly but luminously the Christian concept of the universe and the profound meaning of the spiritual life: "All are yours, and you are Christ's, and Christ is God's."[1] What a marvelous gradation! What perfect order! All things are ours. God puts all things into our hands that by using them we may be led to Him. But we go to God through Jesus Christ, who is the Way, the only Way, to reach Divinity; and Christ Himself, in so far as He was man, subjected Himself to God.

And thus the same Apostle reveals to us that when the universal resurrection has taken place, when death, the last enemy, has been destroyed, Jesus Christ will present humanity, regenerate and holy, to His heavenly Father and then God will be "all in all."

By this profound teaching of St. Paul we understand that Catholic doctrine is a universal and perfect concept, that the spiritual life is not something incidental in human existence but something comprehensive and all-embracing because it puts order into everything. The Christian life is the perfect and total ordering of our being.

After ordering our soul, and after establishing a proper relationship with our neighbor (themes we have considered

---

1. 1 Cor. 3:22-23.

in the foregoing chapters), it is necessary to adjust our relations with inferior creatures. Such creatures as wealth, pleasures, honors, and everything that enters the complicated web of our life, all are ours. At our disposal are the ocean, the forests, the fields, and the animals, as well as the joy that we can find in them.

God has willed that as we grow in our physical life we should also grow in dignity, and in some cases, that we should be surrounded with honors. These pleasures of honor and dignity are ours on condition that we are Christ's, as Christ is God's.

Creatures are ours. We can dispose of them, but we are not to use them in a selfish way. We are to use them, as St. Ignatius of Loyola says, that they may help us to the attainment of our end, as a stairway by which we mount to God. Creatures are ours to touch as we would the strings of a lyre, to intone a melodious song to God. That is the way they were used in paradise. In a brief but delightful age of humanity, creatures obeyed man. Man was king of creation; he could dispose of everything on earth. Adam, before his sin, had a profound sense of order and he used creatures as a stairway to lead him to God.

The universe belonged to man; its purpose was to help man to God. Man, in the divine plan, was to take creatures by the hand and present them to the divine Heart; they were to be used to give praise to the Creator. But sin introduced disorder, unbalanced human nature, and upset the whole earth. And now, after the sin, even when we have the right to use creatures, we often do so in a disorderly fashion. To put it briefly, creatures do not always belong to us; many times we belong to them. In God's mind, creatures were to be at man's service; but sin has brought about the monstrous aberration by which man is often at theirs.

The avaricious man is not master of his riches, he is their slave. Wealth in the hands of a miser is not a means of enriching his life and taking him to God, it is rather his idol, to which he renders worship and service. For the glutton, foods are not the means of sustaining his life, of nourishing and strengthening him so that he can glorify God; the glutton is the slave of his food. It can be said, not that food is his, but that he belongs to his food. The sensual man does not use pleasure in the measure ordained by God, as a help and compensation in the sacrifices that duty imposes on him. The sensual man is the servant of pleasure. Pleasure does not belong to the sensual man; rather, he belongs to it. Examples like these could be multiplied. Sin has introduced disorder into the world, and for many men creatures are not steppingstones to God, but bonds that enslave, cruel masters which force man into their service when he should be their king.

Our Lord Jesus Christ came to repair the disorder introduced by sin; to teach us to be free, to be kings again. St. Paul speaks of this "freedom of the glory of the sons of God."[2] The freedom Jesus brought to us is not the freedom of the world, the liberty to behave as we please. This, in reality, is slavery — to the passions, to exterior things. The freedom of Christ consists precisely in placing ourselves above earthly passions; in being masters of ourselves, in disposing of things in an orderly and holy manner, so that creatures may have again their original mission: to help us to God.

But we have within us a terrible obstacle to the proper use of creatures. A shameful complicity on the part of our very self causes them to exercise an inordinate fascination over us. We have inherited from our first parents those three concupiscences which the Apostle St. John says are the essential marks of the world: the lust of the flesh, the lust of the eyes,

---

2. Rom. 8:21.

and the pride of life.[3] They are the deep traces left in human nature by original sin. No longer is there balance in our faculties, no longer are the inferior subject to the higher. We feel in the depths of our being that constant struggle of which we have heard St. Paul speak, between the law of the spirit and the law of sin. These concupiscences, these disordered inclinations to pleasures, to honors, to riches, prevent us from using creatures moderately, and hold for us a pernicious attraction.

To recover our place and reconquer our kingdom, to break the chains that tie us to earth and to feel the liberty of the sons of God, we need to use creatures in an orderly manner. But to do this, we must first acquire interior peace.

The Holy Spirit accomplishes this work in us. He penetrates to the depths of our souls, to the innermost part of our being, controlling our concupiscences and subjecting our interior faculties to reason and to faith. There are virtues and gifts to accomplish this work. Temperance and the related virtues bring about the moderation of our passions; the gift of fear breaks the bonds that enslave us to creatures; the gift of knowledge gives us the true understanding of creatures and a profound vision of all those things that God has placed at our disposal. The divine ordering is completed within us by these works of the Holy Spirit.

But, to repeat: wherever the virtues and the gifts produce perfect order, at least an order relative to the stage through which the soul is passing in the spiritual life, there is to be found a heavenly consolation, a fruit of the Holy Spirit. And for this order in our relation with exterior things, which makes us use them moderately and subjects our desires, there are three corresponding fruits of the Spirit: modesty, continency, and chastity.

---

3. Cf. 1 John 2:16.

The name of the first fruit appears a little strange to us. We are accustomed to consider modesty simply as a virtue that moderates our exterior, the virtue that directs our movements, our glances, our carriage; but in the first Christian centuries the word modesty had a broader application. The Apostle intends this in the Epistle to the Philippians when referring to that order that ought to exist in all our exterior life: "Let your moderation be known to all men."[4] He is not referring simply to the way we should bear ourselves, but to the norm of moderation and sweetness by which all our actions should be inspired. He uses the word modesty in this sense in his enumeration of the fruits of the Spirit. Modesty is the moderation and harmony which should mark our relation to all creatures. It means control in the use of riches, of honors, and in our whole exterior behavior.

Continency and chastity are the fruits of the Holy Spirit that proceed from control and moderation in the personal inclinations of our soul; that is, from that orderly disposition of our passions indispensable for recovering our liberty and our grandeur. Just as modesty guides us in the use of exterior things, so chastity and continency bridle the concupiscences that we inherit from our first parents and establish order in the inferior part of our being.

At first sight we are not able to understand what joys can be found in these austere virtues. Moderation in the use of creatures is a very fine thing, a very holy thing, but it seems rather difficult to practice. We are inclined to use everything without order, without measure, without limitation; we want to seek unlimited wealth and we want to use it freely.

To moderate ourselves, to establish norms, seems very hard and very much like servitude. And we feel a still greater austerity in those divine norms that control our concupiscences,

---

4. 4:5.

that channel our inclinations in the path of order and harmony. Is it possible to find comfort and happiness in such severity?

It is true that when we look superficially at the matter, moderation in the use of exterior things and restraint of our passions seem indeed like slavery. But if we look deeply, we find that the contrary is true. It is the one who lets himself be carried along by his passions who is in servitude; it is the one who has no norms in the use of exterior things who has lost his real character of king of the universe, that character given to him as he came forth from God's creative hand.

The man who has learned by the ordering of the Holy Spirit how to dominate his passions, how to use creatures well, has broken the chains, become master of himself, recovered his true greatness. He possesses some of the signs that were proper to the state of original justice in the garden of paradise. And because the Holy Spirit makes us free, we feel exquisite joys: the joy of liberty, the joy of a holy sovereignty. These are the joys that the Apostle calls modesty, continency, chastity; the last three fruits, the fruits that free us, that break our chains and reinstate us as kings of creation. This is not exaggeration or hyperbole. It is a profound truth. If we reflect, we will understand it.

* * *

If we have followed properly St. Paul's heavenly doctrine on the fruits of the Spirit, we shall understand one thing: the spiritual life is not sad; it is not so austere or burdensome as it appeared at first sight. Many, even among Christians, believe the life of piety to be unbearable! "They seemed, in the view of the foolish, to be dead...but they are at peace."[5] For those who do not understand the spiritual life, it is a certain kind of death; the saints, to them, seem to live in this world as if dead, as if without joy or consolation, as if oppressed

---

5. Wis. 3:2-3.

under the weight of overwhelming abnegations. Thinking thus, such people deceive themselves. The just are dead in the eyes of the foolish, but they live in peace. They carry celestial treasures and joys in their hearts, for whoever lives the spiritual life in its fullness bears within him the fruits of the Holy Spirit.

Let us repeat it — Jesus Christ did not want to suppress pain: it is so beautiful, so fruitful, so full of hidden delight. He performed a more prodigious work than if He had destroyed it. He enfolded it in divine sweetness and brought forth from its bosom both joy and consolation.

The spiritual life has the Cross for its symbol. But around the Cross there is light, the light of consolation, because there is love. The spiritual life is sown with divine solace. Here and there, on the side of the road, are found the rich trees that bear the celestial fruits of the Spirit: first, the fruits of which we have just spoken, chastity, continency, modesty; then benignity, goodness, mildness, and faith. In the superior part of the soul and in the last stages of the spiritual life are the divine consolations of love and pain: charity, joy and peace, which are the fruits of love; patience and longanimity, which are the consolations of pain.

These divine joys, besides being exceedingly sweet consolations for soothing our pain, fortifying our spirit, and expanding our hearts, are also like anticipations of the eternal kingdom, breezes from the heavenly land which blow over us in our exile to refresh our brow and soothe our spirit with the exquisite perfume of heaven. May we some day enter triumphantly into that celestial region, that eternal fatherland, where there is no grief, no tears, no bitterness; where God reigns forever in His everlasting joy.

PART IV
THE BEATITUDES

INTRODUCTORY

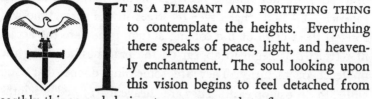

IT IS A PLEASANT AND FORTIFYING THING to contemplate the heights. Everything there speaks of peace, light, and heavenly enchantment. The soul looking upon this vision begins to feel detached from earthly things and desires to soar upward, to fly.

The true heights are beyond death in the eternal fatherland, in the fair region where God is all in all; where purified souls meet and love each other in the immense heart of God, in the joy of eternal brightness, in the fullness of unfailing peace.

God, who is rich in goodness and mercy, willed that before attaining eternal life, souls who love Him and who have left all things for Him should receive even in this life the hundredfold which Jesus promised. Thus we have the beatitudes that the Master preached on the mountain; and although we view them through the shadows of imperfection which can never disappear totally in this exile, they are the true heights of perfection and felicity.

Let souls that long for love and thirst for happiness behold them. Let souls that are strong in the endurance of pain sigh for them. Let them dream of living there in the realms above, breathing the tranquil atmosphere of the high places; and let them be valiant and confident in climbing the steep crags that the Gospel defines for us with divine precision.

The beatitudes are a marvelous chain of mountains of which each peak is a steppingstone in the sublime ascent that leads to God.

Each one of the beatitudes, St. Thomas says, is something perfect and excellent — a summit in itself; and at the same time it is a beginning of future happiness even in this life. The beatitudes are not remote presages of the eternal fruits, like the rich, full buds that cover the trees in the springtime and foretell the wealth of the coming autumn; they are the actual first fruits that begin to appear on the branches, awaiting the opulence of maturity. They are something divine that God willed to deposit on earth. They are "heavenly-colored hyacinths brilliant in the muddy water of this mortal and transitory life."

All the beatitudes are lofty mountaintops, but there is a constant ascension from the first ones to the last, which seem to touch the very sky. What a sublime vista! First, the joy of detachment, the sweetness of tears; then the fullness of justice and the gentleness of mercy; and very near to heaven, the light of purity, the peace of love, the ecstasy of martyrdom!

Let us try to obtain an over-all view of this exceedingly beautiful panorama; and to keep from getting lost, let us continue to follow the eagle eye of St. Thomas Aquinas.

When Jesus opened His lips to reveal to us the mysteries of the beatitudes, He gave us a picture of the royal ascent to happiness; He uncovered the secret of all felicity.

The first step to be taken by one who wishes to attain the mountaintop is to abandon the road that leads downward. Thus, the first thing we must do if we are to reach the blessed life described in the beatitudes is to renounce, sincerely and fully, the deceptive joy of what the world offers.

For twenty centuries the anathema against voluptuous living, against the deceitful happiness of riches, honors, and pleasures, has stood in the Gospel pages: "But woe to you rich! for you are now having your comfort. Woe to you who are filled! for you shall hunger. Woe to you who laugh now! for you shall mourn and weep. Woe to you when all men speak well of you."[1] But men do not know how to read the Gospel.

---

1. Luke 6:24-26.

Fascinated as they are by the world, they do not take the divine truths seriously. That is why there are not many happy people on earth. Very few have the courage to be happy. It is difficult to tear the heart away from the things of earth, from riches, from honors. Yet happiness is not outside us, in these things: "The kingdom of God is within you."[2] "For the kingdom of God does not consist in food and drink, but in justice and peace and joy in the Holy Spirit."[3]

Jesus teaches this truth to us in the first beatitude: "Blessed are the poor in spirit, for theirs is the kingdom of heaven."[4] It is the first peak, the total detachment that liberates, purifies, elevates, and plants divine treasures in our soul. We find God where we leave creatures.

But if happiness is within us, it is not because of ourselves; it is higher and deeper than anything we possess. After becoming detached from exterior things, we must free ourselves *from ourselves.* There are two beatitudes that liberate us so, elevating us above our misery: the beatitude of sweetness and that of tears. The first makes us master of ourself because it shatters the tyranny of wrath; the second opens our heart to divine consolations, having let loose a holy torrent of tears. Pleasure is deceitful because it promises a happiness that does not exist; tears are true because they express the vanity of human things. Pleasure is the enemy of love because it is egoistic; tears either come from love or lead to it.

"Blessed are the meek, for they shall possess the earth." "Blessed are they who mourn, for they shall be comforted." We reach two peaks by dying to ourselves; and from this death springs forth a new and happy life.

The first three beatitudes teach us to die; they disclose the secret of the death — which gives sweetness and joy — of

2. Ibid. 17:21.
3. Rom. 14:17.
4. Matt. 5:3.

that which the Scriptures call "the old man," the formidable enemy of happiness.

The last four beatitudes contain the secret of life; they reveal to us how, from the tomb of the old man, the new man rises, created according to the will of God in justice and holiness of truth.

Happiness on earth is not and cannot be anything but the germ, the pledge of heaven, the fruit that appears on the fertile branches and awaits the ripening of eternity.

But heaven is contemplation and love; therefore the height of earthly happiness is the contemplative life of which Jesus spoke when He said: "Mary has chosen the best part, and it will not be taken away from her."[5] The active life is good, but it has many miseries. It is worked out in the midst of those earthly struggles so trying for the soul that was born for heaven. The contemplative life, on the other hand, unfolds its clean and powerful wings in a very serene, very high atmosphere.

Undoubtedly, activity is part of the way to happiness in that it prepares us for contemplation. We are purified and elevated by activity and become worthy to draw near to God. Rest is the fruit of work; it is bought only at the price of struggle. But activity can also be an obstacle because it can hinder contemplation. Multiplicity of cares and exaggerated solicitude about mundane things may disturb the divinely ordered simplicity of Mary. There is nothing so difficult to achieve as moderation in the active life and its confinement within proper limits. We should learn that divine plan by which activity, without losing its order and efficiency, becomes a steppingstone to contemplation, and nothing more.

The Master revealed a precious truth to us in the beatitudes: "Blessed are they who hunger and thirst for justice, for they

---

5. Luke 10:42.

shall be satisfied. Blessed are the merciful, for they shall obtain mercy."[6] Justice and mercy! They are the two substantial foundations of all our activities, and they assure the soul of the unspeakable gifts of fullness of contemplation and ineffable mercy by which God brings us near to the ocean of His light and love.

We now reach the final peaks of perfection and of happiness. How far away is the earth as seen from these heights — how close is heaven! Upon these summits only two things remain to be done: to see and to love.

Here, we see with a pure, simple, profound, luminous glance that finds only God; a glance that plunges into an abyss of light and, through a divine prism, contemplates the entire universe bathed in a new, unfamiliar brilliance. Here, we love. It might be said that life has changed into love possessing all the tenderness of which our heart is capable and all the strength communicated by the Spirit of God. Our soul loves God, who is infinite Love, and in Him we love everything.

But light springs from purity. To catch a glimpse of the heights, the soul must be clean and diaphanous like a crystal, must let itself be penetrated by God's most pure glance. Not only must evil disappear from the soul, but all lowness, the earthly, the mortal, as well. Purity, which comes from God, which is God Himself in essence, must penetrate with its celestial whiteness into the most interior parts of the soul. Therefore Jesus has said: "Blessed are the clean of heart, for they shall see God."[7]

The mystery of love is accomplished in peace. Love pacifies and, in so doing, deifies. Love transforms: it unites, it unifies, it makes the creature disappear, so that the glory of Jesus

6. Matt. 5:6-7.
7. Ibid. 8.

shines alone; it leads to the consummation of unity, the description of which is found in the glorious cry of St. Paul: "It is now no longer I that live, but Christ lives in me."[8] "Blessed are the peacemakers, for they shall be called children of God."[9] Thus the mystery of happiness is completed.

St. Thomas teaches that we arrive at these high summits by the exercise of the virtues, but principally by the work of the gifts of the Spirit. The hierarchy of these seven beatitudes corresponds to the hierarchy of the gifts. The beatitude of detachment corresponds to the gift of fear of God; meekness, to the gift of piety; tears, to that of knowledge; justice, to fortitude; mercy, to counsel; light, to understanding; the beatitude of love, to the gift of wisdom. The gifts are the roots, the beatitudes are the most sweet fruits which one enjoys in the shadow of the Beloved.

The eighth beatitude, which is the beatitude of pain and martyrdom, is a summary and consummation of all the others. Pain is the final word of love on earth, as unfailing joy is of love in heaven. The beatitudes are love's triumphant march, the delicate shades of its splendid rainbow, the exceedingly full scale of its divine harmony. If love steps majestically over the seven mountain peaks, pain must tint them with its mysterious color. Pain is the richness of poverty, the refinement of gentleness, the divine touch of tears, the grandeur of justice, the unction of mercy, the purity of light, and the fullness of love. "Blessed are they who suffer persecution for justice' sake, for theirs is the kingdom of heaven."[10]

If we would express the Sermon on the Mount briefly, it could be reduced to the two profoundest words in the human language: love, the most divine of heavenly things, and pain, the holiest of the things of earth.

---

8. Gal. 2:20.
9. Matt. 5:9.
10. Ibid. 10.

And if we would symbolize those divine realities that hold the secret of happiness, we could have as emblems the Dove of eternal love and the Cross of immortal pain, united in the divine Heart of Christ: that Heart burning and torn, whose wide wound is the only door through which is poured onto the earth the celestial torrent of felicity.

THE FIRST BEATITUDE: "Blessed are the poor in spirit, for theirs is the kingdom of heaven."

THE BEATITUDES ARE EIGHT IN number, but they treat of one perfection, they offer only one happiness. As the seven colors of the spectrum, each with its own shade and properties, are fused in a single beam of white light, so in Christian perfection the colors of all the virtues and the hues of all the gifts of the Holy Spirit are fused into one celestial light, which is participation in eternal light.

Each one of the beatitudes tells us of some aspect of perfection, and all of them form a wondrous stairway whereby the soul ascends to God. At the foot of this divine flight is total detachment from earthly things, the principle of which is fear of God. This fear has for its reward the kingdom of heaven, that is, the possession of celestial good.

Poverty of spirit, according to St. Thomas Aquinas, is total and voluntary detachment from exterior goods, namely, honors and riches. On many occasions Jesus Christ taught us the necessity of detachment: "If thou wilt be perfect, go, sell what thou hast, and give to the poor, and thou shalt have treasure in heaven; and come, follow Me."[1] "So, therefore, every one of you who does not renounce all that he possesses, cannot be My disciple."[2] What could be more clear, more final, than this? The majority of men, like the young man of the Gospel, sadly turn away when they hear this teaching of Jesus. Earthly things cling so tightly to the poor heart! The soul has so

1. Matt. 19:21.
2. Luke 14:33.

deeply rooted in it the deceitful idea that the passing goods of this world contribute to happiness! It does not know that when it leaves Jesus it separates itself from happiness; that when it closes its ears to the world of life, the doors of its heart are closed to the very good that it desires.

Detachment in itself is already happiness. Those who are detached know the joy of being free, of being pure, the incomparable joy of finding God. Of course creatures can lead us to God. The divine Artist who contemplates creation through the magic prism of His ardent love has made the perfume of the flowers, the song of the birds, the mysterious murmur of sister water, that we may ascend by means of them to uncreated Beauty. Was it not creation that served as a basis of human wisdom from which the Eagle of Aquino soared aloft to heavenly wisdom? Have not earthly kingdoms led many saintly kings to the eternal kingdom?

But in order to use things as a means of ascent to heaven we must not tarry with them; we may rest our feet upon them, but not our heart. The Church asks God in the Mass of the Third Sunday after Pentecost: " ... that with Thee for our Ruler and Guide, we may so pass through the good things of this world as not to lose those of the world to come."

We ought, then, to use creatures in accord with the direction and guidance of the divine will. If we let them detain us, instead of serving as steps to lead us upward they change into obstacles; if we give our heart to them, they become chains that bind and enslave us. They take away the liberty of the children of God, at the same time losing their own by being deprived of their proper function, and therefore they groan, according to the expression of St. Paul, sighing for liberty.[3]

To be happy we need to be free, and holy detachment is the soul's first cry of freedom: Blessed are the poor in spirit.

---

3. Cf. Rom. 8:21-22.

Poverty of spirit makes us also begin to feel the happiness of being pure, not only with the special virtue of purity, but with purity in its broadest sense: remoteness from evil and closeness to God, the supreme good.

The symbol of purity is light. We think of light as without admixture of anything earthly. It seems to us so clean that, touching everything, even the mire of this earth, it is never stained. "God is light,"[4] says the Apostle St. John; and in order to explain the mystery of justification to the faithful of Ephesus, St. Paul tells them: "For you were once darkness, but now you are light in the Lord."[5]

To become light, to pass from glory to glory until we are transformed into the image of God, this is the whole path of perfection. But many purifications are necessary until the last is completed. First the darkness of sin, then the murk of worldliness, must be driven out of the soul. Even so, he who would be clean needs that the Master should wash his feet. When we appear stainless to human eyes, the eye of God still discovers in us indescribable remnants of darkness which His merciful hand removes in order to make us worthy of heaven.

It is necessary for the heart to be lifted up above earthly things in order to be pure.

Detachment does not consummate the marvelous work of our purification, for only on the high peak of the sixth beatitude is the soul bathed in the fullness of light. But already on the mountain of poverty the soul senses that it begins to be diaphanous; it beholds from afar the sad valleys of earthly things covered with shadows. What happiness to be light, which is to draw near to God.

And precisely in this approach to God is the reward of poverty of spirit promised by the first beatitude. The kingdom

---

4. 1 John 1:5.
5. Eph. 5:8.

of heaven is the possession of God, which will be full and unending after death, but which begins on earth as the sweet dawn of the eternal day. The door to this happiness is detachment. As soon as the heart is empty of creatures, God fills it with Himself. As the waters of the ocean fill the hollows of the rocks hidden in its vastness, so the ocean of the charity of God which surrounds us fills the depths of our souls when they are empty.

Ernest Hello tells a beautiful story about the celebrated mystic Tauler and a poor beggar who was lying at the church door. When the mystic discovered that the beggar had attained intimate union with God, he asked him: "Where did you find God?" The beggar replied: "Where I left creatures." These few words are a sublime commentary on the words of Christ: "Blessed are the poor in spirit, for theirs is the kingdom of heaven."

But it is clear that to attain the divine prize of detachment which is the fruit of the virtues, is not enough; we also need the holy divestment effected by the gifts of the Spirit. The virtues teach us to make good use of creatures; the gifts take riches and honors out of our heart in such a perfect and definitive manner that we become wholly unmoved by them; we feel about them like those who have passed beyond the frontiers of death.

St. Thomas says that the first beatitude corresponds to the gift of fear of God and to the virtue of hope. The virtue, setting before us eternal goods, pulls us away from temporal things, and the gift, making us perfectly subject to God, removes us from everything contrary to that happy subjection.

Do not think that, being founded on fear, the beatitude of poverty is alien to love. The gift of the Spirit is not that servile fear that flees from pain, but filial fear which is terrified at the thought of separation from God whom it loves. Like all the gifts, the gift of fear has its root in charity, and the Scriptures say that it is the beginning of wisdom, that is, of that "honorable wisdom" which is "the love of God."[6]

Poverty of spirit is love that commences, that initiates, the work of despoiling and of pain; for love is as strong as death. It separates, it pulls out, it destroys, in order to transform. Love is poor and very rich, opulent in its marvelous nakedness. It rids itself of all because it gives all. Love is Jesus Christ Crucified, prodigy of nakedness and abyss of riches. To find love we must strip ourself of everything and seek the rich treasure of the divine nakedness of Jesus. "Blessed are the poor in spirit, for theirs is the kingdom of heaven."

---

6. Ecclus. 1:14 (Douay transl.).

THE SECOND BEATITUDE: "Blessed are the meek, for they shall possess the earth."[1]

WHEN A STICK OF WOOD IS thrown into the fire it is destroyed, or rather, it is transformed; it ceases to be what it was before and is turned into something igneous and luminous. This transformation begins on the outside, on the bark, which burns and becomes very brilliant; then, as the fire penetrates more and more through all the layers of the wood, burning every fiber, and finally the pith, the wood is changed from its former dark and heavy condition into splendid, glowing fire.

This is a symbol of the transformation that love works in the soul. The change begins on the surface and, if the soul is faithful, continues to invade every layer until it reaches the innermost of all. First, it breaks the hard bark of the soul, detaching it from exterior things, then it enters into the soul itself, transfiguring all its powers.

The first stage of this intimate transformation is the perfect meekness which the second beatitude holds up to us. Poverty of spirit prepares the way for it, because it stops up the most fertile source of anger, that desire to possess things by which wrath is enkindled in human hearts. Thus the Apostle St. James teaches: "Whence do wars and quarrels come among you? Is it not from this, from your passions, which wage war in your members? You covet and do not have; you kill and envy, and cannot obtain. You quarrel and wrangle, and you

---

1. Matt. 5:4.

do not have. . . . "[2] When the desire to possess is quieted, the soul is ready for the tranquillity of meekness.

St. Augustine attributes the beatitude of meekness, or sweetness, to the gift of piety. According to St. Thomas, the gifts of counsel and knowledge as well as that of fortitude contribute to its perfect accomplishment.

The gifts of counsel and fortitude, directing and elevating our practical knowledge, shed their light on the beatitudes of the active life, which are the first five enumerated by St. Matthew; and these gifts are indispensable guides in this stage of the spiritual life. The gift of fortitude also conduces to perfect meekness, because it moderates the passions of the irascible appetite. But the immediate production of beatifying meekness belongs to the gift of piety. Thus meekness is the daughter of light, strength, and unction.

It is the daughter of light because in man there is no virtue, no action, that need not be directed by knowledge. In the natural order, acquired prudence illuminates and directs all the natural virtues. In the supernatural order, all the virtues are directed by infused prudence; and in that same order, on the superior and more perfect plane of the gifts, all the operations of the active life are ruled by the indefectible light of the gifts of counsel and knowledge.

What a difference between the light that our reason, although illuminated by the virtues, pours into the practical life and that which the gifts and the counsels shed upon it! "The deliberations of mortals are timid, and unsure are our plans,"[3] runs a Scripture text that we have noted before. These natural imperfections put their stamp, so to speak, even on the virtues. How long and painful the process of reason! How many shadows, how many uncertainties, how many conjectures! But

2. 4:1.
3. Wis. 9:14.

the light of the gifts excludes uncertainty and error. "Happy the man whom You instruct, O Lord, whom by Your law You teach."[4]

Meekness is also daughter of the gift of fortitude, since by this gift the irascible appetite is disposed to receive the influence of the Holy Spirit. The soul which exercises only the virtue of meekness restrains its irritation over some offense; but when perfected in the gift of fortitude, it not only renounces vengeance, but with marvelous serenity rejoices in the injury received.

To those who have attained such perfect meekness Jesus has promised the earth as a reward. What does this possession of the earth mean? There is only one reward of holy works, one treasure that beatifies: God. But since this reward is infinite, we obtain possession of it by degrees, which increase indefinitely without ever being exhausted. Each reward of the beatitudes contains the divine treasure in divers degrees and under multiple aspects that correspond to the merits. To those who are detached from the things of earth is given the right to the kingdom of heaven; to those who pass beyond this perfection and attain the serenity of sweetness is given the title to that "land of the living" so often spoken of in Scriptures, signifying the firm reality of the eternal possession.

Possession implies tranquillity and solidity; to possess the earth is to enjoy eternal goods in peace and with certainty. Men struggle and give in to excessive anger in order to assure the possession of earthly goods. The Master teaches us that by the power of sweetness souls attain the possession of eternal goods.

But why does the gift of piety, which fills the soul with filial affection toward God, and orders our communication with others, have an immediate influence on the second beatitude?

---

4. Ps. 93:12.

Meekness has two aspects: it perfects us and it makes our relations with others peaceful. In this second aspect, meekness depends on the gift of piety. The influence of this gift on the second beatitude is more clearly understood if we examine the different motives that belong to the virtue and the gift for suppressing anger. While the virtue is founded on the human good to which anger is opposed, the gift of piety cleanses the soul of all movement of indignation in a divine manner, through filial reverence for God, as if the ineffable meekness of God were poured upon the soul like a heavenly unction, filling it with sweetness. Under the influence of the gift of piety the soul is meek, because God is. Jesus appeared on earth full of gentleness, pouring out everywhere His unctions with the meekness of a victim that does not complain when it is immolated, and that prays for its executioners on the altar of sacrifice.

Daughter of light, of purity, and of unction, the meekness of the second beatitude brings us sweet peace, as the Master has said: "Learn from Me, for I am meek and humble of heart; and you will find rest for your souls."[5]

This perfect meekness makes us sweet in our relations with God, upon whom we look as a Father; sweet in our contact with our neighbor, whom we consider our brother; and sweet with our own soul, because we discover in it the splendor of the divine countenance and the breath of the Almighty.

Who can say how this sweetness helps the spiritual life? Its fullness is heaven, but its reward begins on earth. As the waters of a lake undisturbed by the wind reflect clearly and splendidly the image of the sky, so the souls of the meek, never troubled by gusts of wrath, possess without ever losing Him, God, the lover of silence and of peace.

---

5. Matt. 11:29.

When the soul possesses God, it possesses itself in holy sweetness. Anger makes us lose control of ourselves, disturbs the peace and harmony of our interior kingdom. Sweetness maintains unchanging peace within the confines of that kingdom; so that the soul, without fear, can sit down tranquilly beneath the fig tree like the Israelites of old and taste the fruits of the Beloved.

The powerful influence of sweetness extends even outside of us. It attracts souls and draws in its wake the hardest hearts, like the magic melody of Orpheus which made the trees of the forest march along in his triumphal procession.

Marvelous sweetness, which seems to be weakness and is strength; which attains everything without violence and without noise; which keeps peace without struggle; and which draws after it, caught in its indestructible and gentle bonds, not only men but even God, who never resists its enchanting violence!

THE THIRD BEATITUDE: "Blessed are they who mourn, for they shall be comforted."[1]

WHEN THE SOUL HAS REACHED the high plane of detachment and is at peace in the unction of sweetness, it sees things in a new light. No longer does it look up at the heights clothed in their veil of mysterious cloud; now it views from above the whole broad valley of life deeply penetrated by the light of God.

Of course, in all the steps of its laborious ascension, the soul has been guided by light. How could it travel in darkness? In this stage of the spiritual life, as we have said, the light comes from the gift of knowledge. The soul looks upon the things of earth as despicable and is inspired by the light with perfect poverty of spirit; it knows sweetness and possesses eternal goods. But in the serenity of the heights is the empire of the light, which throws its brilliance unimpeded over the whole extent of human life, and, filtered by the clean and diaphanous atmosphere wherein the soul begins to live, penetrates to the depths of things and reveals their secrets.

Therefore the third beatitude is characterized by the luminous explosion of the gift of knowledge. Under the influence of this gift, the soul attains a new vision of life, discovers the profound sense of things on earth, and beholds with astonished eyes its own depths laid bare. As it bathes in this light it is deeply stirred. Tears come — tears crystalline as the light, bitter as pain, and gentle as messengers of love, which produce in the soul the miracle of consolation.

---

1. Matt. 5:5.

Terrestrial things take divers forms according to the light that colors them. In the deceitful light of the world they are clothed with fictitious charms that captivate the poor human heart and produce in it what the Scriptures call the "witchery of paltry things."[2] When the light of God begins to shine in a soul, illusion vanishes, and things, divested of their gaudy trappings, present only their native nothingness to eyes illuminated by the Spirit. The soul knows creatures as they are: ephemeral, empty, incapable of satisfying its desires; and, undeceived, it detaches itself from them, at first with resignation because it had loved them, then with joy because it realizes they are worthless.

But the light of God grows; no longer is it the brightness of dawn as in the beginning of the spiritual life, but the fullness of splendid day. The sight of created things becomes desolating, repugnant, intolerable; abysses of misery in the pristine half-light, they are revealed in all their horror under the powerful illumination of Divinity.

The soul feels emptiness and darkness all around it. The concept that it formerly had of human things is overthrown. Knowledge, wealth, honor, affections, without their old adornment are sad ruins that inspire only fear. The very depths of the soul have been transformed by the light.

Let us imagine that by a miracle the flesh of all human bodies had disappeared before our eyes and we saw nothing but dry skeletons; that our glance pierced marble tombs and we saw the corruption in all of them; that we contemplated under the magnificence of our grand cities the ill-smelling sewers. Could we behold all this and live?

Something analogous happens in the soul that is filled with the love of God: earthly things when seen under a heavenly light reveal incredible miseries; because only God is

---

2. Wis. 4:12.

greater and more beautiful the more He is revealed. Not by cold arguments of reason, nor by the always imperfect observation of experience, but by divine and profound intuition produced by the gift of knowledge, the soul comprehends the profound truth that all things are vanity and affliction of spirit.

Then it sees its own misery clearly as well as the vanity of all that is created. It comprehends vividly what it was when it lived in sin and what it is in spite of the gifts of God. So repugnant does the spectacle of human life in its sad nakedness appear, so intolerable the sight of the soul itself, that it seems as impossible to live such a life as to live in a tomb. This holy disillusionment fills the soul with a deep sadness and bitter tears, tears that we might say are shed over its own grave. For, in truth, it has died mystically, it has died to earth. It lies dead in the light in which the fragile wings of its illusions were burned, to rise afterward to a new and transfigured life where God will dry its tears and attach other delicate and celestial wings that will take it soaring to the very summit.

Blessed tears that carry in their flow the remains of human life! Fruitful tears that fall on the tomb of the old man, as those of Christ fell on the fetid tomb of Lazarus, and like them, produce the prodigy whereby life comes from death!

Happy are those who weep because of a holy disillusionment about earthly things. They shall be consoled.

The consolation that Jesus Christ promises to those who weep is not like human consolation, superficial and ephemeral; nor like what we ordinarily call divine consolation, which is truly precious but transitory. No, the consolation of this beatitude is the fundamental consolation.

Human consolations are a combination, more or less happy, of the earthly things that alleviate the pain of loss. If we have lost health, friendship will console us. If the bonds of a sweet

friendship have been broken, perhaps we shall find forgetful-
ness in science or art. But when all has been lost, when our
complaint is one complete disillusionment with life, when all
earth has a bleak, wintry covering where formerly it had been
for us a springtime landscape, what can possibly console us?

As Noe's dove found no place to rest in the flood, so the
soul illuminated by the gift of knowledge does not look upon
earth with its welter of miseries as a solid support. But precisely because it does not find a resting place upon the earth,
it takes its flight toward heaven. Below, there is emptiness;
but above, there is consolation that is not passing but eternal;
not a consolation that quiets our desires for a time but one
that fulfills them. It is the only fundamental consolation:
it is God.

Holy Scripture attributes to each one of the three divine
Persons the power of consoling. St. Paul says: "Blessed be
the God and Father of our Lord Jesus Christ, the Father of
mercies and the God of all comfort, who comforts us in all
our afflictions."[3] And in this same Epistle the Apostle adds:
"For as the sufferings of Christ abound in us, so also through
Christ does our comfort abound."[4] Jesus Himself in the sermon at the Last Supper said to His own: "I will ask the
Father and He will give you another Advocate to dwell with
you forever."[5]

God, it is true, is pleased to pour out on the souls He loves
an ineffable sweetness and joy immeasurably superior to earthly
joys, which, in spiritual language, is called divine consolation.
But these irradiations are not constant. When the earth is
sinning beneath its feet the soul calls upon God with the irresistible language of tears, and God responds lovingly to its

3. 2 Cor. 1:3-4.
4. Ibid. 1:5.
5. John 14:16.

pressing cry, and makes the Gift of Himself, who is the fundamental, the only consolation.

Did not the soul possess God before it wept? Undoubtedly it did; but there was not room enough, so to speak, for the Gift of God in the soul because it was not totally empty of self and of earthly things. When light had hollowed out an abyss within the soul, God rushed in like an ocean and filled it. Blessed the soul that weeps because it knows its immense emptiness; it shall have the consolation of being filled with God.

Life will change for the soul thus consoled; upon the ruins of the life that is ended, there will rise a new one, spiritual and mysterious, in which God will be all in all. Nature will be transfigured before its illuminated eyes, as it was transfigured before the eyes of St. Francis of Assisi. Upon the misery of creatures there will be the reflection of God, the light that shines in darkness. Creation will have a new meaning for the soul, profound and divine. The murmur of sister water will seem a prayer; the perfume of flowers, the incense of adoration; the mysterious harmony of the woods, a song of praise; the noise of the ocean, a triumphal hymn; the heavens, a poem of light, silent and deep, to the divine glory.

Everything will have meaning, because everything will speak of God and invite to love. Everything will be a ladder by which to mount to Him: knowledge and poetry, friendship and persecution, smiles and tears, roses and thorns, joy and sorrow, that mysterious trace that Christ left in passing through the earth, which still preserves His divine fragrance. And more than all else, the soul will be aware of its own transfiguration, for in the intense obscurity of its misery, which still remains intact, the illuminated image of God will stand out in the most beautiful contrast. The soul will even find satisfaction in its own nothingness because that makes the divine beauty more prominent; it will rejoice in being small in order to lean upon the divine greatness; it will not wish to lose its weakness for thus it can feel the joy of clinging to the divine strength.

This divine transformation of things will attain its fullness in the fair fatherland where the gift of knowledge, in its noonday splendor, will reveal to the blessed all the profound meaning of creation and will help them to understand that God is all in all. Perhaps in the new land that will follow the universal resurrection, God will show the elect the precious relics of their earthly progress.

But the day of eternity begins already in exile; it is like a beautiful dawn for holy souls. The solace of tears is a prelude to eternal joy. This fundamental consolation encourages the just in the combat of life and at times makes them forget the miseries of exile and gives them a supernatural strength to work without tiring, to suffer without failing; for their eyes and heart are fixed on that paradise whose substance they penetrate by faith, whose reality they already possess through hope, and whose joy they begin to taste through love.

THE FOURTH BEATITUDE: "Blessed are they who hunger and thirst for justice, for they shall be satisfied."

THE SOUL THAT HAS FOUND TRUE consolation upon the peak of the third beatitude sees God everywhere; it carries Him in the intimacy of its being like an ineffable treasure, and finds Him in all things, now clothed for it in divine beauty.

But light engenders love, and love enkindles desire, and desire is the spur that tortures and prods, that starts us to act, to work, to sacrifice, with the sweet restlessness and the strong desire of the lover. Urged on by this holy madness of desire, the soul comes out of itself and goes through the world like the spouse of the Canticles, asking everywhere if, perchance, the Beloved has passed by.

But has it not found Him already? Yes, that is precisely why it feels the ardor of desire. The more we possess Jesus, the more we desire Him. Whoever partakes of that divine delicacy becomes more hungry, and whoever drinks that generous wine suffers a still greater thirst. When the soul was far from God, when its eyes had not yet opened to infinite beauty and its heart had not yet thrilled to the divine touch, it lay motionless in the sad lethargy of one who does not love. But its eyes saw Him upon the mountain of light, its heart was moved with love; and now, like the wounded stag, it restlessly seeks to assuage the fire within.

Where are the cool, crystalline waters that cure the wounds of love? If one could but see the Beloved in the clear light of perfect contemplation; if one could be united with Him in a never-ending embrace! In the boldness of its desire the soul exclaims with the ardent Sulamite: "Let Him kiss me with kisses of His mouth."[1] But possession must be bought at the price of sweat and blood. Effort and suffering are the only refreshment of the soul while it awaits the moment of complete happiness.

Now begins a period of untiring work; fourteen years of hard labor seem to the soul, as they did to Jacob, a small price to pay for the happiness it desires. In this period of the spiritual life it performs good works in overflowing abundance. It resembles the warm earth in the springtime when all the seeds that have been sleeping under winter snows begin to grow. Hunger and thirst express very well the vehemence of its desire. It literally hungers and thirsts for justice; for justice, signifying the conjunction of all holy works, the accumulation of all heavy labors, that the jubilant and great-hearted soul undertakes as a refuge, so to speak, from its longings.

The scene is wonderfully described in the Canticle of Canticles. The Bridegroom knocks on the garden gate and puts His hand through the opening to touch the bride. Her heart thrills with love. She rises to open to Him; there is the aroma of the purest myrrh. But alas, when she swings back the gate, the Bridegroom has gone. She looks for Him and does not find Him; she calls and He does not answer. She hurries forth in search of Him whom she loves, and while she goes through all the city the guards wound her and those who keep watch on the wall take away her mantle. Not caring, she pleads with the daughters of Jerusalem, if they should find her Beloved, to tell Him that she is dying of love.

It is in the garden of contemplation that she will find her Beloved when He comes to cut lilies. But it is not quite time for the loving interview; the enamored soul must travel over

---

1. Cant. 1:2.

the long and rocky road of the active life. "Those who wish to take the citadel of contemplation must first exercise themselves in the field of action," says St. Gregory. The garden where the union between the Beloved and the soul takes place is the soul itself. The deep silence of the open fields must reign there before He can come down to the bride; the ripe fruits must scatter their delicious fragrance, and the lilies must attract Him with their dazzling whiteness.

The active life prepares the place for love by the exercise of the virtues and the divine flowering of the gifts. This work of intensive cultivation is the work of justice, which the soul undertakes with ardent longing.

Although the active life contributes to the soul's own perfection, says St. Thomas, it consists principally in all that which is ordered to the good of others. For this reason the spiritual work proper to this beatitude is called justice. In the previous steps the soul has worked for its own good, but in this one it forgets itself in order to think about others, and laboring for them, obtains a greater perfection as the reward of generosity.

How ardently the soul undertakes this work of justice is told in these words of the Gospel: it hungers and thirsts for justice. A person who has a simple, unhurried need of a thing looks for it peacefully; but one who has a pressing necessity strongly desires to relieve it, permits himself no rest, is not hindered by fatigue, and presses on with passionate eagerness to his goal.

Thus the soul spurred on by love, whose measure is to have no measure, seeks impatiently for the justice that it desires, not considering its own power because it counts on the power of God. Nothing stops it, because it knows it can do all things in Him who strengthens it.

The origin of this astonishing boldness is the gift of fortitude, which has now attained its full development. The *virtue* of justice lives in a moderate and tranquil atmosphere; its norm is reason, its procedure is human. The *gift* of fortitude has a divine norm; it seeks justice in God's way; its atmosphere is that of fire produced by the Holy Spirit.

Under the empire of the virtues the soul measures undertakings by its own meager strength; under the influence of the gifts the soul has a divine strength. The horizon of its desires widens, and it throws itself into action with amazing audacity. Impelled by love and sustained by fortitude, it hungers and thirsts for justice.

This magnificent flowering of the gift of fortitude was admirably prepared for in the previous stages. Light opened the way to strength. Before leaning on God with the bold confidence that the gift of fortitude produces in souls, it is necessary to have two profound knowledges: we must know ourselves and we must know God. Knowledge reveals our own nothingness to us in such an absolute way that we can never forget it, and the same light makes us see God in the depths of our soul. We are nothing; God is everything. There is in us an abyss of misery; but there is also in us something divine. Disappointed in our own strength, we lean on that infinite strength that offers itself to us.

To our confidence in the divine power is added the sweet unction of piety that makes us look upon God as a Father and upon our neighbor as a brother. The holy fire of charity enkindles our desires and increases our boldness. Thus a hunger and thirst for justice, the character of this beatitude, is produced in our soul.

How could God fail to reward such arduous labor? As in the tropical regions the fields are covered in a very short while with heavy vegetation and plants come up everywhere, their

branches growing and interlacing, while the atmosphere is
filled with their pleasing fragrance and delicate flowers slowly
drop their petals so their fruits can expand, in like manner
in the secret garden of the soul, life is diffused, good works
multiply with a divine rapidity, and the perfumes from all the
virtues fill the air. Let the Beloved come into His garden!
exclaims the soul satiated with justice. The flowers have appeared, the fruits now hang from the weighted branches, and
all the perfumes borne by the gentle winds encourage the
sweet intimacies of love.

The soul is filled because everything in it is harmony and
peace. Gradually the noise of action fades away; a celestial
silence, the herald of a better life, sweetly invades it. Action
has prepared it: the hour of contemplation draws near.

Complete satisfaction is not for this life — who could expect it? Perfect justice is only in heaven; only in the loving
bosom of God is the soul at peace with Him, with others, and
with itself. Everything there will be harmony because everything will be order and love and truth. And this substantial
harmony, if one may speak thus, will be the "new canticle"
intoned by the just through the eternal centuries.[2]

But the saints begin that eternal song in this life in spite
of the dissonances which abound. The heart of the just is a
canticle, a living harmony, that exalts God in joy and praise,
as did the holy Virgin in her glorious outpouring of love:
"My soul magnifies the Lord, and my spirit rejoices in God
my Saviour."[3] Mary typifies the soul satiated with justice,
which is perfect fullness and consummate harmony. She sings
with inspired accents to Him who is powerful, whose name
is holy, to Him who brings down the proud and exalts the
humble, to Him who fills the hungry with divine nourishment.

---

2. Cf. Apoc. 5:9.
3. Luke 1:46 ff.

And in the train of this Queen follow all generous souls who, at the cost of painful labors and torturing desires, attain the fullness of justice in the serenity and harmony of their interior garden.

The Beloved will not come yet. The soul must ascend two more mountain peaks before it reaches the heights where the mystery of pain is perfected.

THE FIFTH BEATITUDE: "Blessed are the merciful, for they shall obtain mercy."

AFTER THE WORK OF JUSTICE HAS been completed in the soul, there remains a still more divine work, if one may so express it, namely, the work of mercy. Certainly, the soul that hungers and thirsts for justice goes beyond the limits of human reason and is just according to the manner of God; yet the concept of justice can be perceived by the human intelligence. But mercy is something celestial, something divine, that Jesus brought from the bosom of the Father. Mercy consists in looking for tribulations, in loving them, in making them our own, in taking them to our heart; the tribulations not only of those we love, but even of those who hate us; not only of people who delight us with their charms, but also of those who repel us. Such is the mercy that the pagans did not even suspect, that man could not invent.

It is human to take to ourselves the miseries of persons we love; but it is divine to assume those of others, even our enemies. It is easy to compassionate certain types of human trouble — the weakness of the child, the frailty of the maiden, the delicate tears of sublime grief; but to bend to the misery that seems to force itself on us, and lovingly to kiss repugnant wounds, tenderly to embrace souls that lie in the disgusting mire of all human abjection, is a thing that is not natural to the egoistic heart of man.

But it is proper to the Heart of God. Only He who is superabundantly rich can give without asking; only He who is boundlessly happy can find joy in making the unfortunate happy; only He whose Heart is an overflowing ocean of all perfection can descend to the abyss of all miseries in order to fill it with the opulence of His plenitude.

God is merciful because He is infinite; we are egoistic because we are limited. Mercy requires a certain divine touch; it is an imitation of God. Therefore Christ said to us: "Be merciful, even as your Father is merciful";[1] and while speaking to us of justice: "Unless your justice exceeds that of the Scribes and Pharisees, you shall not enter the kingdom of heaven."[2]

There is a human and a divine justice. There is only one mercy: the divine mercy which, by imitation, is reflected in men.

The soul that ascends the ladder of the beatitudes carries within itself because of the gifts something truly divine. In all the stages of its ascent, it has broken the narrow human molds. On the last step, it throws itself into action with all the impatient ardor of its desire and, avid of justice, passes the landmark of the human and accomplishes a work which is not of earth.

But it is not satisfied yet. To be united with God it needs to *become* divine. And now before its eyes open out the divine horizons of mercy within which the active life will attain its consummation.

Again the field of human miseries spreads out before the soul, desolate and immense, because another, clearer light than that of the gift of knowledge pours its brilliance upon the barren plain.

But the soul does not now live under the illusion which it suffered on the mount of tears; now it looks at trouble as God looks at it: to understand it, to know it, to alleviate it. An immense compassion tortures the soul, as it did the Heart of

1. Luke 6:36.
2. Matt. 5:20.

Christ; it feels the sorrows of all those who suffer, and sheds the tears of all those who weep. A new pain, profound and full of unction, penetrates its whole being. But it is not oppressed, because the waters of that ocean of misery cannot extinguish the fire of charity with which it burns. Rather, they intensify it. Because such love is divine it begins to spread out, after the manner of infinite Charity, in order to fill the emptiness with abundance, to water the dryness with tears, to anoint the wounds with consolation, to warm the coldness with its ardor.

The light that guides the merciful soul is the light of the gift of counsel, a more vivid light because it is higher, nearer to the purest sources of light. By it the soul contemplates misfortunes as God does. What is strange about its attempt to do what God does, to essay the divine policy of mercy?

It is an arduous undertaking: because of it, Jesus sweat blood in Gethsemani and became a victim on Calvary. But is it not precisely the difficult, the heroic, that the soul seeks in the unrestrainable ardor of its loving desire? For such a tremendous work, it has the supernatural strength that the gift of fortitude conferred in the fourth beatitude; and it feels, in this new stage of its active life, the divine irradiation of the gift of counsel, a sure guide in difficult things and a heavenly light over the most tortuous paths.

With that light and strength added to the wealth of love which, together with all the cortege of virtues, is constantly increasing in the soul, it will throw itself into the world of miseries as Jesus did when He walked upon this earth. It will go down into the abysses without stain, like the light that descends into the mire and remains immaculate. It will become all things for all, because it will carry within the burden of all, and it will pour out on all with divine munificence the treasure of the consolations received from a higher Mercy. Giving without measure, it will not diminish its wealth, but marvelously increase it.

It is understandable that this difficult and generous exercise of mercy should enrich the soul. As the little rock that is carried by a furious torrent, after countless frictions and violent jarrings comes out of the river bed clean and smooth, the soul moved by the torrent of merciful love is polished with the friction of all human woes, relinquishing in its rapid and laborious course whatever remains in it of earth, of lowliness, of dissonance, and appearing finally more resplendent, more brilliant.

The soul's strength has been greatly increased in this labor. Each day it finds fatigue more pleasant and pain sweeter; it feels the strength of God as its own, and trusts more fully in the inexhaustible Goodness; it penetrates more and more into the miseries of others, sure of the power that sustains it; and in order to alleviate these woes, it finds each day more ingenious and fruitful resources in its heart, united to the merciful Heart of Christ.

When charity pours itself out, it increases. Fire is like that: the more it burns, the more intense is the flame. In a conflagration stirred by a strong wind, the dry stalks tremble, cross over each other, and the victorious flames throw themselves on this fuel, spreading rapidly in their eagerness to soar upward. So with the soul touched by the flame of merciful love; when the wind of the Spirit of God blows over it, it is on fire within, bursting forth with uncontrollable strength, enfolding the miseries of others; and the more it goes out of itself, the more it burns; the more it does for its neighbor, the nearer to heaven rise the flames of its love.

To alleviate the miseries of others the soul forgets itself. But there are eyes that watch it, the eyes of God. There is a

Heart that allots mercy to it as it shows mercy to others, the Heart of Him who said: "Amen, I say to you, as long as you did it for one of these, the least of My brethren, you did it for Me."[3] "Blessed are the merciful, for they shall obtain mercy."

And what mercy! The soul that gives itself to helping a neighbor in trouble has also its own pressing tribulation: a love unsatisfied. If misery is emptiness, then there is none like the misery of this soul; if misery is desire, then no one is so profoundly wretched: if it is torture, there is no word in human language to describe this misery. For what other is rooted, like this, in the very depths of one's being? The soul has had the boldness to set its eyes on infinite Good — and who will give it this Good? It has had the madness to deliver its heart to a Beloved who dwells in light inaccesible — and who will lead it into those radiant abysses? A love like this is not bought, nor is it merited; only the hands of Mercy can grant the gift.

In its incomprehensible misery of love the soul, enlightened by the gift of counsel, had understood that only mercy can attract Mercy; that in order to appeal to Mercy, it was necessary to be like it, to learn its language. Thus, with intimate compassion and fruitful work for the unfortunate, it called to that Love who, in order to give Himself to creatures, must be merciful. And Mercy came because it cannot resist its own summons, and the voice that can never be confused with any other rang in the ears of the soul: the voice of Love. And it spoke a word which in its profundity seems to exhaust all human language: Come!

And the soul felt gentle hands taking it up with the delicacy of a mother who lifts her little child, and it seemed that those hands raised it up very high, above the mountain of justice and the peak of mercy; above that region in which

---

3. Matt. 25:40.

the active life is carried on in the midst of human miseries; and that they placed it gently in the crevice of a very high rock, where the great eagles that look at the sun have their nest.

Now the winter is past, happy soul! The rain is very far away, down below. A new life, the life of contemplation, opens its immense horizons to you. Enter. Does the gate seem narrow? If you could but know where it leads! Does the mysterious region seem obscure? It is because the new light, so vivid, so intense, dazzles your imperfect eyes.

Little by little they will become adjusted to the heavenly light, because that light itself will purify and heal them. And when they have forgotten their former manner of seeing, when they open serenely on the new light, the divine clarity, you will contemplate ecstatically that which for a long time you have desired with a deep desire to contemplate: the Beloved who in heaven is called Love, and who, in order to show His beautiful face to you, needs must be called Mercy.

THE SIXTH BEATITUDE: "Blessed are the clean of heart, for they shall see God."

IF WE HAD A DEEPER UNDERSTANDING OF things, we would be able to comprehend the intimate relation that exists between purity and light, and perhaps we would comprehend with some astonishment that light and purity are two aspects of one same divine reality. The Greeks produced an admirable word to express graphically the idea of holiness: "hagios," meaning without earth. To be pure is to be without earth; that is, to be free of all that is not God. The greater the estrangement from all the lowly things symbolized by earth, the greater and more perfect is purity.

God is the infinite Purity whom the saints praise in the eternal Trisagion because He is substantially and infinitely removed from all that is earthly; because He is sufficient unto Himself in His divine and incomparable simplicity. God is the purest Being, the purest Thought, and the purest Love. He is so pure and so simple that He is who is; He contains within Himself nothing foreign to Himself. He does not have, nor can He have, a trace of earth, because He is who is.

His thought is as pure and simple as His being; He reaches out over all infinity without going out of Himself. He is enclosed, if it may be so expressed, in the fullness of His simplicity. Understanding all things He but understands Himself, for all that He sees in Himself is divine, is Himself. His love, the perfection of His life, is the perfection of His simplicity. His purity encloses, so to say, the circle of His life without anything foreign being able to enter within His bosom, which is utterly simple and yet inconceivably immense in the richness of its perfection.

God is so far above His creation, He is so contained in His simplicity, that while giving Himself without measure and communicating Himself without reserve to His creatures, even to degrees of union that astonish us by their intimacy, He remains in that mysterious union infinitely superior to them, infinitely apart from them.

God is Purity; the mystery of the Trinity is a mystery of purity. Thus, the eternal canticle of the blessed heard by Isaias and St. John is a song of purity: "Holy, Holy, Holy."[1] And because God is purity, He is light. St. Thomas teaches that immateriality is the foundation of cognoscibility. In the natural order, the hierarchy of intelligent beings is the hierarchy of their degree of remoteness from matter. In the supernatural order, another hierarchy raises itself above the natural; it is in reality a new ascending stairway of purity which marks another step upward from earth. On the highest peak of all is infinite Light, infinite Immateriality, infinite Purity which unites all things to itself without becoming fused with them, in the immensity of divine simplicity.

Thus the Scriptures say that "God is light"; the Church sings of the Word, "Light of Light," and she calls the Holy Spirit "Most happy Light."

For souls to be bathed in light, to become light, they need to be purified. Justification, which is sinlessness, is a mystery of light: "For you were once darkness, but now you are light in the Lord," says St. Paul. For souls to be transformed into the image of God, passing from glory to glory, they must ascend from purity to purity in the continuing effort to become, more and more, glowing crucibles.

Therefore the sixth beatitude brings the reward of light because it has purity for its merit: "Blessed are the clean of heart, for they shall see God."

---

1. Isa. 6:3; Apoc. 4:8.

Each beatitude contains a degree of purity, as has already been observed, and the soul that has traversed this ascending path is so far from mundane things, has so purified itself from all that is earthly, has been so polished in the work of the active life, that it is ready to open itself to the effusions of light. Now it is time for the gift of intelligence to shine resplendent as the sun in the heaven of the soul that has become transparent with purity.

Thus does St. Thomas teach, explaining that cleanness of heart means not only freedom from the incitements of the passions — a cleanness presupposed by the perfect active life — but freedom from errors, imaginations, illusions, all of which those striving for divine contemplation ought to shun. St. Augustine had interpreted cleanness of heart in the same way.

To understand this intellectual purification, we must analyze the reward promised to the clean of heart: nothing less than the vision of God.

This promise will be fulfilled in heaven because the blessed will know that God is there; their eyes, fortified by the light of glory, will penetrate the divine essence without ever exhausting its infinite treasure. But on earth the supreme vision of God, granted to the perfect, consists rather in knowing what God is not than in knowing what He is; in seeing that He exceeds all contemplation and all knowledge; in understanding in a vivid and profound manner that God is nothing of that which exists outside of Himself.

It is impossible for the soul to be lifted to this supreme height of knowledge of God if it does not rid itself beforehand of the human mode of knowing; because this mode is founded on that analogy with sensible things above which it is necessary to be elevated in order to know that God exceeds everything we can comprehend.

Faith itself, without the aid of the gifts of wisdom and knowledge, cannot communicate to the intellectual vision that superior and divine mode of knowing that makes it possible to look at God as incomparable and as transcending all knowledge. The soul must be purified of all sensible images, of all intellectual processes such as judgments and reasonings, which use sensible things.

This purification was begun in previous stages, when the light of contemplation began to appear in the soul as the day dawns in the east — heroism of action cannot be attained without the contemplative light shining in the soul. But the bright day of contemplation begins in the sixth beatitude, and its work is consequently the intense and perfect purification of the spirit. With it the soul will go on acquiring little by little a new knowledge, an intuition which encloses marvelous riches in its simplicity, an utterly simple gaze that penetrates into the treasures of divine things and, as it becomes purer, plunges into the inaccessible light where God dwells.

When the soul begins to see in this way, it feels disconcerted. Like the weak pupils of nocturnal birds opening slowly in the shadows when the sun shines in the heavens, the eyes of the soul, dazzled by the splendor of light, seem to behold darkness. In vain the poor intelligence, groping in this darkness, pursues the familiar image in order to seize it; in vain its vacillating steps search for the beaten paths of discourse. In the mysterious night, images fail and paths have disappeared. Ethereal wings are needed here to move about, and steady eyes to gaze upon this light.

This transformation goes to the deepest roots of our intelligence. It cannot be explained; it has no analogy with anything we have ever experienced. A profound stupor overtakes the soul when it penetrates into the unknown. It seems that in broad daylight, all light has suddenly been blacked out;

all divine truths, that appeared so bright and beautiful, are hidden in a stupendous eclipse. Neither God, nor creatures, nor its own truth are discerned by the intelligence in the deep darkness; and with obscurity, the cold of death seems to penetrate the astonished soul. By an inescapable law of our psychology the heart must follow all the oscillations of the intelligence; and now the soul's sweet and ardent affections of yesterday are paralyzed. A deep-rooted impotence hinders it from moving as it formerly did in the flowery fields of goodness and love. Not a ray of light in the desolate night, not a familiar face in the immensity of the silence; its lips cannot form a prayer, nor is its desire fulfilled in a single palpitation of love.

Where is it? Has the sweet voice that called, deceived it? Has it been victimized by some terrible illusion, or guilty of some enormous infidelity because of which it may fall from the heights into a wretched abyss, never to come out?

No, eternal love does not deceive, because it is eternal truth. But all purification is painful, more, it is radical and profound, tearing out of the soul the last vestiges of earth.

Little by little the soul feels that God approaches in the sacred darkness. It had never suspected that it would be thus; in its dreams it had seen Him, gracious and most sweet, but in a human way, and in the boldness of its love, the confidence of its tenderness, it had forgotten that the Beloved of its heart is infinite Majesty. Now it perceives Him, great, immense, incomprehensible; so great that it feels annihilated, that it would like to disappear, to plunge into the abyss so as not to be overwhelmed. It seems to itself a very black spot before that Holiness, and filled with shame, contemplates the repugnant rags of its own misery. It has often realized this nothingness, but never penetrated so far into the depths as now, when it compares itself with the Infinite it is glimpsing. Many times it has trembled with horror at the remembrance of its sins, but now that it evokes the shameful memory while so near to Holiness, it feels that it must die of anguish. This Greatness cannot love it; this Majesty cannot unite Himself with its misery; the holy and terrible God who approaches in the darkness can only punish it, spurn it away. How could it be otherwise if He is that One of whom the Scripture says that He looks at the earth and makes it tremble, that He touches mountains and they smoke?

A terrible purification, this, in which God Himself seems to snatch from the soul all that remains in it of earth! The more the eyes of the soul are cleansed, the more they are filled with heavenly light. The Greatness is seen to be incomprehensibly vast; Majesty unfolds itself to the soul's vision as in the beginning of time the enormous firmament unfolded. But Greatness appears as Goodness, Majesty as Beauty, the Infinite as Love.

Who can explain what the soul experiences when it beholds the Beloved rising in the midst of the shadows that change into light. It *is* the Beloved, but so great, so beautiful, so irresistible, so divine, that the soul seems to see Him for the first time; it is the same One to whom it gave itself utterly — but it did not even suspect the beauty of His face, the sun of His glance, the heaven of His smile, the ocean of His goodness, the abyss of His love. Mortal powers cannot bear to contemplate such beauty — an ecstasy so intense as that which the divine vision produces, does not belong in the fragile vase of the human heart; and the soul faints before the mighty invasion of light and love.

These apparitions are rapid and fleeting, because the natural weakness of the soul could not support them. The Beloved goes away leaving in the soul the fire of charity and the ardor of desire; He returns again, filling the soul with such celestial delights that it knows its anxieties and its sacrifices were nothing in comparison with such a reward.

THE SEVENTH BEATITUDE: "Blessed are the peacemakers, for they shall be called children of God."

EVERY EARTHLY AFFECTION, EVEN that which seems to be the deepest, is superficial. Our hearts were not made for created things, although these things attract us in as much as they are reflections of the divine. But they neither satisfy nor pacify human hearts, nor produce in them the interior movement proper to profound love, the love of God.

If men really knew what love is! If they knew that after years spent in devoting to creatures what they think is a deep and wonderful love, they are still ignorant of the first rudiments of the divine science; they have not even begun to taste the holy delights of a love so profound that it touches the roots of our being, so great that it fills the immense emptiness of our souls, so ardent that it carries us out of ourselves, so sweet that it enraptures us, so strong that it transforms us, so lasting that it is immortal!

No love equals the love of the soul that has had a glimpse of God in the midst of the gloom of earth. For this fortunate soul has not found love, but Love; it has not experienced a slight refreshment for its unquenchable thirst, but has attained the good that satisfies thirst forever.

It is a love that contains all beauties, that surpasses all unions. The soul touched by this feels that all its multiple and varied desires are fused into one single, tremendous longing for the infinite beauty it has seen and which rises toward it like a great flame rushing forth from all the volcanoes of earth.

The fire has pierced to the center of the soul, to depths unknown and unsuspected, where only the Beloved can enter. A new life, the life of love, the silent and sweet kingdom of charity, begins. The soul seems to itself now to love for the first time because it considers all former loves as child's play before this ineffable attraction, as strong as death and as sweet as heaven. The presence of the Beloved at times overwhelms it like an ocean surging formidably over its great bed; at other times it feels an immense vacuum and suffers a deep, fiery-red wound of love because the Beloved has withdrawn.

The wound awakens desire, and desire provokes union, and union in turn deepens the wound. Joy and sorrow follow each other, making harmony in the new life where love grows with marvelous rapidity.

The seventh beatitude is the peak of love.

But in these marvelous regions love stems from light, and light emanates from the bosom of love. The gift of intelligence increases charity, and from its fire rises a new light, the most splendid that shines on earth, the light of the gift of wisdom.

We repeat, the soul received all the gifts of the Holy Spirit together with charity when it received grace; but these divine seeds gradually acquire their full development accordingly as the soul prepares itself for this in the different stages of the spiritual life. The gift of wisdom in a certain manner directs all the gifts, as charity, which is intimately united with it, directs all the virtues. It was wisdom that directed the fear of God from the time that the work of the first beatitude began. In the beginning of the contemplative life it illuminates the soul in darkness, for if it belongs to the gift of understanding to purify the spirit, it is wisdom that is the splendid and indispensable light in contemplation. But the full and divine flowering of the first of the gifts corresponds to the ardent period of the first of the virtues, because wisdom must have for its development an atmosphere filled with the fire of charity.

There are two ways of knowing things: one, by explanations and theories; the other, by an intimate experience. Learned discourses can tell us what love is, but the theories never equal the intimate teaching that love itself gives us when we have it in our souls. The impression of beauty that invades us as we contemplate a work of art is worth more than the most admirable description of that work. For theories teach us about things by analogy with other things that are known and sensed, while intimate experience makes us savor things in themselves.

This observation is applicable in a special manner to God and divine things, which hardly have even an imperfect analogy with human things. They are on another plane and possess a character so much their own that they are inimitable and indescribable.

Now, knowledge of divine things communicated by the gift of wisdom is the intimate experience of those things, not a remote and imperfect approach through symbols. To have this divine knowledge it is necessary to bear God in the soul, to be intimately united with Him, and to be able to exclaim in the divine ecstasy of possession: "I found Him whom my heart loves; I took hold of Him and would not let Him go."[1]

Only love can realize a happiness so complete; only love can give such sweet possession. This is the power that draws down the God of heaven and binds Him to our misery, that chains Him to our heart with indestructible chains and makes Him cleave to us in a manner so perfect that we are one spirit with Him.

---

1. Cant. 3:4.

Therefore the gift of wisdom is the gift of love; it is the light of souls that look through the eyes of the Beloved. And the seventh beatitude, which is love at its highest, is also the very summit of wisdom.

The fruit of wisdom and love is peace. But have we not said that peace was produced in the soul by the virtues and gifts proper to the earlier stages? Did not the first three beatitudes bring peace by tearing out of the soul the roots of restlessness? And did not justice and mercy establish proper relations with others?

The work accomplished by the active life was indeed a work of peace, but it was negative. It was the war that prepared the peace by shattering the enemies; it was the relentless sickle that prepared the harvest by cutting down the weeds; it was the strong wind that hurried the dark clouds along so that the sun might shine.

Pure peace is something divine that only wisdom and love can produce. To be peaceful, it is not enough to live in sweet concord with our brother; it is not sufficient to have all our powers in tranquil harmony under the empire of the will. Rather, all the desires of the soul must be fused in one single divine desire, all flowing as one great torrent, with no scattered currents of affection anywhere. The soul must be simple as God is simple, so that all things can be unified.

What but love can produce this work? — love which by its essence simplifies, which is the divine seed of unity, which intimately unites us to God and, as far as that is possible, transforms us into unity and into eternal Simplicity?

It is proper to the happy lover to have peace, and it is wisdom that produces peace. St. Augustine has profoundly said that peace is the tranquillity of order; but order is the simplification of the multiple; thus the peaceful soul is the one who rests tranquilly in divine simplicity. Love engenders peace; but simplification, which is tranquil order, is the fruit of wisdom. The philosophers have told us that it is proper to wisdom to put things in order because its single and simple light illuminates the universe and simplifies it in unity.

Faith reveals the mystery to us more profoundly. Order is the reflection of that unique and rich thought which is the Word of God, substantial Wisdom. Peace is the tranquillity of that reflection in nature and in the spiritual world. But free will has the terrible privilege of hindering the divine irradiation of wisdom in souls; for this reason, peace is a difficult thing to acquire in the world of the spirit.

But in both worlds, wisdom produces peace; and peace is always the undisturbed image of the Word. In the inferior world, wisdom produces peace through the operation of causes subject to necessary and precise laws. In the spiritual world, souls themselves are the glorious ministers of the Word. They must produce peace in themselves, and in order to do this they receive, as intelligent and free causes, an active and fruitful "impression" of uncreated Wisdom. In the natural order this "impression" is acquired wisdom, the marvelous source of peace.

But it is love that engraves in nature and in souls the image of the Word. It is love that seeks union, it is love that writes tenderly wherever it will the name of the Beloved. In the heavens, it does so with the scintillating stars; on earth, with the gigantic contours of the mountains, with the harmonious colors of the flowers and the moving crystal of the immense oceans; in souls, with the opulence of the virtues and the divine fullness of the gifts. On earth peace is the daughter of light and love, as in heaven the Word and the Holy Spirit are the eternal founts of the peace that emanates from the bosom of the Father.

While the soul's charity is yet imperfect and the gift of wisdom unceasingly pours out its celestial brilliance, the image of the Word appears and disappears in the soul like the reflection of the sky that is barely visible in the flowing crystal waters of a lake. But when the waves are at peace, the sun and the sky are clearly outlined upon its smooth mirror. Thus in the soul, when charity is perfect and wisdom is its ever-shining beacon, the divine image no longer oscillates, because the soul has become fixed in peace; it is now so clear, so diaphanous, so pure, that the human imperfection disappears under the triumphant splendors of the divine.

We have already noted what St. Paul says of this transformation: "We all, with faces unveiled, reflecting as in a mirror the glory of the Lord, are being transformed into His very image from glory to glory, as through the Spirit of the Lord."[2] Contemplation and the Spirit wrought that divine transformation. Love has attained in the peaceful soul its highest degree, which St. Bernard describes as "embracing the Beloved in perfect security." Christ has already put His left hand under the head of the spouse, and with His right He embraces her, adjuring the daughters of Jerusalem not to awaken her nor disturb the sweet peace of her dream of love.

Who can separate the soul from its immortal love? The Beloved is all in all to it and it is all in all to the Beloved. They are no longer two but one. Love has accomplished its divine work of unity. Have you ever seen a delicate, hazy cloud bathed in the sun's rays? Its opaque substance has vanished before the invasion of light; it is no longer cloud, it is splendor, it is brilliance. It has been transformed into sun. This is indeed a lowly comparison to explain the divine mystery of love. Sensible things are too gross to convey divine operations. By love's magic, the old physiognomy of the soul has vanished.

2. 2 Cor. 3:18.

The light of the Word penetrates it, imparting a new brilliance to it, transforming it into the Word Himself. Look at it: it *is* the Word. Do you not see His glance, His smile, His majesty, His sweetness? Do you not see His strength, His unmistakable and divine zeal? In a mystic but real manner, He comes again to live on earth in order to reproduce the poem of His divine mysteries. It is the Jesus who was born while angels' hymns resounded, who grew in silence and scattered the celestial fragrance that enraptures the Father. It is the Jesus who spoke words of life, who startled men with His prodigies. It is the Jesus who wept over human miseries, who transfigured in His Heart all the sorrows of earth, who immolated Himself as a victim to divine justice and primordial love. Finally, it is the Jesus who perfects His work in the wondrous and deep silence of the Eucharistic life.

Nothing pleases the Father but the Son, His Jesus. The Father wishes to behold Him always, in heaven and on earth. He wishes to receive the song of His praise, the incense of His love, and the perfume of His sacrifices. And not satisfied with Jesus of the Tabernacle, the Father is pleased to reproduce Him in souls transfigured by the sanctifying fruitfulness of the Holy Spirit. The Church is a Thabor where the mystery of the transfiguration of souls is constantly produced. Jesus reappears in His saints, dazzlingly bright; the luminous cloud of the Paraclete enfolds Him, and the voice of the Father repeats: "This is my beloved Son, in whom I am well pleased."[3]

The Church teaches us in her liturgy that the perfect adoption of the sons of God is announced by the mystery of Thabor. To be an adopted son is to reproduce the image of the eternal Son. It is to be wisdom participated, as He is the infinite Wisdom of the Father. Whoever has grace is an adopted son because he has the divine resemblance to the Word. But souls

---

3. Matt. 17:5.

transformed into Jesus, converted into living images of the eternal Wisdom, will attain the perfection of divine adoption: they will be called the children of God.

It is obvious that this last stage of the perfect life cannot be completed on earth. Souls that ascend to it are living a celestial life; their feet hardly touch the earth; their brow is haloed with light and is lost in the heights with the heart of the Beloved, in the bosom of God. But the divine work is not yet consummated, for the last purification, the last sacrifice, the supreme act of love, is lacking: death. Transfigured souls sigh for it with unutterable groans, as exiles sigh for their fatherland, as we all sigh for happiness, as love sighs for its eternal consummation.

Therefore, in the heavenly and exalted life in which transformed souls live, above the delights of union and the ineffable torments of love, arises the incomprehensible shout of desire, the cry of heaven and earth, which is like the last word of the Scriptures: "And the Spirit and the bride say, 'Come!' ... Amen! Come, Lord Jesus!"[4]

---

4. Apoc. 22:17, 20.

THE EIGHTH BEATITUDE: "Blessed are they who suffer persecution for justice' sake, for theirs is the kingdom of heaven."

THERE IS ONLY ONE PEAK HIGHER than the seven we have contemplated. It is that of Calvary, where Jesus, the divine model of perfection and incomprehensible type of happiness, is crucified. "Nothing is greater in the universe than Jesus Christ, and nothing is greater in Jesus Christ than His sacrifice," wrote Bossuet profoundly.

The sanctity of Jesus is above the perfection of the virtues and the gifts, as the fullness of the grace that He received and the unique grace of the hypostatic union are above that which we have received. Therefore does the Church sing in the Gloria of the Mass: "Thou alone art holy!"

Jesus possesses the divine substance of the virtues and the quintessence of the gifts because in the person of the Word He possesses the sanctity of God who in His sacred Humanity has assumed the form of a creature. St. Paul teaches us that when Jesus appeared, benignity itself, the grace of God our Saviour, came to earth.[1] Jesus is the very sanctity of God, the source and model of all sanctity; and He contains the divine substance of all the virtues and gifts with which it has pleased Him to enrich our souls.

All through His mortal life Jesus, who came to teach us to be holy, let the perfume of the virtues and the irradiation of His sanctity escape from the depths of His being; and He

---

1. Cf. Tit. 3:4; 2:11.

let fall on the earth the crumbs from the sumptuous banquet of perfection and happiness which His soul enjoyed.

But as He neared the climax of His life, the consummation of His sacrifice, He broke the vase that contained the perfume, He made transparent the shade that covered the radiant light, He opened the doors of the divine Cenacle so that the world might see the delights of the intimate feast.

The most exquisite, the most sublime, and the holiest work of Jesus is His sacrifice. The grace of God appeared on the Cross in its supreme manifestation. There, divine sanctity was scarcely veiled in the thinnest and most transparent gauze that the divine can have on earth: the veil of sorrow. Jesus Christ Crucified is human sanctity at its peak because He is divine sanctity in the abyss of its annihilation. It is the incomprehensible nakedness of divine simplicity, discovered in the greatest human nakedness. It is divine love made human; it is human love made divine. And this happens in the only crucible that can fuse them: sorrow.

A river running along its bed enlarges its volume as it flows, and when it is full, merges in the ocean with all the other rivers. Virtues also become enriched by degrees, and in their highest and divine fullness, are marvelously united in an ocean of sorrow which is Jesus Christ on the Cross.

The mystery of the Cross is the compendium of the beatitudes. In it are found, in the unity of sorrow — the most perfect unity that exists after the unity of love in the bosom of God — the virtues and the gifts which the beatitudes produce in an incomparable and divine degree of perfection. The divine nakedness of the Cross is the consummation of detachment. The unutterable state of Jesus as victim, totally surrendered to divine justice in the sacrifice of Calvary, is the height of meekness. The immense desolation of Christ on the Cross is the depth of the holy sadness of those who weep.

The immortal victim is supreme justice and supreme mercy united on earth in an ineffable kiss of pain, as they are united in heaven in the divine kiss of love. The holy, the unfathomable and infinite purity of the nakedness of Christ Crucified is the divine summit of purity on earth, as in heaven nakedness, divine simplicity, is infinite purity. And the sublime monument upon the top of Calvary is the last word of love, both human and divine, on earth.

When we contemplate Christ on the Cross with the enlightened eyes of the heart, we grasp this most profound and fundamental truth, that there are only two consummations of sanctity because there are only two unities: that of love in heaven and of pain on earth. Sanctity is simplification. God is most holy because He is infinitely simple; souls are holy because they are simplified in God. In the discourse at the Last Supper, when He asked the Father for perfect holiness for His own, Christ said: "That they may be one, even as We are one."[2] The Father and the Word are joined in the unity of the Holy Spirit, that is, in the unity of love. Souls are united in the Cross of Christ, in the unity of pain.

Perhaps it is for this reason that in heaven, the home of exalted holiness, there are only two songs: the eternal Trisagion that the mysterious animals sing to the Holy One seated upon the throne, and the song that the blessed intone to the Lamb who, by virtue of pain, broke the seals of the book of life and showered upon the earth the seven spirits of God.[3]

Can it be that pain, by dissolving, immaterializes, and, by purifying, simplifies? that pain is the new and earthly name of love? Can it be that God who sits on the throne of love in heaven has chosen the Cross for His throne on earth?

Why scrutinize the mystery? What is certain is that the supreme manifestation of sanctity on earth is Jesus Crucified,

2. John 17:22.
3. Cf. Apoc. 7:9 ff.

and consequently, that the supreme consummation of sanctity in souls is to glory in the Cross of Christ, to be crucified with Him, to be another Christ.

Sanctity, as the seventh beatitude shows it to us, is this: to be holy is to be Jesus. To say it more completely: to be holy is to be Jesus Crucified; to be, like Him, naked with only the royal purple of pain. To be holy is to be victim, it is to offer oneself as a sacrifice of adoration, as a holocaust of love to the heavenly Father; to offer oneself immaculate through the Holy Spirit as victim, altar, and priest. . . .

This is why the eighth beatitude — which is the beatitude of persecution, of pain, of martyrdom; in a word, of the Cross — is the consummation and the manifestation of all the others, containing and perfecting them. All the virtues and gifts of the Holy Spirit converge toward it as the rivers flow to the ocean. The supernatural organism that sprang from the Cross, as a divine seed, tends to reproduce its parent tree, to renew in souls the mystery of the Cross.

And by a divine logic it is necessary to deduce that Jesus Christ Crucified is the prototype of felicity, for He is the prototype of perfection. His Cross, which encloses all the merits of the beatitudes, must contain all the rewards as well.

But since the rewards of the beatitudes begin here in this mortal life, can it be possible that even on earth the greatest happiness is to become Jesus Crucified? Did Jesus always have in His sorrowful Heart the secret of the joy that stems from pain? Did that joy become greater as the pain on Calvary became more intense? Let us ponder the mystery through the mind of St. Francis, the Little Poor Man of Assisi, on fire with love of God, by remembering again his explanation of the secret of perfect happiness: "This does not consist in giving good example, in performing miracles, in knowing all sciences and the Scriptures; it does not consist either in converting all infidels to the Faith of Christ, but in suffering all things with patience and with happiness, thinking of the pains of the Blessed Christ, which He had to suffer for love of us." The mystery of perfect happiness is the mystery of the Cross.

All the degrees of happiness given us by the beatitudes harmonize to form the unique and celestial tint of supreme happiness on earth that is hidden in the Cross. The first three beatitudes give to the soul the happiness of being free; but the supreme liberty is pain. The fourth and the fifth illuminate; but the light of pain is the most splendid on earth. The last ones purify and transform; but pain is purity that emerges triumphant from the miseries of earth, it is the purity of heaven groaning under the filth of the world. Pain is the supreme transformation of the soul into God, because it is the supreme transformation of God into man.

The only desire that seemed to disturb the divine serenity of Christ with its ardor was the desire for His sacrifice. The vehemence of His words and the emotion of His accent betrayed His soul: "I have greatly desired" — the Douay wording is *"With desire have I desired"* — to eat this passover with you."[4] Which passover did He mean? There are two, the Eucharistic passover and the bloody passover: essentially the passover of pain and of love.

What divine enchantment did Jesus find in the abyss of His sacrifice? Happiness is the perfume of love, and its highest form must stem from the supreme satisfaction of the greatest love. The love of Jesus is undoubtedly supreme love; His love for the Father, His love for souls. From the time that He came into the world He began to satisfy that love — for the two are really one. He always pleased the Father and He

---

4. Luke 22:15.

never ceased to save souls. Therefore He had at all times the secret of His happiness in the depths of His own soul.

But that happiness was disturbed during thirty-three years by a torturing thirst. If all love is insatiable, what must be said of Christ's love?

In the solemn evening of His life, He found full satisfaction for His love, for His infinite desires. As His hour drew near, Jesus was disturbed in spite of His divine serenity. Was it the disturbance of pain or of happiness? To immolate Himself for the Father: To offer Him an infinite homage! To return to Him a love like that which He had received, as well as a bloody, painful, mortal love because He was human; to be able to say to the Father the supreme word of love: "I love Thee to the death!" To be able to offer to infinite Justice and primordial Love the annihilation, the sacrifice, the total immolation, of a divine victim; to be able to say to all the souls of all the centuries: "As the Father has loved Me, I also have loved you"[5] — this is perfect happiness, consummate joy, this is the supreme satisfaction of supreme love!

Complete happiness is described for us in these words of St. Paul, which are perfectly realized only in Jesus: "Through the Spirit [He] offered Himself unblemished unto God."[6] The symbols we use to express this are the Dove, the emblem of happiness of heaven, because it is the emblem of eternal love; the Cross, which is the sign of earthly happiness because it signifies pain; the sorrowful and most happy Heart of Jesus, in which are fused two loves in an ineffable and eternal kiss.

And Christ did not reserve His Cross as He did not reserve His love, His life, or His happiness. All that He has He has given to us; we receive everything from His fullness.

---

5. John 15:9.
6. Hebr. 9:14.

His Cross must be our Cross. We all fit onto it. The same nails fasten us to the tree of life, the same thorns crown us, the same lance pierces our heart. And when we have touched all the peaks and arrive finally upon the divine Calvary and consent to be lifted on the Cross and immolate ourselves with the holy victim in His unique sacrifice, our souls, trembling with pain and happiness, find in the arms of the Cross the supreme secret of human life, the secret of perfect joy.

ACKNOWLEDGMENTS

The pages listed below contain material quoted or para-
phrased by Archbishop Martínez from various sources. Where
it has been possible to supply a standard English translation or
reference for these, such sources are indicated. In other cases
(except for those brief phrases or sayings which may be called
common property), the English text is that of the translator.
Material formally quoted is used with the permission of the
respective publishers, here gratefully acknowledged:

All direct quotations from the *Summa Theologica* are taken
from: *The Summa Theologica of St. Thomas Aquinas*, literally translated by Fathers of the English Dominican Province.
Burns Oates & Washbourne, London, 1920-1935; Benziger
Brothers, New York, American publisher and copyright owner.

All direct quotations from St. John of the Cross are taken
from: *The Complete Works of St. John of the Cross, Doctor
of the Church*, translated and edited by E. Allison Peers. The
Newman Press, Westminster, Maryland, 1953.

The quotation from Thomas à Kempis given on page 204
is taken from: *The Following of Christ, by Thomas à Kempis*,
edited by the Rev. J. M. Lelen; page 180. Catholic Book Pub-
lishing Co., New York, 1941.

page 3:
St. Augustine: *De Moribus Eccl.*,
XV.

St. Thomas: IIa IIae, q. 45, a. 6,
quoting Aristotle, *Metaph.*, I,
20.

page 11:
De Trinitate, XV, 19.

page 12:
St. Thomas: IIa IIae, q. 45, a. 6,

St. Augustine: *De Trinitate*, IV,
20.

page 13:
IIa IIae, q. 45, a. 6.

page 19:
Ia IIae, q. 68, a. 2.

page 21:
Ia, q. 38, a. 2 ad 3.
Ia, q. 43, a. 3 ad 1.

317

page 22:

Ibid., a. 5 ad 2.

Ibid., q. 38, a. 1.

page 24:

*Thoughts and Teachings of La-
cordaire.* Art and Book Co.,
London, 1902, page 271.

page 30:

Elevations. II, page 437.

page 31:

Ia, q. 43, a. 5 ad 2.

page 32:

Ibid., quoting *De Trinitate,* IV,
20.

Ibid.

page 33:

Ibid. ad 1.

page 35:

Esquisse d'une Vie de Tauler, by
G. Thery, O. P., in *La Vie
Spirituelle,* March, 1927, page
147.

St. Thomas: Ia, q. 43, a. 7 ad 6.

page 40:

Cf. Ia IIae, q. 68, a. 1 ad 1; also
ibid., aa. 2, 4, 5, and 8.

Cf. *In III Sent.,* d. 34, a. 3.

page 50:

Ia IIae, q. 68, a. 5.

page 56:

Cf. Peers, II, *Ascent of Mount
Carmel,* book II, 1, 2.

page 58:

Cf. Ia, q. 82, a. 3 ad 3.

page 59:

IIa IIae, q. 20, a. 3.

page 62:

Peers, III, *Living Flame of Love,*
I, 28.

Ibid., 3.

Peers, II, *Spiritual Canticle,*
stanza 19.

page 63:

Cf. Ia, q. 82, a. 3 ad 3.

page 71:

Peers, III, *Living Flame of Love,*
II, 34.

page 73:

Ia, q. 38, a. 2 ad 3.

Ibid., a. 10.

page 75:

Ia IIae, q. 111, a. 2.

In Epist. ad Rom., 8, 14.

page 76:

Cf. Peers, III, *Living Flame of
Love,* prologue, 3.

page 80:

IIa IIae, q. 45, a. 6 ad 1.

page 87:

De Trinitate, IV, 20.

page 99:

Peers, II, *Spiritual Canticle,*
stanza 5.

page 102:

Cf. *Tract. in Joan.,* 26.

page 105:

Cf. op. cit.

pages 106-107:

Letter to the Romans.

page 109:

St. Teresa of Jesus, *Autobiography,* chap. 40.

page 114:
Cf. Peers, I, *Dark Night of the Soul,* book I, 8 ff.; *Ascent of Mount Carmel,* book II, 5.

page 125:
Cf. Ia IIae, q. 68, a. 2.
Ibid.

page 126:
Pensées, II, 17, 5.

page 145:
Spiritual Exercises, #339: Rules for the Distribution of Alms.

page 146:
Cf. IIa IIae, q. 27, a. 6.

page 150:
Ia, q. 2, a. 2 ad 1.

page 152:
Cf. Ia IIae, q. 68.

page 170:
Peers I, *Ascent of Mount Carmel,* book II throughout.
Cf. supra, page 99.

page 173:
Cf. Butler's *Lives of the Saints,* 1956, II, page 418.
Cf. *St. John of the Cross,* by Paschasius Heriz, O. C. D., 1919, pages 171-172.

page 175:
Cf. *Annotations,* #20.

page 177:
St. Thomas: Cf. Ia, q. 38, a. 2 ad 3.
St. Ignatius: Cf. *Spiritual Exercises,* #23: Principle and Foundation.

page 182:
Cf. IIa IIae, q. 113, a. 9 ad 1.

page 188:
Div. Nom., II, quoted by St. Thomas Aquinas, IIa Iˣae, q. 45, a. 2.

page 189:
Cf. Ia, q. 82, a. 3 ad 3.

page 194:
Sermo XV, *In Cant.,* n. 5-6.

page 205:
Cf. *The Little Flowers of St. Francis of Assisi,* I, 8.

page 208:
Cf. supra, page 182.

page 223:
Cf. Ia IIae, q. 70, a. 3.

page 229:
Cf. Ia IIae, q. 70, a. 3 ad 7.

pages 229-230:
Cf. *St. Ignatius: The Pilgrim Years,* by James Broderick, S. J.
Farrar, Straus and Cudahy, New York, 1956, page 329.

page 233:
Cf. *Enchiridion,* II.
Cf. *De Moribus Eccl.,* XV

page 234:
Cf. *Autobiography,* chaps. 20-21.

page 239:
Cf. *Canticle,* stanza 5.

page 241:
Cf. IIa IIae, q. 182, a. 3.

page 242:
Cf. IIa IIae, q. 188, a. 8.

page 253:

Cf. *Spiritual Exercises*, #23: Principle and Foundation.

page 261:

Cf. Ia IIae, q. 69, a. 2, and q. 70, a. 2.

page 262:

Quoted from Albertus Magnus on Luke, *Commentaries on the Gospels* (vols. 20-24) in the *Opera Omnia*, edition of Abbé Auguste Borgnet.

page 266:

Cf. Ia IIae, q. 69, a. 1.

page 268:

Cf. ibid., a. 3

St. Thomas: Cf. IIa IIae, q. 19, a. 9 ad 1, and a. 12.

page 274:

St. Augustine: Cf. *De Serm. Dom. in Monte*, I.

St. Thomas: IIa IIae, q. 121, a. 2; cf. also Ia IIae, q. 69, a. 3 ad 3.

page 286:

St. Thomas: Cf. *In III Sent.*, d. 35, q. 1, a. 3.

page 297:

Cf. Ia, q. 14, a. 1.

page 298:

Cf. IIa IIae, q. 8, a. 7.

page 305:

Cf. *De Civ. Dei*, XIX, 13.

VISIT, WRITE or CALL your nearest ST. PAUL BOOK & MEDIA CENTER today for a wide selection of Catholic books, periodicals, cassettes, quality video cassettes for children and adults! Operated by the Daughters of St. Paul.
We are located in:

ALASKA
750 West 5th Ave., Anchorage, AK 99501 **907-272-8183.**
CALIFORNIA
3908 Sepulveda Blvd., Culver City, CA 90230 **213-397-8676;**
 213-398-6187.
1570 Fifth Ave. (at Cedar Street), San Diego, CA 92101
 619-232-1442; 619-232-1443.
46 Geary Street, San Francisco, CA 94108 **415-781-5180; 415-781-5216.**
FLORIDA
145 S.W. 107th Ave. Miami, FL 33174 **305-559-6715; 305-559-6716.**
HAWAII
1143 Bishop Street, Honolulu, HI 96813 **808-521-2731.**
ILLINOIS
172 North Michigan Ave., Chicago, IL 60601
 312-346-4228; 312-346-3240.
LOUISIANA
423 Main Street, Baton Rouge, LA 70802 **504-343-4057.**
4403 Veterans Memorial Blvd., Metairie, LA 70006 **504-887-7631;**
 504-887-0113.
MASSACHUSETTS
50 St. Paul's Ave., Jamaica Plain, Boston, MA 02130 **617-522-8911.**
Rte. 1, 450 Providence Hwy., Dedham, MA 02026 **617-326-5385.**
MISSOURI
9804 Watson Rd., St. Louis, MO 63126 **314-965-3512; 314-965-3571.**
NEW JERSEY
561 U.S. Route 1; No. C6, Wicks Plaza, Edison, NJ 08817
 201-572-1200; 201-572-1201.
NEW YORK
150 East 52nd Street, New York, NY 10022 **212-986-7580.**
78 Fort Place, Staten Island, NY 10301
 718-447-5071; 718-447-5086.
OHIO
616 Walnut Street, Cincinnati, OH 45202 **513-421-5733; 513-721-5059.**
2105 Ontario Street (at Prospect Ave.), Cleveland, OH 44115
 216-621-9427.
PENNSYLVANIA
168 W. DeKalb Pike, King of Prussia, PA 19406 **215-337-1882;**
 215-337-2077.
SOUTH CAROLINA
243 King Street, Charleston, SC 29401 **803-577-0175.**
TEXAS
114 Main Plaza, San Antonio, TX 78205 **512-224-8101.**
VIRGINIA
1025 King Street, Alexandria, VA 22314 **703-549-3806.**
CANADA
3022 Dufferin Street, Toronto, Ontario, Canada M6B 3T5
 416-781-9131; 416-781-9132.